The Politicizing Presidency

STUDIES IN GOVERNMENT
AND PUBLIC POLICY

The Politicizing Presidency

The White House
Personnel Office, 1948–1994

Thomas J. Weko

University Press of Kansas

© 1995 by the University Press of Kansas
All rights reserved

Published by the University Press of Kansas (Lawrence, Kansas 66049), which was
organized by the Kansas Board of Regents and is operated and funded by Emporia State
University, Fort Hays State University, Kansas State University, Pittsburg State University,
the University of Kansas, and Wichita State University

Library of Congress Cataloging-in-Publication Data

Weko, Thomas J.
   The politicizing presidency : the White House Personnel Office,
1948–1994 / Thomas J. Weko
     p. cm. — (Studies in government and public policy)
   Includes bibliographical references and index.
   ISBN 0-7006-0695-5 (cloth)   ISBN 0-7006-0696-3 (pbk.)
   1. United States. White House Presidential Personnel Office.
2. Presidents—United States—Staff. 3. Presidents—United States.
4. Patronage, Political—United States. 5. Executive power—United
States. 6. United States—Officials and employees—Selection and
appointment. I. Title. II. Series.
JK518.W45   1995
353.03′13—dc20   94-41099

British Library Cataloguing in Publication Data is available.

Printed in the United States of America

10 9 8 7 6 5 4 3 2 1

The paper used in this publication meets the minimum requirements of the American National Standard for Permanence of Paper for Printed Library Materials Z39.48-1984.

To my parents, Dorothy and Stephen Weko,
and my children,
Noah, Ruth, and Madeleine

Contents

Preface

"Taken by and large," Edward Corwin wrote at midcentury, "the history of the presidency has been a history of aggrandizement." Nowhere has the aggrandizement of the modern presidency been more plainly revealed than in the efforts of modern presidents to centralize authority in a vastly expanded White House Office and to politicize (or "presidentialize") the federal bureaucracy by pushing presidential loyalists deep into operating agencies and bureaus.

Though routinely decried — and defended — centralization and politicization have been subject to surprisingly little systematic study; we know little about either their causes or consequences. My book aims to shed light on these developments, posing two principal questions. First, why have presidents tried to centralize authority in a vastly larger and more specialized White House Office? Second, what are the consequences of centralization: has it made the executive branch more responsive to presidential leadership, or simply yielded a bloated and unmanageable White House Office?

In my judgment, presidency scholarship should yield presidency theory, and theories (as opposed to descriptions) are best constructed by emphasizing simplicity and parsimony. Hence, I address these questions by conceiving of presidents as leaders who act purposefully in pursuit of policy and electoral aims — and whose calculations about how best to achieve their aims are shaped by an institutional setting that defines the alternatives available to them and the consequences of their choices.

Among presidency scholars it is often supposed that presidents themselves shape the office they inhabit, importantly influencing its evolution. Thus, my study examines an alternative account of the aggrandizement of the White House Office: that its evolution is substantially rooted in the habits and orientations of individual presidents, rather than in the institutions they inhabit.

Drawing upon White House files, archives, and personal interviews with more than one hundred veterans of the executive branch, I test these explanations for the evolution of the modern White House Office against the experience of the White House Personnel Office, a primary instrument through which modern presidents have pursued centralization and politicization.

I begin the study by tracing the institutional factors that have propelled presidents to centralize control over political appointments in an expanded White House staff. In Chapter 2 I show that the attenuation of political parties did significantly increase the attractiveness of building a Personnel Office within the White House, as rational choice accounts claim. However, most of the staff's expansion took place after 1968 — well after parties had lost virtually all their leverage over presidents and the shape of the White House Office. In Chapter 3 I show that the staff's aggrandizement during these years, 1968 to 1988, was rooted largely in the waning significance of cabinet departments and the policy networks with which they are allied — an institutional development about which rational choice accounts are largely silent.

In Chapter 4 I conclude my analysis of the presidency's institutional setting by turning from the atrophying of traditional constraints to the creation of new constraints, both inside and outside the White House. These constraints, I argue, have yielded a White House Personnel Office that differs significantly from the predictions of rational choice accounts. In recent years the Personnel Office has not grown inexorably; instead, hemmed in by internal constraints, it has grown scarcely at all. And, although freed free the claims of party, the Personnel Office is not a simply an instrument of administrative leadership; rather, it is deeply engaged in meeting the claims of the organizations which have come to dominate contemporary, post-party electoral politics in the United States.

In Chapter 5 I put presidents at the center of the analysis. What difference do presidents make in the evolution of the White House? Can presidents accelerate, retard, or even reverse the systemic forces pushing towards centralization? I address this question by examining the experience of the two presidents who wished to most sharply alter the White House Personnel Office, Richard Nixon and Jimmy Carter. Their experience offers strong evidence, I conclude, that presidents may reshape their White House Office only at the margins — unless they wish to pay dearly for the changes they introduce.

In Chapter 6 I examine whether the dramatic expansion of the president's appointments staff has expanded White House control over political appointments — and whether this control has actually permitted presidents to assemble a team of men and women who are responsive to their leadership. I explore the question of responsiveness by examining how two Republican presidents, Richard Nixon and Ronald Reagan, used political appointments to tame a bureaucracy they believed to be antithetical to their political concerns and policy aims — the Department of Health, Education and Welfare.

Next, I turn my attention to the unintended consequences of White House aggrandizement. Here I show that presidents have gotten a good bit more than they have bargained for: the centralized control over political appointments in an expanded White House staff has created a new set of problems with which Bill Clinton and his successors must wrestle.

In Chapter 7 I conclude by discussing theoretical and practical implications. I begin by discussing the study's implications for rational choice theories of the presidency, arguing that the study confirms the central insight of these accounts but calls into question some of the ways that rational choice accounts have chosen to characterize the institutional setting of the modern presidency. Drawing upon the study's substantive findings and the implications of rational choice institutionalism, I critically evaluate recent proposals for reforming political appointments and the Presidential Personnel Office.

The research for this book was made possible by a host of institutions, most importantly, the Brookings Institution, which awarded me a Brookings Research Fellowship. Additional support was provided by the University of Minnesota, which awarded me a Special Dissertation Travel Grant and a McMillan Fellowship; and by the University of Toledo and Juniata College, which awarded me faculty development grants.

I am deeply grateful to more than one hundred respondents from eight administrations who generously consented to speak with me. The staffs of four presidential libraries (Truman, Eisenhower, Kennedy, Johnson), the Nixon Collection of the National Archives, the Brookings Library and Archive, and the Columbia University Oral History Collection were indispensable in helping me ferret out documents and interviews. Fellow presidency researchers Bradley Patterson, Jr., Richard Schott, and Samuel Kernell graciously shared some of their own interviews with White House staffers. Paul Light, former director of the National Academy of Public Administration, made available to me data, interviews, and reports from the academy's Presidential Appointee Project.

Many colleagues provided advice and encouragement throughout the research and writing of the book, including John Aldrich, David Canon, Mark Kessler, David Menefee-Libey, James Pfiffner, David Sousa, Steven S. Smith, Charles Walcott, and Joe White. I am most deeply indebted to my wife, Bess Gonglewski, who has been a gracious editor and an indefatigable supporter of my work.

1
A History of Aggrandizement

Since the middle of the twentieth century, presidents have struggled to extend their control over the national government by aggressively centralizing authority in a vastly expanded White House staff and by politicizing the federal bureaucracy — by pushing presidential loyalists deep into the agencies of the Executive Office and the executive branch. The cumulative results of their efforts are profound.

The White House Office, conceived as a small, anonymous group of aides — the "eyes and ears of the president"[1] — has become a large, specialized, and decidedly visible bureaucracy of nearly six hundred individuals.[2] More important, as the White House Office has grown, it has accumulated enormous power and now has hold of many of the prerogatives that once belonged to other leaders in the Washington community, including party officials, the president's cabinet, and career civil servants.

Politicization has reshaped Washington politics as well. During the 1930s, the upper echelons of the federal bureaucracy were populated by only a few dozen presidential appointees, many of whom were veterans of party politics who were far more interested in quiet sinecures than galvanizing the bureaucracy to support a presidential program. The president's appointees, civil service reformers lamented, were merely "idling cogs in the national machine."[3] Now, after half a century of sometimes feverish politicization, the executive branch has been fundamentally altered by the men who have served as president. Three thousand political appointees blanket the executive branch, reaching deep into the bowels of the federal agencies, and the men and women who occupy these posts are no mere "idling cogs." Often they are keenly loyal to the president they serve and aggressively push his policies and political concerns.

Not surprisingly, these developments have sparked sustained and sometimes acrimonious debates that revolve around two issues. Why have presidents

1

centralized political authority in a burgeoning White House staff and politicized the executive branch? Have these developments jeopardized the administrative capabilities and constitutional integrity of the national government, or do they permit presidents to overcome the unresponsiveness of the administrative establishment?

Centralization and politicization, some people contend, are caused largely by presidents — that is, these developments stem from the personalities and preferences of presidents themselves. It was Lyndon Johnson's prodigious appetite for control and his "impatience with the traditional machinery of government,"[4] Richard Nixon's suspicious and secretive turn of mind,[5] and Ronald Reagan's simpleminded yet deeply felt conservatism[6] that led them to draw decisions into a vastly expanded White House Office and to people the bureaucracy with men and women loyal to them (or to their policy agendas).

Other people, though, argue precisely the opposite: the personalities or aims of individual presidents have little to do with centralization and politicization. These developments, they argue, are the product of inexorable forces — a set of incentives and constraints that envelop the presidency and shape the actions of all presidents regardless of their personality, work habits, or ideology. In the estimation of these observers, all presidents are faced with a tremendous disparity between the public's expectations for performance and the office's modest leadership resources. Hence, presidents have no choice but to centralize and politicize in order to right the imbalance between the two.[7]

The consequences of centralization and politicization have evoked still more debate, it seems, than the causes. In the years since the Watergate affair, many journalists and scholars have offered a sharply critical assessment of centralization and politicization. The centralization of political responsibility in a vastly expanded White House and Executive Office of the President (EOP), they note, has undermined traditional leaders in the Washington community, including cabinet and party officials. In the place of these leaders stands a new bureaucracy — a greatly expanded White House — staffed by zealous presidential loyalists and removed from the normal avenues of scrutiny, such as congressional confirmation and oversight. Thomas Cronin, for example, describes the modern White House and Executive Office as a

> powerful inner sanctum of government, isolated from traditional, constitutional checks and balances. It has become common practice for anonymous, unelected, and unratified aides to negotiate sensitive international agreements that are free from congressional oversight . . . [or] wield fiscal authority over billions of dollars that Congress appropriates yet a president refuses to spend, or that Congress assigns to one purpose and the administration routinely redirects to another — all with no semblance of public scrutiny.[8]

Not only has the expansion of the modern White House undermined customary and constitutionally established centers of power, critics contend, but it has also failed to make the executive establishment more responsive to presidential leadership. Rather, the expansion of the White House has created an enormous staff that presidents find increasingly difficult to manage,[9] and it has reproduced within the White House Office the same sort of importunings and centrifugal forces that presidents found so onerous within the executive branch.[10] "As with the ships of the Spanish Armada," observed two veterans of the Carter administration, "size is a crippling handicap, not a source of strength."[11]

Politicization of executive agencies and the EOP, its detractors allege, has done little to make the government more responsive to presidential leadership: political appointees are too numerous and transitory to be an effective instrument of presidential leadership. Because appointees are "birds of passage,"[12] agencies are led by men and women whose commitment to the president's agenda is considerable,[13] but whose time horizons are short, and whose commitment to the long-term well-being of the agencies they lead is slight.[14] Because appointees are numerous, they "are beyond the ability of any President or White House to directly oversee" and may actually "dilute the President's ability to develop and enforce a coherent program."[15] The proliferation of appointees has, instead, "distance[d] the President and his principal officials from those with the most relevant experience" and "discouraged talented men and women from remaining in the career service, or entering in the first place."[16] Though presidents may have sought to make the executive branch more responsive to their leadership through politicization, they have succeeded instead in damaging the continuity, competence, and integrity of the federal administrative establishment.

Many people contend, though, that politicization has been a beneficial development, one that has increased the responsiveness and accountability of the federal administrative apparatus. Neither federal courts nor Congress, they suggest, can supply responsible political leadership to the administrative state. Congress has the capability to exercise tight control over the activities of administrative agencies, but congressional committees and subcommittees — where control over administrative agencies is actually vested — are too fragmented and too closely tied to special interests to supply responsible leadership to the bureaucracy.[17] Federal courts, too, are ill suited to bureaucratic leadership. In contrast to the "political branches," unelected judges do not transmit popular sentiments about the performance of bureaucracies; rather, they clarify and enforce statutorily established rights and police administrative procedures — while disregarding administrative feasibility, fiscal constraints, and public concerns.[18] Given the inadequacies of Congress and the courts, the only way that "popular control over the bureaucratic and technocratic power centers"[19] of the national government can be established is through presidential leadership. Only the president has the incentives and the capabilities to push the concerns of broad, national constituencies into administrative policymaking.[20] By exercising careful control over the selection of political appointees and drawing budgetary and regulatory decisions into a powerful and politicized Office of Management and Budget (OMB), Reagan was able to forge the essential "link between the political ideas that win elections and the policies of the government."[21] Seen in this light, Reagan's attempts to gain control over the executive branch through politicization and centralization were a triumph of democratic leadership.

Centralization, too, has its defenders. By increasing the competence and reach of the president's staff, Bradley Patterson argues, centralization yields a presidency that is more capable of meeting the exigencies of world affairs and acting as "a countervailing magnet to the atomizing particles in the polities of the nation."[22] Dick Cheney, chief of staff in the Ford White House, argues: "I don't think we should place artificial constraints on the president. If the president says he needs 500 people to do the job, give him 500; if he needs 700, give him 700. It is a minor price to pay for having a president who is the leader of the free world."[23]

Controversy about centralization and politicization is inescapable. Clashes about their causes are rooted in dissimilar theoretical habits and research strategies: some scholars emphasize the role that leaders play in shaping the presidency, while others focus on how larger forces outside of the office constrain the actions of its occupants.[24] Arguments about the consequences of centralization and politicization spring from clashing ideological and partisan perspectives on the development of the modern presidency. Conservative scholars and politicians, bitter foes of presidential aggrandizement during the New Deal epoch, came to appreciate the virtues of centralization and politicization during an era of Republican presidents and Democratic Congresses. Given the nearly hegemonic Democratic control of Congress in the past six decades, the only way to translate conservative victories in presidential elections into conservative policies is to aggressively push centralization and politicization of the executive branch. For liberals, circumscribing the reach of the White House and EOP means that decisions about development and administration of policy rest in the hands of career civil servants rather than presidential loyalists who are hostile to Democratic programs or the agencies that administer them.

Although controversy is inescapable, ignorance about the fundamental features of centralization and politicization is inexcusable — and surprisingly widespread. Consider, for example, political appointments. Alone among the Western democracies, the United States entrusts the leadership of its national administrative agencies not to career officials, but to hundreds of presidential appointees. Political appointments are widely acknowledged to be the primary means by which presidents leave their mark upon the executive branch, and the proliferation and centralization of political appointments is taken to be a hallmark of the modern "administrative presidency." There is tremendous confusion and ignorance, though, surrounding presidents' use of political appointments. How rapidly has the number of appointees grown? How much control do presidents (and their staffs) exercise over appointment choices? How does the White House put its control to use?

Louis Cordia, the Heritage Foundation's expert on political appointments, writes, "While the need for political direction and leadership [of the bureaucracy] is greater than ever . . . at present [1988] the number of senior management positions is less than in 1968."[25] The Volcker Commission, a blue-ribbon panel convened to combat the "deteriorating quality and performance of the federal bureaucracy" found precisely the opposite—that politicization has sharply accelerated in recent decades: "From 1933 to 1965, during a period of profound expansion in government responsibilities, the number of cabinet and subcabinet officers appointed by the president and confirmed by the Senate doubled from 73 to 152. From 1965 to the present, a span when total employment and programs were more stable, that number more than tripled to 573."[26] Which account is correct? Both are wide of the mark. But no matter how they are defined, "senior management positions" have not diminished in number over the past two decades—nor have senior policymaking posts more than trebled between 1965 and 1988.

Distinguished scholars of the presidency have fared little better in assessing the degree to which presidents (and their aides) have managed to seize control over political appointments. "Ronald Reagan has achieved what Nixon contemplated: White House staff control of all appointive jobs," observed presidency scholar, Richard Neustadt.[27] Contemporaneous accounts from White House aides offer a very different picture: one of a circumscribed White House role. Commenting on the influence of the president's personnel aides during Reagan's second term, a senior White House aide observed, "Everything is supposed to be cleared with [the] White House Personnel [Office], but [Caspar] Weinberger wouldn't go to them on a bet."[28] Personnel aides conceded their limited influence, describing their frustration with the State Department in these terms: "Their whole attitude was they're better than the White House, and they just don't even understand why they should be responsive to the White House. . . . Schultz's attitude was, 'This is different country. Just buzz off.' "[29]

How has the White House put its control over political appointments to use? Since the collapse of party control over presidential nominations, argues Terry Moe, presidents have been freed from the necessity of repaying electoral obligations with appointments. Instead, presidents are now free to put appointments to use "as a mechanism of [policy] control," choosing appointees according to their loyalty, ideology, or programmatic support.[30] Nonetheless, those who work in the White House have described a job in which narrowly political constraints loom large: "The PPO [Presidential Personnel Office] is a political organization, and it has to be. That's what it was designed for, and that's what it has always been, and you must make it that [or fail]."[31] Senior executives in departments, too, often describe the staff as one that is narrowly "political." A deputy secretary of defense from the Carter administration voiced a typical opinion: "We would have had a bunch of stooges who represented some constituency that some politico thought important" had appointments rested in the hands of the PPO.[32]

In sum, the debate that has raged about a central feature of the modern presidency—centralization and politicization—is based upon the weakest of empirical foundations. This book seeks to shed light on two questions at the center of the debate. First, why have presidents tried to centralize authority in a vastly larger and more specialized White House Office? Second, what are the consequences of centralization—has centralization made the executive branch more responsive to presidential leadership? Or, have the most important consequences of centralization been those that presidents have neither anticipated nor sought, such as a "dilution of the president's ability to develop and enforce a coherent agenda"?[33]

To address these questions I first review how scholars have explained the evolution of the institutionalized presidency, focusing in particular on the leading account of its aggrandizement, "rational choice institutionalism." Then I describe how I will test this account of the presidency's institutional evolution.

WHY AGGRANDIZEMENT? PRESIDENTS AND INSTITUTIONS

> *The relationship between the president and the presidency, the individual and the institution has long been the central analytic problem [in the study of the presidency].*
> —Joseph Pika[34]

Presidents and the White House

The simplest explanation for the aggrandizement of the White House Office begins with the obvious: presidents organize the White House to suit their own needs. The structure and evolution of the White House staff is a product of the presidents themselves—of their work habits, their orientations toward the office, their personalities, and their political aims.[35] Seen in this light, the institution of the White House is best understood as "the lengthened shadow of the man."

For both journalists and practitioners of Washington politics, president-centered explanations come naturally. Journalists are not "conceptualizers or generalizers"[36] but typically view politics as a competitive struggle for power among individual politicians.[37] Thus journalists view the evolution of the White House in these terms: "The orbits of advisers and agencies that revolve around the President do not, like the heavenly bodies, follow a fixed and settled course. To some extent, their paths are determined by Constitution and custom; but to an important degree, the President himself, as central occupant of the executive galaxy, shapes the pattern of government [i.e., the White House]."[38] Veterans of Washington politics, whose survival and advancement depend upon their ability to assess "who is doing what to whom," and whose focus is on the short-term,[39] are equally inclined to point to individual presidents as the chief forces shaping the institutionalized presidency. In Henry Kissinger's estimation, for example, the prominence of the National Security Council staff during Richard Nixon's presidency was a product of Nixon's determination "to conduct foreign policy from the White House, his distrust of the existing bureaucracy, coupled with the congruence of his philosophy and mine and the relative inexperience of the new Secretary of State."[40] The members of the Tower Commission (the President's Special Review Board), empaneled to investigate the Iran-Contra affair, reached a similar conclusion about the National Security Council (NSC) staff. After reviewing the staff's history, they concluded that "the NSC staff is used by each president in a way that reflected his individual preferences and working style. . . . [The NSC staff] has remained the president's creature, molded as he sees fit, to serve as his personal staff for national security affairs."[41]

Not only journalists and Washington insiders have explained the evolution of the White House in personalized terms, though. Smitten by behavioralism, a generation of presidency scholars has viewed "the presidency as a presumptively personal institution."[42] This preference for personal explanation is most obvious among studies that adopted an explicitly psychological approach to the study of presidential leadership, such as James David Barber's *Presidential Character*. The assumption that the White House Office is largely shaped by presidents recurs, implicit and unarticulated, throughout studies of the presidency and public administration. If one examines reforms proposed by these scholars one notes a common theme: presidents are urged to shun the centralization of authority in a large White House Office and to reinstitute a modest White House staff typical of mid-century presidencies. Contemporary presidents, Philip Henderson implored in *Managing the Presidency*, must restore "the Eisenhower era primacy of the Cabinet" and "reverse the trend toward the enlargement of the immediate White House staff."[43] The National Academy of Public Administration also recommended that "the trend toward enlargement of the immediate White House staff should be reversed. Rigorous efforts should be made to keep this staff small."[44] "Trimming the presidential staff," writes Stephen Hess, "is a relatively simple matter for Presidents, if there is the will."[45] Implicit in each of these recommendations is the assumption that presidents — not in-eluctable institutional forces — have created the modern White House and that presidents may choose to undo the handiwork of their predecessors.

Taken by itself, however, a president-centered explanation yields little in-sight into the long-term growth of the White House: the aggrandizement of the White House has persisted for decades now, in spite of presidents of vastly different work habits, policy aims, and conceptions of their office. Consider the case of the president's political appointments staff: since 1960 its growth has been nurtured by presidents of thoroughly dissimilar work habits (Lyn-don Johnson and Ronald Reagan) and policy aims (John Kennedy and Richard Nixon). Hence, one must look elsewhere — to forces outside of the Oval Office that have pushed all modern presidents in the same direction — to explain the long-term evolution of the White House.

Institutional Forces: Demands and Workload

Those who searched outside the Oval Office for the forces that have fueled the aggrandizement of the White House Office have typically pointed to the burgeoning demands and workload imposed upon the presidency as the source of the office's growth.[46] As Thomas Cronin argues: "There is no single villain or systematically organized conspiracy promoting this expansion [of the White House]. A variety of factors is at work. [The most important of which are] an increase in the role of the presidency itself [and an expansion of] the business of government."[47] Stephen Hess, too, locates the growth of the White House Office in the vastly expanded workload of the presidency:

> It is not necessary to impute malevolence or a dictatorial impulse to the growth of the White House. Generally it has reflected a greater participa-tion by the United States in world affairs since World War II, a wid-ened concept of what services government should perform, . . . popular support for an increasingly activist concept of the presidency, more com-plicated interrelationships between government programs, and new of-fices imposed on the White House by Congress.[48]

There can be no disputing that the workload of the presidency has grown significantly over the past four decades — and that organizations typically adapt to an increased workload by increases in size and complexity. None-theless, the burgeoning workload of the presidency does not satisfactorily ex-plain the growth in the White House staff. Consider, for example, the case of political appointments: between 1965 and 1985 the number of presidential ap-pointments to policymaking posts increased by about 25 percent, growing from 420 to 527.[49] However, during the same period the president's appointment staff mushroomed from seventeen staffers in 1965 to fifty-five in 1985 — an increase of 325 percent—adding a formal designation (the Presidential Personnel Office) and layers of hierarchy, and expanding its division of labor and specialization. The same observation might be extended to other units of the White House Office, such as the Office of Policy Development, the growth of which is only weakly related to the size of the president's legislative program.[50] In short, the president's workload and staff have both grown, but the relationship between the two is far from regular and predictable.[51]

Moreover, these explanations are theoretically unsatisfying because they do not tell us how these institutional changes are linked to presidents' choices. Why, for example, have presidents chosen to handle their new responsibilities in-house, rather than delegate them to others outside the White House, such as executive agencies or the party's national committee. Presidents *could* have chosen to cope with an increase in the number of political appointments by relying upon the expertise of their departments or the political acumen of politicians at the party's national committee—as their predecessors did. But as the efflorescence of their staff reveals, presidents have chosen otherwise. Why? Accounts that focus upon the demands and workload of the presidency cannot supply the answer. What is needed instead is some means of showing how institutional changes have reshaped the incentives and resources of presidents and how presidents, in turn, have reshaped the modern White House Office.

Rational Choice Institutionalism

One way to link political institutions to individual choices is to construct an explanation that is anchored in rational choice theory. Seen from a rational choice perspective, political institutions induce preferences in officeholders, and officeholders, in turn, act upon these preferences to shape the political institutions they inhabit. For example, the institutional structure of congressional elections—highly decentralized, member-centered elections—induces among members of Congress a preference for a legislative assembly in which power is broadly dispersed among a set of standing committees, rather than concentrated in the hands of party leaders.[52] Changes in the structure of congressional elections—such as the enhancement of candidate organizations and the continued atrophying of party organizations—alter members' preferences about the structure of Congress, leading them to prefer a still greater dispersion of power and electoral resources within the institution, such as "subcommittee government."[53] Seen from this perspective, the White House Office is the product of presidents—not presidents who are sui generis, but rather generic actors whose preferences about the White House Office are induced by the institutional setting they inhabit. What sort of preferences about the White House Office (and, more generally, the institutionalized presidency) are induced by the institutional setting of the modern presidency?

All modern presidents, Terry Moe argues in his germinal essay, "The Politicized Presidency," are induced "to seek [centralized] control over the [policymaking] structures and processes of the government."[54] Although "presidents have differed widely in personality, style, and agenda,"

certain basic factors have structured the incentives of all modern presidents along the same basic lines. The president has increasingly been held responsible [by the public] for designing, proposing, legislating, administering, and modifying public policy, that is, for governing. Whatever his particular policy objectives, whatever his personality and style, the modern president is driven by these formidable expectations to seek control over the structures and processes of the government.[55]

Although by this logic presidents would like to initiate institutional reforms that allowed them to monopolize the policymaking processes of the government, they obviously cannot. The separation of powers and a host of other constraints prevent them from doing so. Rather, the institutional changes that presidents actually pursue are determined by "the resources they can marshal" and the "flexibility with which these resources can be put to use."[56] Presidents are faced with severe constraints both internal, such as time pressures and inadequate knowledge, and external, including congressional and bureaucratic resistance, and institutional inertia. Thus, a president's efforts at reform are channeled into "the structures and resources closest to him and least controlled by outsiders."[57] In short, the institutional setting of the modern presidency induces each president to "centralize" and "presidentialize" — to "centralize the institutionalized presidency in the White House" (to draw problems and issues once handled elsewhere into the hands of a larger and more elaborate White House staff), and to "presidentialize," that is, to embed his concerns in institutions with other agendas and loyalties by increasing "the number and location of political appointments" and by "appointing individuals on the basis of [personal] loyalty, ideology, or programmatic support" rather than other criteria.

In spite of presidents' ceaseless efforts to "right the imbalance between [the public's] expectations and capacity" through centralization and politicization, an immense gap between expectations and capacity remains. Thus politicization and centralization show no signs of abating. Moe concludes that

there is no reason to think that the future will be different from the near past. Barring some fundamental and unforseen changes in American institutions, the gap between expectations and capacity will continue to characterize the presidency, as will the serious constraints on presidential resources and the consequent attractiveness of politicization and centralization. There will likely be no turning back from the general path of historical development thus far.[58]

Among the accounts of the presidency's institutional evolution, none is as elegant or parsimonious as "The Politicized Presidency," and none has had a greater influence on scholars' understanding of the presidency's development. Although widely cited and reprinted, "The Institutionalized Presidency" — like other rational choice accounts of the presidency — has not been carefully documented.[59] Rather, its central insights — that the presidency is best understood by "omitting personal factors," and that its evolution is inexorably in the direction of politicization and centralization — remain untested claims. In the chapters that follow I test the claims of rational choice institutionalism, matching its theoretical observations against the evolution of the White House Personnel Office from 1948 to 1994.

THE WHITE HOUSE PERSONNEL OFFICE, 1948–1994

If scholarly resources and the patience of readers were limitless, one might test these accounts of the presidency's evolution by examining the entire White House Office over nine or ten modern presidential administrations, linking changes in the institutional setting of the presidency and the characteristics of presidents to the evolution of the White House Office and tracing the repercussions of centralization. However, studying the entire White House Office over the past half-century, not to mention the environment that has shaped its development, is a task that cannot be managed within the compass of a single book.[60] To cut the problem down to size, I could either focus on the entire White House Office over the course of one or two administrations, or focus on one facet of the White House Office across the full range of modern presidencies. Because I cannot capture sufficient variation in the institutional setting of the presidency — or presidents themselves — by studying only a handful of administrations, I have chosen the latter strategy. My book examines one facet of the larger White House Office, the Presidential Personnel Office (PPO), the staff within the White House Office that screens and recommends to the president candidates for political appointments. Drawing upon White House documents and interviews with over one hundred White House aides, I trace the aggrandizement of the PPO across four and a half decades (1948–1994) and ten presidential administrations.

Among the dozen specialized staffs within the modern White House Office, none provides us with a clearer insight into the evolution of centralization than the PPO. Political appointments are central to the exercise of presidential leadership — and to our understanding of it. "In affecting the everyday work of the government," Hugh Heclo notes, "these hundreds of personnel selections add up to a cumulative act of choice that may be as important as the electorate's single act of choice for the president every four years."[61]

Appointments are theoretically crucial as well: virtually all studies that explore the politicization of the institutionalized presidency or the aggrandizement of the White House place the president's use of political appointments at the center of their analysis.[62] The president's appointments staff is not only important, but representative of other staffs within the White House. Its rapid growth is typical: from two aides with largely clerical responsibilities at midcentury to a staff ranging from sixty to one hundred aides during the first Reagan administration. The causes of the PPO's growth and its impact on the political process are also typical of other specialized staffs, such as the Domestic Policy Office or the Political Affairs staff. Hence, explanations and conclusions about the PPO are applicable to other units within the White House Office. Lastly, the president's appointments staff stands at the center of the "Washington community." Each member of this community — congressmen, clientele, civil servants, and party officials — seeks to influence the PPO's choices. Hence, long-term changes in the staff illuminate basic changes in the working relationships between the president and other members of the Washington community, changes that are the hallmark of the "postmodern presidency."[63]

Guided by the logic of rational choice accounts, I pose two questions about the evolution of the president's appointments staff. First, what caused the explosive growth in its size and prerogatives? Was the aggrandizement of the PPO increasingly attractive to presidents as a result of changes in the institutional setting of the presidency? Or is centralization primarily the result of presidents themselves — the aims and habits they bring to office — rather than changes outside of the Oval Office? The second focus of my study is the consequences of growth. Has a burgeoning appointments staff permitted presidents to centralize control over appointments choices and, ultimately, to assemble an administration whose members are a responsive instrument of presidential leadership? Has the aggrandizement of the White House Office yielded what rational choice accounts claim for it?

2

Loosening the Ties That Bind: The Decline of Party and the Creation of a White House Personnel Office, 1948–1974

How has the atrophy of party organizations shaped the Presidential Personnel Office? To address this question I trace the evolution of the president's Personnel Office across three Democratic presidencies (Truman, Kennedy, and Johnson) and two Republican presidencies (Eisenhower and Nixon). Spanning a quarter century, these presidents faced parties that were steadily less capable of providing or withholding assistance. Their personal predilections notwithstanding, they responded to their party's waning leverage by expanding — haltingly — the size and managerial capabilities of their White House Personnel Office at the expense of their party and its prerogatives.

PARTIES AND PRESIDENTS

What do the leaders of party organizations[1] want from appointment politics? The major political parties in the United States have been concerned first and foremost with winning elections; they have been far less programmatic and ideological than parties in the European mold.[2] For the leaders of American party organizations, political appointments have *not* been exploited as a means by which to shape the policies of the government. Instead, they have been seen as a means to maintain and enhance their organizations and, ultimately, to win elections. Appointive posts, such as ambassadorships, are a currency through which key financial backers and campaign workers are rewarded.[3] Appointments are also used to nurture the careers of promising party figures or to reward defeated office-seekers.[4] Moreover, appointments may be used to demonstrate a party's solicitude for crucial electoral constituencies whose loyalties it hopes to solidify.

If they could, party leaders themselves would exercise control over each electorally valuable appointive position, that is, they would establish a "property right" to most federal jobs. In reality, however, a host of participants are endowed with the incentive and the capacity to influence appointment choices — including the president, White House aides, members of Congress, organized interests, cabinet officers, and party officials. Thus, party officials have not been able to exercise a property right to all appointive posts, or even the bulk of them. Rather, they have claimed the right of *access*: to learn of pending vacancies, to submit candidates and have them receive serious consideration, and to review (and if necessary, veto) candidates who are under consideration for appointment. Access allows party figures to block choices that are seen as damaging to their interests (such as awarding a coveted post to an opposition party contributor); it enables them to claim credit for helping contributors and workers secure desired positions; and it allows them to participate in allocating patronage among competing claimants, thereby nurturing their party's electoral coalition.[5]

Presidents want different things from political appointments than party leaders do. Presidents are held accountable for the performance of the government and are thus concerned about the competence and responsiveness of the men and women who will act on their behalf. Simply stated, presidents are compelled to care about governance; party leaders are not.

Like party leaders, presidents are concerned about the political consequences of appointment choices. However, presidents' political interests are *not* identical to those of their party. To one degree or another, a president's supporting coalition is dissimilar from that of his party. Consider, for example, the relationship between Richard Nixon and his party. Campaigning as the candidate of the minority party in 1972, Richard Nixon assiduously courted Independents and Democratic voters, recognizing that he would need their support to win reelection.[6] Nixon distanced himself from the Republican party and mobilized Democratic voters by creating his own campaign organization, the Committee to Re-Elect the President, rather than by relying upon the Republican party.[7] The election over, Nixon and his aides aimed to solidify his hold on the loyalties of southern and urban ethnic Democrats by rewarding prominent supporters from these constituencies with visible appointments — at the expense of Republican party stalwarts.[8] In short, there is an inevitable tension between presidents and their parties over the handling of political appointments, a tension that is rooted in dissimilar incentives that guide presidents and party leaders.

This tension was not lost on presidents who governed during the first half of the twentieth century. Presidents and their aides, concerned with governance, surreptitiously expressed their frustration with the caliber of the job seekers that party leaders proffered or political calculations of party notables. One aide remarked, "They [party leaders] don't know anything more about how to run the government than a chair would." Nonetheless, presidents respected the prerogatives of party and honored its claims. Throughout the first half of the twentieth century presidents permitted the party's national chair to serve as the Postmaster General, a post that afforded control over the single largest source of job patronage in the national government to the party's titular head.[9] Moreover, presidents granted an extraordinary measure of access to party claimants. Even Dwight Eisenhower, who chafed at the demands of partisan politics, acquiesced to his party's claim to access. Eisenhower's appointments staffer recalled, "Every day, invariably, I would walk across the street to the Republican National Committee headquarters at Farragut Square and sit down with Len Hall (RNC Chair) and his staff." Each day the president's aide would solicit recommendations from Hall, clear candidates with him, and elicit political intelligence about prospective appointees.[10]

Presidents acceded to the claims of party, granting them access to their staff and control over appointments, because it was in their interest to do so. There were costs to permitting party leaders to have their say — presidents ceded opportunities to exercise policy leadership in the executive branch. But these costs were outweighed by the benefits of cooperation: the leaders of party organizations were valuable allies during elections and between them, and presidents could not afford to alienate them or incur their ire.

By the late 1960s and early 1970s the position of party claimants was dramatically different. Presidents freely poached on the prerogatives of party officials, ignoring even the smallest courtesies that were once extended to parties, such as notification of pending appointments. Simply stated, in just over two decades party representatives had moved from a position of privileged access to one of insignificance, while the White House appointments staff had come from insignificance to prominence.

"MY GREATEST ALLY": PARTY AND APPOINTMENTS IN THE TRUMAN PRESIDENCY

In 1950 Harry Truman presided over an executive branch that had roughly twenty-two thousand presidentially appointed posts, yet only two White House aides assisted him in staffing the executive branch. How could Truman, who had to fill far more presidential posts than Ronald Reagan, manage with a staff a fraction the size of Reagan's? Quite easily, because virtually all of these appointments were "presidential" in name only. In reality, most decisions about staffing the executive branch were made outside the White House. During the Truman administration, as in past administrations, most political appointments were the product of negotiations among cabinet secretaries, congressmen from the president's party (particularly senators), party officials, and clientele groups, and their bargaining was structured by well-defined norms about "who gets what" and backed by powerful sanctions.

Appointments to posts in the field offices of federal agencies, such as postmasters and U.S. attorneys—which constituted the vast majority of presidential appointees—were chosen not by the president, but by senators and officials from the president's party. Senators or, in their absence, state and local party leaders, nominated candidates directly to departments. And departments, in turn, submitted slates of candidates to the White House, which "confirmed" the senators' choices: the constitutional order was stood on its head.[11] Only a thin layer of subcabinet appointments, roughly 100 posts at mid century,[12] linked the president to the Washington bureaucracy. Here, too, the role of the president was very modest, confined largely to ratifying choices made by politicians outside the White House.[13]

What, then, was the role of the president and his White House staff? Mid-century presidents, hemmed in by those outside the White House with a stake in appointment politics, played a highly circumscribed role in appointment politics. Presidents eschewed attempts to promote policy leadership of the executive branch through the centralized control of political appointments.[14] Instead, they confined their attention to "meeting the demands of those who stakes were political in nature,"[15] that is, to managing the claims of party, clientele, and fellow partisans on Capitol Hill in order to build support or, at a minimum, to avoid conflict. Hence, White House appointments staffs were rudimentary and their responsibilities were modest.

Truman's role was sufficiently modest that staff work was initially vested in the hands of a single White House administrative assistant, Donald Dawson.[16] In keeping with his responsibility for "meeting the [political] demands of others," Dawson devoted his time to three activities: placing candidates, clearing candidates, and patronage management. Although presidents were not responsible for selecting most appointees, presidents nonetheless had to "manage patronage." They had to determine whom to consult (that is, which politicians were authorized to offer candidates) and how to allocate patronage "among those whose recommendations are entitled to be given weight."[17] Thus, much of Dawson's attention was devoted to keeping "track of what we had done for certain people, certain states, certain state chairmen, and certain members of Congress," allocating jobs according to a sponsor's importance and loyalty to the president, and answering politicians' complaints that they had been slighted.[18] Dawson described the management of patronage and its benefits to the president:

> Patronage is essential to governing. It's a way a President can get leverage, rewarding people and things like that. . . . We broke the country down geographically and by type of political endorsement given the man. You wanted sectional spread and you wanted to keep track of who'd already got what by way of patronage; maybe the Banking Committee chairman in Congress already had a lot. We paid attention

to the partisan coloring, not so you ended up with someone from the wrong factions.[19]

Much of Dawson's time, too, was devoted to placing candidates proffered by Democratic politicians, campaign contributors, and clientele groups, an activity that Dawson and his boss deemed to be particularly valuable. Finally, Dawson was responsible for clearance: ensuring that candidates nominated by the president met with the approbation of powerful Democrats and brought no politically embarrassing "skeletons in the closet" to confirmation hearings.

Presidential appointments to field positions were handled outside of the White House. The Post Office Department or Justice Department consulted directly with Democrats on Capitol Hill and local party organizations and presented Dawson with a slate of candidates for his endorsement.[20] Candidates for appointments to policymaking posts, such as undersecretaries, assistant secretaries, or bureau chiefs, would receive slightly more scrutiny, though here, too, Dawson's aim was mitigating conflict with other politicians and avoiding embarrassment to the president, rather than scrutinizing the policy predispositions of the candidates. Dawson would "look over their resume and call some references to make sure everything was OK," consult with other Democratic politicians about the candidates' sponsorship, and double-check the candidate's acceptability to Democratic leaders on Capitol Hill.[21] And, in a bow to the politics of Senator McCarthy, Dawson and Friedman routinely solicited FBI field investigations of candidates to ensure that there were no surprises, such as politically embarrassing links to leftist political groups or personal scandals.

In handling each of his appointment responsibilities — patronage management, clearances, and placing candidates — Donald Dawson worked intimately with the chairman and staff of the Democratic National Committee (DNC). Dawson found the DNC to be a valuable ally, an extension of the president's staff. The DNC assisted Dawson by receiving, winnowing, and evaluating the claims of state and local Democratic organizations, by helping him with strategic decisions about the management of patronage, and by clearing candidates with Democratic organizations around the country and, in many cases, with Democratic politicians on Capitol Hill. DNC representatives enjoyed an extraordinary measure of access to Dawson. "I would never do anything," Dawson averred, "without checking with them."[22] Access was not granted grudgingly, but willingly, and proudly. As Dawson recalled, "They had better service out of the White House than they ever had before."[23] Democratic politicians with whom Dawson worked confirmed his judgment. India Edwards, vice chair of the DNC during the Truman years, was responsible for placing deserving Democratic women in the government. She described her relationship with Dawson this way: "I couldn't have done anything without Donald Dawson. He was my great ally. Don and I worked very closely together."[24]

Departing from the Status Quo?

These highly traditional arrangements worked reasonably well for Truman during the first years of his presidency, but by the winter of 1950 Truman and his aides concluded that they were no longer adequate. In the winter and early spring of 1950 Truman's approval rate had sunk to a dismal 37 percent, and there seemed to be no prospect for second term.[25] "Everybody," one aide recalls, "had written us off."[26] Moreover, the Truman administration was beset by corruption scandals and harassed by Senator Joseph McCarthy's allegations that it was a haven for communists and communist sympathizers. Under these conditions capable men and women stayed away from the administration in droves, and replacing departing members of the Truman team became very difficult.[27] Something had to be done to find competent men and women to serve in the administration.

In March 1950 Donald Dawson assembled a "Committee on Executive Personnel" to devise improvements in the staffing of the executive branch. The committee consisted of five assistant secretaries, "young men on their way up who were bright, vigorous, not afraid of new ideas, and who did not particularly come out of a political milieu" (in other words, they were not representatives of Democratic machine politics).[28] The committee was instructed to "formulate plans to locate and catalogue men and women of outstanding leadership ability from which the president may choose in making key appointments."[29] The committee's members, assisted by academic experts,[30] met regularly throughout the spring and summer of 1950, and by October 1950 they had completed their work: a plan to assist the president in staffing the government, which they dubbed "Operation Best Brains."

Though the committee's final report no longer exists, preliminary proposals by the committee's two most active members, Assistant Secretary of Labor Philip M. Kaiser and Assistant Attorney General H. Graham Morison, provide a clear picture of the changes they had in mind. Both Kaiser and Morison's proposals called for the expansion of the White House personnel staff to four staffers. Kaiser, for example, proposed to "establish in the White House, under Donald Dawson, a personnel unit headed by a staff director and composed of several top-flight assistants" and file clerks. Both anticipated that this staff would create an inventory of presidentially appointed posts in the executive branch and keep track of vacant posts. The staff would solicit recommendations from political and civic leaders around the country (and leaders within the executive establishment), and winnow this "talent bank" down to manageable proportions. When vacancies in the executive branch arose, then, the staff would submit a slate of candidates to the president. Morison's plan was more frankly partisan than Kaiser's: he proposed that recommendations be solicited only through Democratic party organizations and Democratic personnel commissioners within the civil service, while Kaiser recommended that recommendations be solicited from *"all* (Republican and Democratic) Senators, Congressmen, governors, mayors, party officials, and leaders of national organizations." Morison also proposed to include the DNC chairman as an ex officio member of a committee that winnowed down candidates from the president's consideration. Kaiser, in contrast, acknowledged that the chairman of the Democratic National Committee had a right to be consulted but did not include him as a member.[31]

Throughout its deliberations the committee was keenly aware that party officials were "watching us with a jaundiced eye,"[32] and it continually weighed the possible reactions of party leaders to its proposals. Philip Kaiser, for example, worried about his proposal to solicit recommendations from all politicians, Democrats and Republicans, recognizing that it was "highly controversial" and likely to meet with criticism from Democratic party figures.[33] Hence, the committee was careful to keep its proposals confidential, "because of the controversy that its recommendations might have aroused" among party officials.[34]

As the committee neared the completion of its work, its staff prepared talking points for a cabinet presentation of their proposal. Again, as the talking points show, Dawson assiduously sought to defuse the fears of party officials. His planned talk did not begin with a statement of the changes "Best Brains" would introduce but with an inventory of what the plan would *not* do:

> First let me tell you about several basic things that the plan recommended by the Committee *does not do*. (1.) It does not provide for the selection of appointees by anyone but the president. (2.) It does not locate candidates for cabinet positions. (3.) It does not alter the requirement of political acceptability or circumvent the Democratic National Committee in any way. (4.) It does not substitute technicians for leaders.[35] [emphasis in original]

Dawson never presented this talk or the committee's final report to the cabinet. As the committee completed its study, party officials weighed in with their views, making it clear that they saw the committee's plan for a fortified presidential staff as a threat, an unwanted "layer of expertise interposed between the national committee, the congress, the local and state political organizations, and the president."[36] In light of this response, the president's staff rejected the study's recommendations and decided it would be unwise even to *reproduce* the report.[37] They concluded that its plans were "too ambitious" and threatened to create "too much of an intermediary [staff] layer between the president and responsible officials."[38] As Truman's assistant, Donald Dawson recalled: "Our ultimate conclusion was that there would be too much professionalism, too much ivory tower approach, and you would ignore the practical aspects of party discipline, party reward, and party penalties [if new staffing arrangements were adopted]. We came to the realization that you had to be *practical* about presidential appointees and use them for political advantage . . . and [to] build up the party."[39] William Boyle, chairman of the Democratic National Committee, could have described the plan's shortcomings no better.

In the months that followed, Dawson and the committee did decide to create a "talent bank," but it was a shadow of the proposals they had initially discussed. The president's staff would simply serve as a repository for names presented to it — from its traditional sources — and it would classify these names according to occupational categories. The machinery they established was described this way: "[Dawson aide Martin L.] Friedman personally maintained a simple card index classified by job categories. When he heard of someone who might make a good appointee, he would classify him according to the various presidential positions for which he should be considered. When a vacancy occurred he would draw from this index and other sources the names and biographies of candidates and assemble them into a 'black book.' "[40] This was a truly insignificant accretion to the president's staff, no more than a clerical tidying-up of the status quo. It did nothing to fortify the president's capabilities as a participant in staffing his administration, but it did have one virtue: it kept the president and his staff from violating the expectations of those whose support was essential, leaders of the Democratic party.[41]

The White House Constrained

Why did the president and his staff conclude that it was "unwise and impractical to systematize the recruitment of presidential appointments"[42] under the leadership of an expanded presidential staff? Or, stated otherwise, why did the anticipated costs of extending presidential control over appointment choices in an expanded White House staff outweigh its expected benefits? The answer lies in the importance of the political parties to mid-century presidents.

At mid century, state and local party leaders remained the dominant participants in presidential nomination politics. Most delegates to the national convention were chosen through state and local conventions, processes that were dominated by party officials.[43] Although just nearly half of all delegates were formally chosen in party primaries — 46 percent in 1952 — far fewer were legally committed to supporting a particular candidate (only 18 percent of Democratic delegates and 24 percent of Republican delegates). In many primary states, "primaries were mere 'beauty contests,' with no direct bearing on delegate selection. In several states delegates were directly elected, but their election was insulated from national political currents by legal means, including prohibitions on the identification of prospective delegates' candidates on the primary ballot. In other states . . . a tradition of 'favorite son' candidacies often effectively barred outsiders from competing in primaries."[44] In sum, presidential primaries played quite a limited role in the nomination of presidents, providing an arena in which candidates could demonstrate their electoral strength to the party leaders, who actually controlled the convention.

Party organizations not only dominated nomination contests but loomed large in general election campaigns as well. At mid century presidential candidates had neither the incentive or opportunity to build their own campaign organizations.[45] Rather, candidates relied upon "a maze of state and local [party] organizations" to do the work of the campaign in the field,[46] while they used their party's national committee to provide them with political intelligence and advice, to act as a financial intermediary,[47] and to marshal the activities of state and local parties.

Although American parties have chiefly been electoral organizations, during the middle decades of the twentieth century they provided valuable services to presidents *between* elections, linking presidents to party elites inside and outside of Washington, D.C. In the 1940s and 1950s state and local party organizations in "traditional party states" such as Ohio and Pennsylvania possessed considerable influence over congressional careers. Thus, state and local party leaders were useful allies in organizing governing coalitions in Washington, D.C., and the party's national committee, as its Washington agent, served as the president's conduit to these organizations. As President-elect John F. Kennedy prepared to take office in 1960, he was advised by Democratic sage Clark Clifford, a veteran of the Truman presidency, that "the National Committee and its staff are an important instrument for the president. They assist the president in getting his views to the party leaders and receiving a return flow of support, and help on patronage and other personal problems with members of Congress and party leaders."[48]

In short, Democratic party organizations remained central to Truman's electoral fortunes and his prospects for governance, and they also played a central role in his 1948 reelection bid. Louis Johnson, treasurer of the Democratic National Committee, was Truman's financial intermediary to campaign contributors,[49] and the party's national committee provided much of the staff work for Truman's campaign, including advance work and speechwriting.[50] Suspicious of scientific opinion polling, Truman relied heavily upon politicians at the National Committee (and a coterie of party officials throughout the country) to supply him with intelligence about his electoral prospects. Truman consulted men like Leslie Biffle, "a Truman crony [and secretary of the Senate] who set out on a truck trip through West Virginia, Kentucky, Southern Ohio, and Illinois disguised as a chicken farmer to sound out grass roots sentiment."[51] Finally, Truman leaned heavily upon state and local Democratic organizations to furnish workers for the campaign[52] (rather than "issue activists") and the party's national committee to coordinate their work.

Truman looked to Democratic party organizations between elections, too. Beyond assisting the president's aides in the handling of political appointments, the party's national committee provided the president with assistance in nurturing support among organized groups within the party's coalition,[53] and, to a lesser degree, it assisted the president's staff in building support among members of the president's party on Capitol Hill by servicing the needs of congressmen (e.g., drafting speeches, securing job patronage).[54]

In short, given the electoral and governing assistance provided by the president's party, the potential costs of expanding his staff's size and capabilities — thereby undermining party prerogatives and alienating party notables — were considerable. Scrapping "Operation Best Brains," in contrast, denied Truman an opportunity to leave *his* stamp on the Truman administration by reaching out beyond the pool of candidates who put themselves forward or were put forward by traditional sources of candidates — departments and Democratic politicians. Nonetheless, Truman could muddle through the last eighteen months of the administration with a fairly large number of posts vacant or staff his administration with careerists who were largely sympathetic to the New Deal/Fair Deal agenda. That is what Truman did, relying more heavily than any previous administration on the career civil service to fill the political ranks of the executive branch.[55] This choice may have meant that Truman would forgo the political leverage and skills that "the best brains" from outside of government could have provided, but this was far less costly, and far more certain, than risking the political antagonisms that might have been created by the adoption of "Best Brains."

Exactly one decade later, in the spring of 1960, John F. Kennedy and his staff would be faced with the same choice: whether to expand the size and influence of their appointments staff, threatening the prerogatives of party officials, or to eschew this course. They reached the opposite conclusion and chose to build a White House staff for political appointments that was remarkably similar to the outlines of "Operation Best Brains." Lyndon Johnson, in turn, accelerated Kennedy's initiatives, rebuffing the protests of party notables, and by the mid-1960s the president's appointments staff had grown to more than a dozen aides, and its aggrandizement was hailed as a "change of permanent significance for the power position and the institutional apparatus of the presidency."[56]

THE EBBING FORTUNES OF PARTY: KENNEDY AND JOHNSON

Why were Kennedy and Johnson able to expand the size and reach of their White House staff in ways that Truman's aides could only furtively contemplate? What happened to make the expansion of the president's staff more attractive? The answer lies in the sharply reduced leverage of party figures. Between 1950 and the mid-1960s the role that parties played during elections and between them diminished appreciably.

The weakening hold of party organizations over presidential nominations was due, in part, to the expanding role of primary elections in the selection of convention delegates. Between Truman's election of 1948 and Johnson's in 1964, the proportion of delegates chosen through primaries grew gradually, from 36 percent (1948) to 51 percent (1964). More important, the institutional barriers that effectively prohibited candidates from seeking delegates though primaries, such as favorite son candidacies and "beauty contest" primaries, were eroding, and by 1964 fully 41 percent of all delegates were committed to candidates by primary contests.[57] These changes, coupled with the increased prominence of new campaign technologies such as opinion polling produced an important shift in nomination politics, substantially weakening the control of party leaders over nominations and strengthening the hand of individual candidates, primary voters, and the mass media. As early as the mid-1960s, prescient observers noted that "for the past twenty years a remarkable transformation in the process of nominating presidential candidates has been taking place in the United States. Since World War II, the presidential primary elections have become a major and sometimes crucial factor in capturing a party's nomination in an open presidential race."[58]

General election campaigns, too, had become much less heavily influenced by parties in the dozen years separating the Truman and Kennedy election contests. By 1960 both John Kennedy and Richard Nixon were far less dependent upon the fundraising capabilities of their parties than presidential candidates had been in the past. For example, the Democratic National Committee raised roughly three million dollars on Kennedy's behalf, but the candidate's own campaign organizations raised slightly more ($3.27 million).[59] Democratic party organizations were becoming less important, too, as a source of volunteers. In many areas of the country nonparty organizations (especially organized labor)[60] and political amateurs[61] had become equally important.

Moreover, candidates increasingly turned to professional pollsters and public relations consultants rather than party notables disguised as chicken farmers for political intelligence, political strategy, and campaign propaganda. Truman would not deign to base his campaign strategy or tactics on polls; John Kennedy, though, was a avid consumer of polls. Kennedy had Louis Harris conduct nearly fifty polls between the Democratic convention and the general election, and he used Harris's polls to make decisions about his campaign itinerary, advertising, campaign speeches, and policy positions.[62] Although Kennedy was compelled to rely upon state and local Democratic parties (and organized labor) for the routine work of campaigning, he was reluctant to cede control over the his campaign in the states to local parties, and he was loathe to let his party's national committee manage his national campaign.

Hence, Kennedy relied heavily upon personal emissaries to supervise and coordinate his campaign in the states,[63] and he assembled his own organization to manage the national campaign — the first campaign organization "staffed primarily by candidate loyalists rather than party regulars."[64] The party's national committee, meanwhile, was "relegated to a poor place in the shadows."[65]

Between elections, too, the president's party found that its fortunes were waning. The very same technologies that had begun to reshape electoral politics in the 1960s — professional public relations and public opinion polling — were becoming more important to governance as well. The ability of the national committee to meet these new presidential demands was limited: it had neither an extensive polling apparatus, nor a large public relations staff.[66] Significantly, Kennedy and Johnson chose not to develop these capabilities at their party's national committee — an organization that was only partly under their control — but to institutionalize this assistance in the White House Office. Although Kennedy and Johnson did relatively little to build a public relations apparatus within the White House Office[67] (at least in comparison to their successors), both were eager consumers of public opinion polling, and "after 1961 . . . the White House became a veritable warehouse stocked with the latest public opinion data."[68] Kennedy retained Louis Harris to provide him with a steady stream of postelection polls, and Johnson established the first "in-house" White House pollster, Oliver Quayle.[69]

Although the National Committee remained a "tool for getting his [the president's] view to the party leaders and receiving a return flow of support," its role as a liaison between presidents and members of their party was slowly being eroded by the accretion of political assistance within the White House Office. John Kennedy's Office of Congressional Relations (OCR), headed by Larry O'Brien, was substantially larger and more active than any of its predecessors,[70] and it absorbed two vital responsibilities once vested in the party's National Committee: servicing Capitol Hill patronage requests and keeping track of — and allocating — presidential favors. When, for example, Representative Bonner (D-N.C.) wanted to place "some people in janitor-level jobs at a Voice of America installation in Eastern North Carolina,"[71] he plied his case with Henry Hall Wilson, an O'Brien OCR aide responsible for southern Democrats, rather than with the party's national committee. And, naturally, as the White House Office absorbed this responsibility, it became the scorekeeper as well, rather than the national committee.[72]

Responsibility for liaison with state and local leaders, too, was gradually shifting away from the national committee and into the White House — into the hands of the president's appointments staff, Office of Congressional Relations,[73] and an informal coterie of political advisers headed by Kenneth O'Donnell, Kennedy's appointments secretary. As the reach of these aides expanded, party professionals around the country recognized that the Democratic National Committee was "out of the loop" on political appointments.

They quickly adapted and "went down the hall to Kenny [O'Donnell]" with many of the complaints and requests they had once carried to their party's national committee.[74] Reflecting on these developments Larry O'Brien observed: "The DNC was playing no meaningful role in advising the president. And, in a sense Dick Maguire and others [on the White House staff] were usurping the role that the DNC should have had. There was a flow of responsibility across the driveway there into the White House Office."[75]

Finally, the weakening claims of party were exacerbated by the evolution of the federal bureaucracy itself. As the executive branch grew in the postwar years, the thin layer of political posts atop the bureaucracy proliferated, and the thick bottom layer of federal field appointments was sharply reduced by spasms of reform. The number of assistant secretary posts doubled between 1910 and 1950, and doubled again in half the time between 1950 and 1970 (from 55 to 113).[76] Conversely, presidential appointments to field positions, which accounted for 98.5 percent of presidential appointments at the outset of Franklin Roosevelt's administration, were virtually eliminated by the 1960s.[77] For the leaders of party organizations, who "would rather have twenty-five labor jobs at a naval ordnance plant than three assistant secretaries"[78] — and whose reputation for supplying candidates of probity and competence was modest — the changing structure of federal appointments was especially important. On the one hand, the incentives for party organizations to protect their claims on the appointment process diminished. On the other hand, the incentives for presidents to exclude them grew, since the policy costs of losing control over assistant secretaryships are far greater than the costs of ceding control over postmasterships.

The Consequences of Ebbing Constraints

With the election of 1960 over and the Kennedy transition under way, Democratic party veterans did what they had always done: they set up an office at the headquarters of the Democratic National Committee and prepared to receive a deluge of importunings from Democratic contributors, campaign workers, and officials. Presidential confidants Clark Clifford and Richard Neustadt, looking back on the experience of the Roosevelt and Truman administrations, urged President-elect Kennedy to allow the DNC to take the lead, at least publicly, in the management of political appointments. Neustadt advised the president-elect that the Democratic National Committee should "be out in front to take the heat, pass the work, fend off the importunate, and soothe the disappointed."[79] Clark Clifford warned that "the flood of job-seekers will be enormous" and reminded Kennedy that "the National Committee will give the president a place to divert pressures."[80]

However, Kennedy spurned the assistance of his national party organization and instead created a personal organization for staffing the government, much as he had relied upon a personal political organization in his campaign to reach the White House. By relying upon his own staff rather than the assistance of the Democratic party, Kennedy hoped to put his own stamp on appointments in a way that none of his predecessors had. As Kennedy aide Larry O'Brien recalled: "We approached this administration asking, 'How do you get control over this massive bureaucracy—control in the sense that it is directed in its activities to the president's interests?' If we can get control of the top 600 or 400 or 300 jobs, if we can only get this, get these people properly placed, then we will have some degree of control."[81] Freed to a then-unprecedented degree from the claims of his party—and endowed with a personal political organization with which to carry out the staffing of his administration—Kennedy broke with the experience of his Democratic predecessors.

As the transition began, Kennedy deputized two sets of aides from his campaign organization to begin a "talent search" for presidential appointees. One group of aides, headed by Robert Kennedy, consisted of the president's senior political advisers, the men who had managed Kennedy's ascent to the presidency, including Larry O'Brien, Richard Donahue, and Ralph Dungan (the "Irish Mafia," as journalists dubbed them). Their role was thoroughly traditional: they were responsible for the placement of the men—and, very rarely, women—who had been important backers of Kennedy's campaign, and to winnow, clear, and place candidates who had originated from leaders within party circles. These aides were responsible, as well, for "patronage management," that is, for ensuring that the regional, ethnic, and factional balance was maintained in staffing the administration.

More significant, though, was the other side of the Kennedy "talent hunt," a second team of aides headed by Kennedy's brother-in-law Sargent Shriver. It was they who were charged with finding and placing "New Frontier Types" throughout the Kennedy administration, thereby ensuring that the executive branch would be "directed in its activities to the president's interests." These aides were not party politicians but denizens of Washington law firms, foundations, civil rights groups, and universities who were also members of the Kennedy entourage.[82] Instructed to "comb the universities and the professions and the civil rights movement,"[83] Shriver's group set to work tapping not elected officials but their "egghead constituency." Working together with cabinet officials, "we'd go through our files for the other top jobs in his department. Of course we would stay up all night and work hard as soon as somebody was appointed; we'd know that department was coming up. Then we'd really call everybody so we'd have as much as we could as far down in the department as we could."[84]

Although both sets of aides were housed at the Democratic National Committee and worked alongside party professionals, they quickly overshadowed the DNC, effectively "supplant[ing] the national party organization"[85] in the staffing of the Kennedy administration much as they had displaced Democratic party organizations during the campaign. Predictably, the leaders of Democratic party organizations were less than enamored of Kennedy's actions. As Harris Wofford, an aide to Sargent Shriver recounted, party politicians clearly felt outmanned by Kennedy's talent hunt: "John Bailey [chairman of the Democratic National Committee] summarized it all to us one day. We were having a meeting and he said, 'I know the problem. Your guys are generally better than my guys. I keep telling the people that we'll have no trouble competing with Sarge's gang if we can just get people who are as good as his people. Then our people will have added weight on their side. [But] we can't come up with these guys.' "[86] Bailey and other party professionals, such as Sam Brightman (director of publicity at the DNC),[87] felt not only outmanned but threatened. Nonetheless, their concern did not spill over into active opposition to the talent hunt: Shriver's staff was but one participant among many in the staffing of the Kennedy administration, and the Talent Hunt was short-lived.

By the day of Kennedy's inauguration, the files of Kennedy's talent hunt were unceremoniously dumped in Adam Yarmolinsky's garage, and the talent hunt staff was dispersed throughout the White House and departments. In a reversal of their preinaugural arrangements, Kennedy and his senior aides opted for highly decentralized and haphazard arrangements for staffing the remaining vacancies in the administration: Larry O'Brien, head of Kennedy's Office of Congressional Liaison, would chair a screening committee of Kennedy's political aides and John Bailey, DNC chairman, would winnow candidates for appointment proffered by Democratic politicians. In short, Kennedy's White House staff for handling appointments would be virtually indistinguishable from Truman's.

Not for long. Just months into the Kennedy presidency, voices were raised throughout the administration urging the president to reestablish a significant presidential presence in political appointments — to "put the talent hunt that occurred during the transition on a permanent basis."[88] Adam Yarmolinsky, for example, proposed that a small, expert staff — insulated from narrowly partisan pressures — review the quality of departmental candidates for presidential appointments (and "periodic samplings" of their schedule C candidates), learning thereby "where particular vigilance must be exercised" by the White House staff. Moreover, he suggested, the staff should "receive suggestions of first rate people who should be brought into the administration," thereby "preserving the public image of the Administration that the talent hunt has helped to create."[89] Another junior Defense Department aide, Joseph Califano, was similarly dissatisfied with the narrowly partisan status quo arrangements. Califano pointed out that he had been contacted by "scores of capable young men" who were "inspired by the New Frontier" but bereft of political connections that would permit them to gain the support of the heavily partisan screening group.[90] Others inside the government, including Budget Bureau Director David Bell, White House aide Fred Dutton, and Civil Service Commissioner John Macy — a veteran of the "Operation Best Brains" deliberations a decade earlier — voiced similar concerns. They, too, urged that a new staff be established *outside* of Larry O'Brien's Congressional Relations Office so that political appointments could be "depoliticized" and put to use to serve the *managerial* needs of the presidency.

Kennedy and his inner circle embraced the idea, and by August 1961 the president's senior aides had summoned Dan Fenn from Cambridge and asked him "to serve as a continuing recruiter, picking up where the talent search had left off."[91] In short, they had embraced the choice — an expanded White House presence in staffing the government — that Truman's inner circle had rejected a decade earlier.

Best Brains at Last?

Two weeks after his arrival in Washington, D.C., Dan Fenn offered his boss, Ralph Dungan, this assessment of the role that a presidential personnel staff might play in the Kennedy administration: "In the broadest sense, the objectives of this effort are to . . . suggest highly competent people who share the President's fundamental political and operating philosophy for major governmental positions, thereby to strengthen the president's control over the government [and] improve the management of the government."[92] How to do this, though, was a puzzle; after all, no one had ever built a White House appointments staff of any consequence. Thus, Fenn set to work by soliciting ideas from Washington insiders, beginning with veterans of the Truman White House. Their practices, Fenn quickly concluded, were ill-suited to "strengthening the president's control over the government." Fenn recalls: "We talked to Marty Friedman and Don Dawson [of the Truman personnel staff] and Bob Hampton [of the Eisenhower personnel staff]. . . . It was perfectly clear that it had really been a slapdash operation, depending much more on what was coming in, particularly from the Hill, than on any kind of even semi-conscientious, conscious attempt to say 'Alright, what do we need in this job, and where can we find him?'"[93]

Though Fenn could not rely upon the experience of his White House predecessors, he quickly discovered a group of Washington veterans who were eager to remedy the "perennial underdevelopment of the personnel function of the [White House] office."[94] This group, spearheaded by seasoned Washingtonians like Civil Service (CSC) Chair John Macy and supported by the Brookings Conference on Personnel Management, seized the opportunity they had been patiently waiting for. "I had only been in Washington for about 6 minutes," Fenn recalled, "when John Macy called up."[95] Macy offered Fenn a list of CSC staffers from which he could choose in assembling a staff, as well as his ideas about how to organize a staff, a product of more than a decade of experience with high-level governmental staffing.[96] The Brookings Institution, which had earlier underwritten extensive transition planning, was equally eager to participate. It provided Fenn with its yet-unpublished research on appointment politics, *The Assistant Secretaries*, and organized a series of conferences at which Fenn and his aides could meet with "Fulbright sorts" from previous administrations and the public administration community to discuss the problems of building a more orderly and presidency-centered appointments process.

Over the next few months Fenn repeatedly drew on their assistance and began to carve out a role for himself and his staff within the Kennedy White House. He moved slowly and cautiously, adding only one professional staffer during his first year in the White House, chosen from the staff of the Civil Service Commission, and two others in the second year of his stay, both of whom were veterans of the Budget Bureau.[97] Moreover, Fenn's staff confined its attention to a small number of vacancies, recruiting candidates for approximately thirty-five to forty posts in his first year on the White House staff, approximately a third of open posts.[98]

In fact, Fenn's role is best understood as one defined in antithesis to O'Brien's staff and to his predecessors in the Truman and Eisenhower administrations. Fenn's staff would not handle low-level appointments but confine its attention to either presidentially appointed positions or positions below this level that were of special concern to the president, such as Agency for International Development mission chiefs.[99] In trying to fill these posts, Fenn's operation would not "take whatever was coming across the transom from political sources" or try to find posts for deserving supporters, acting as a placement agency for office-seekers backed by powerful politicians.[100] Rather, the staff worked "from the job to the man": it began by assessing the requirements of the job and its relationship to the president's program and then recruited candidates appropriate to the position. They learned about the demands of the job by leaning heavily on trusted program experts in departments and budget examiners from the Bureau of the Budget. Once this investigation was completed, they recruited the right person for the post. Candidates were recruited and assessed by tapping a "contact network" consisting of a few hundred knowledgeable, trusted, and sympathetic sources located around the country, chiefly journalists, academics, and notables from foundations and leading law firms — not party figures.[101] Finally, staff support would be necessary. In light of the role carved out for the staff, the appropriate place to find a staff would not be the candidate's campaign organization, as it had been in the past. Rather, staff would be drawn from the institutionalized presidency: from the Budget Bureau and Foreign Service. These men would bring a passion for anonymity, deep familiarity with government programs, and a predisposition to act as "honest brokers" between the White House and departments.

Fenn's relationship with the party's national committee was far different than that of his predecessors in the Truman administration. Fenn's staff granted Democratic politicians, particularly those at the DNC, less access than Donald Dawson had. Fenn and his aides were not inclined to solicit the advice or recommendations of party figures at the national committee.[102] Candidates proffered by party leaders met with skepticism and disdain rather than serious consideration. Reflecting on the inability of party sources to provide them with "serious" candidates, Fenn and his aides commented:

Fenn: They [party figures] don't have the people.
Sherman: It is a problem for them to go out and locate a guy who is technically qualified in his field.
Barrett: They don't give a goddamn.
Scanlon: They don't need to.
Sherman: But at the same time they are knocking down the doors to place somebody's uncle.
Fenn: At a GS-9 [a low-level patronage post].[103]

Another veteran of the staff recalls that "John Bailey would always be coming over with a list of names. I'd say, 'Sure, John,' and go about my business without a second thought to his list."[104]

How did Democratic party leaders, particularly the party's national committee, respond to Fenn's efforts? Understandably, they were not champions of Fenn's staff. None offered the sort of encomiums that they had for Truman's appointment aides or described them as "their ally." Rather, Fenn freely acknowledged that "I wasn't one of John Bailey's favorite people."[105] One Kennedy appointments staffer proudly explained why: "John Bailey has a fixed opinion about our office: that we have done him no service in the past, and we will not do him any service in the future."[106]

Nonetheless, the elaboration of a White House appointments staff did not elicit sustained and open opposition of party figures at the national committee and elsewhere: Kennedy's White House aides had made an indirect and rather cautious advance on the prerogatives of party, not a frontal assault. In deference to the constraints that party claimants continued to impose upon the White House, Fenn avoided direct challenges to two remaining bastions of *local* job patronage, the Justice Department and the Post Office Department—the federal appointments that party leaders were most keenly interested in.[107] Instead, Fenn's staff focused its energies on positions that had relatively little electoral value to party leaders.[108] Moreover, Fenn's staff was far from monopolizing White House staff work on political appointments. DNC Chair John Bailey and other party figures were able to find solicitude elsewhere in the White House Office, particularly from a separate patronage staff that was housed within the Congressional Liaison Office.[109] Soon, however, a much more direct challenge to the vestigial prerogatives of party would present itself: the Johnson presidency.

THE JOHNSON ADMINISTRATION

After months of temporizing following Kennedy's death, Lyndon Johnson began to consider how he would assemble a Johnson administration. Johnson spurned proposals by advisers that he draw upon the services of "headhunting" or management consulting firms (such as McKinsey) to assist him in staffing the presidency, arguing that they lacked the political sophistication to help him in staffing the government.[110] Johnson wanted a White House appointments staff that was politically discerning — not a staff that was an appendage of party politics, but rather an appointments staff that was politically sophisticated in the way of *program* politics, that is, capable of ensuring that his appointees were willing and able to lead the bureaucracy in building and implementing Johnson programs. By the time he was elected, Johnson concluded that the solution to his problem was nearby: he would expand and enhance the existing White House appointments staff, but under a leadership with no ties to Johnson's predecessor and rival, John Kennedy.

Five days after his extraordinary victory over Goldwater, Johnson met with the chairman of the Civil Service Commission, John Macy, and asked him to head up his White House appointments staff.[111] Johnson proposed that Macy "wear two hats": that he continue to serve as chair of the Civil Service Commission and also become Johnson's chief talent scout, leading an expanded and rationalized White House appointments staff. Macy, who had been a tireless advocate of efforts to remedy the "perennial underdevelopment" of the president's role in staffing the government, accepted Johnson's offer with alacrity. Within three days Macy had moved into Ralph Dungan's office in the West Wing of the White House. For the next four years Macy would begin his day at the Civil Service Commission, working there from 8:00 A.M. until 2:00, then working at the White House from 2:00 until 9:00 P.M.[112]

In the weeks that followed, Macy met often with Johnson, sometimes traveling to his ranch in Texas, gaining a clear picture of the criteria Johnson wished to follow in staffing his administration, and reorganizing Dungan's staff to fit the needs of its new master. From their discussions three ground rules emerged. First, department heads would be introduced to Macy personally and instructed that Macy's office would be the channel through which *all* candidates and documents must flow to the Oval Office. Macy, the "systematic channel to the president," would "preserve the president's options."[113] Second, Johnson made it clear that senior policymaking officials were to be "the president's people; he is the appointing officer and they are part of his administration."[114] To ensure that appointees would "pass muster as members of the Johnson administration," department and agency heads were directed to collaborate with Macy in "seeking candidates for presidential appointments."[115] Third, Macy would not service partisan constituencies or provide Johnson with narrowly political judgments. "I am aware that your political judgment probably isn't very good," Johnson told Macy. Johnson himself would "make the political judgments."[116] Macy was instructed to provide him with candidates who were highly capable, "committed to the programs that they would be administering," and loyal to Johnson personally.[117]

In keeping with these guidelines, Macy rebuilt the Kennedy appointments staff. Macy began by expanding the size of the staff from four professionals to seven, drawing his staff from the Bureau of the Budget (BOB) and Foreign Service (as Dungan and Fenn had).[118] The BOB "was the best source because [BOB staff members] had been budget reviewers . . . and really knew the departments. And besides that, the Budget Bureau tended to be where the top talent [in the government] was."[119] Macy also moved to upgrade the staff's expertise by introducing a rudimentary division of labor: "I organized the office so that I had two desk officers who divided up the government. Each became a specialist in his part of the government. He knew the key people in those departments and agencies in his sector. He knew the sources of talent for the jobs that had to be filled" and the vacancies that occurred in his area."[120]

Macy reorganized the staff in a second, equally important way: he eliminated the Kennedy patronage staff with the Office of Congressional Relations. The Kennedy patronage staff, directed by Dorothy Davies, had clashed with the Civil Service Commission in Kennedy's term, and Macy, who viewed the patronage staff as "a bunch of political hacks" was eager to disperse it. Given the go-ahead by Johnson, Macy forced the staff members to retire or move to patronage posts in the departments and agencies, and he took over, winnowed, and computerized its files of job seekers.

"A Scarlet Letter around My Neck"

What were the repercussions of Johnson's ambitious moves? Not surprisingly, the way in which Johnson and Macy molded the appointments staff evoked bitter reactions from party professionals. Veteran party figures accustomed to the practices of Roosevelt and Truman, such as Jim Farley,[121] India Edwards,[122] Katy Louchheim, and John Bailey[123] — the titular head of the DNC — were stunned and angry with Johnson's and Macy's disregard for the claims of party organizations. Louchheim, seeking a post in the State Department, blasted Macy's antipathy towards faithful party servants such as she, alleging that Macy had denied her an assistant secretary post in the State Department because she had served in the Democratic National Committee.

"I'm going to say in this book I'm writing," Louchheim vowed. "I felt as if I had a scarlet letter hung around my neck."[124] John Bailey, longtime leader of the Connecticut Democratic organization and DNC chairman from 1961 to 1968, was no less dismayed. Meeting with Johnson after the disastrous 1966 mid-term elections, Bailey argued that Johnson was slighting his party, showing only a minimum of concern for the Democratic National Committee — simply putting it on notice before proceeding with nominations, and often virtually demanding clearances. Appointments in Connecticut, Bailey lamented, were not handled this way. Johnson was unmoved and pointed an accusing finger instead at party regulars and the DNC, who were unable to "furnish qualified persons" that he needed to staff the government.[125]

Still more telling was Johnson's (and Macy's) response to Democratic party figures more closely linked to the president, such as Cliff Carter, hand-picked by Johnson to run the DNC, and Jim Rowe, a longtime political ally and Johnson's chief adviser in his 1960 bid for the Democratic nomination. Carter was quickly dissatisfied with the national committee's meager role in handling appointments. He demanded that Macy send prospective appointees in person to the DNC prior to their nomination, thereby permitting the DNC to engage in more careful screening of presidential appointees — and more credible credit-claiming.[126] Macy and his staff recoiled at the idea and were backed up by Johnson, who quickly rejected it.[127] Throughout the administration Carter remained dissatisfied, and "he constantly bitched," one Macy aide recalled. But in contrast to what happened in decades past, his bitching went unheeded, save for an occasional call from Johnson to Macy pointing out that "Carter really wants this one."[128]

Jim Rowe, who served in Johnson's campaigns of 1960 and 1964 and was a principal adviser for Johnson's abortive 1968 reelection bid, was similarly disenchanted with Johnson's and Macy's disregard for the need to sustain party organizations. After Rowe politely submitted lists of Independents for Johnson-Humphrey and Lawyers for Johnson-Humphrey in January 1964, the former consisting of "*big* businessmen," Rowe heard little from Macy. In the months that followed Rowe peppered Macy's staff (and Johnson himself) with the names of Johnson campaign supporters — to no avail. In April 1965 Rowe wrote a sharp note to Macy, with a copy to Johnson, pointing out that "I still have not been able to get one of the Citizens [for Johnson-Humphrey] people who worked so hard for the president appointed to *anything*. Some of these men are as good or better than the men that you appointed yesterday. [Perhaps some of them can be appointed] or perhaps you can train some of these career men to run the political campaign in 1968. (It ain't as easy as you government people appear to think it is.)"[129] Johnson did not bend but instead defended his staff, and by Rowe's recollection "the president was on the phone the next day giving me hell" for pressuring Macy.[130]

Rowe continued to bombard Macy's office with requests, but his memos were invariably written in a frustrated and cynical voice — asking Macy "not to hold it *against* her" [his candidate for HEW's assistant secretary for education] that she ran Educators for Johnson-Humphrey."[131] Another of Johnson's closest political aides claims that "Rowe couldn't get anybody appointed — except maybe Missy Lehand [FDR's personal secretary]."[132] Rowe's only vindication came after Johnson's presidency: "At least once a month or so since [the end of the Johnson presidency] Rowe told Macy that his 'emphasis on merit ruined the Democratic party,' and that 'we would never have had '68 . . . if Lyndon Johnson had been advised to appoint more out-and-out Democratic politicians.' "[133]

To be sure, Macy's staff was not entirely free from the obligation to service political claims that the president saw as worthy of attention, nor was Macy a political novice. Macy himself recognized the president's larger political needs and sought to accommodate them. "John was a much better politician than we expected," one of his aides recalled. "Johnson would call Macy when he had an important guest — a campaign contributor — in his office and ask Macy to find something for him. Macy would play along and agree, even though no job was open. Then for a year he would correspond with them, finally saying, 'Jeez, no job is available.' Macy was prepared to take the heat, he was super at it."[134] Macy's staff did perform "courtesy interviews" of candidates referred to it by congressional Democrats, the DNC, and White House aides, and it referred candidates to departments and agencies.[135] However, its courtesy interviews were fairly infrequent (perhaps a half-dozen weekly) and its referrals were circumspect. One veteran of the Macy staff describes referrals this way:

We made up our minds very early that unless the White House specifically asked us to *find* a job for somebody, we were simply going to refer them to the agencies, and we made that very clear. The first time I talked to him [Red White, executive director of the CIA] I said, "Red, we're not pushing these people. If we do have one we're pushing, I'll let you know, so that you're aware of it. If you can use these people, fine. If you can't, no problem." And he appreciated that very much.[136]

Moreover, when directed by Johnson, Macy's staff placed supporters to whom Johnson felt obligated. After the dismal showing of the Democrats in the 1966 mid term, for example, Johnson directed Macy to place defeated Democratic incumbents. Of course Macy complied. Nonetheless, in comparison to its predecessors, Macy's staff was neither trained nor organized to serve the claims of other politicians, and it saw these activities as an inconsequential avenue for building political support.[137] More important, Macy committed less of his staff's time and reputation to these activities than did any of his predecessors.

In sum, Johnson was able to slough off the claims of party in a way that Harry Truman would not have contemplated and Dwight Eisenhower would have envied. Johnson's initial calculation—that the costs of poaching on some party prerogatives and ignoring others would be smaller than its benefits— proved to be correct. Free to ignore its prerogatives, Johnson came surprisingly close to creating the *beau ideal* of the public administration community: a White House appointments staff that drew upon the "neutral competence" of the institutionalized presidency to further presidential leadership in the executive branch.

REPUBLICANS, TOO

The attenuation of party claims on the presidency and the aggrandizement of the White House Office at the expense of political parties is not simply a product of the proclivities of Democratic presidents. Rather, a brief comparison of two Republican presidencies, the Eisenhower and Nixon presidencies, reveals that the aggrandizement of the White House Office is rooted in basic institutional changes: the changing shape of electoral politics in the second half of the twentieth century.

Dwight Eisenhower

> *I don't think he [Eisenhower] ever quite got to the point of feeling that the Republican party organization amounted to much.*
> —Bertha Adkins, RNC Vice-Chair

Perhaps no president has more clearly embodied an antiparty animus than Dwight Eisenhower. Eisenhower's disdain for party politics, rooted in a lifetime of military service and his commitment to "corporate liberalism," was thorough and abiding. Moreover, given the extraordinary public standing of Eisenhower in the postwar years, he was able to conduct a more highly personalized campaign—one less rooted in party—than were any of his predecessors. As he began his presidency, Eisenhower signalled that he was going to act on his antiparty animus: he forbade the chair of the Republican National Committee, Arthur Summerfield, from simultaneously serving as Postmaster General and chair of the national committee, as party chairs had done throughout the twentieth century.[138] Moreover, Eisenhower chose not to appoint a veteran of Republican party politics as his aide for political appointments; instead, he installed Charles Willis, a political *naif* who was the cofounder of Citizens for Eisenhower, a nonpartisan group founded to draft Eisenhower.[139] Willis, unsullied by partisan politics, would "handle [appointments] on a quality basis rather than a purely political basis" as they had been handled before.[140]

How, then, would the Republican party organizations gain access to federal appointments — appointments they had been denied during twenty long years of Democratic presidencies? They would have to fend for themselves. The Eisenhower White House would not collaborate with the party's national committee to orchestrate a system of patronage management on their behalf, as the Democratic administration preceding them had done. As Paul Van Riper observed, "There was no political planning. There was no [James] Farley, no organized clearance system for patronage problems, no clear decision such as had been made by FDR, to use the patronage as a 'steel-pointed pic,' and no plan to take care of the faithful."[141] Seen from the perspective of the Eisenhower White House, the strategic management of patronage was not "essential to governing," as Donald Dawson believed, but a liability to be avoided. Eisenhower aimed to shirk the political obligations to which his predecessors had acquiesced — obligations which they sought to turn to their own advantage. The White House would remain above the fray, and its staff would simply act in a ministerial capacity, processing the documents that accompany presidential appointments. If the party faithful wanted to secure appointments, they could go to the Republican National Committee, and the RNC, in turn, could solicit departments and agencies on their behalf. But, Eisenhower cautioned his cabinet secretaries, the Republican National Committee should *not* enjoy privileged access; instead, "suggestions made by [RNC Chair] Len Hall should simply receive the same consideration as others."[142] Eisenhower and Sherman Adams did not embrace a positive, leading role for the White House staff in political appointments, as the "Best Brains" plan had. Nonetheless, it envisaged a negative role for the White House that was equally unsatisfactory from the vantage point of Republican party organizations — a role it was ultimately incapable of carrying through in the face of party opposition.

Quieting the Clamor

These arrangements failed badly. Left to their own devices, the executives who led departments and agencies responded fitfully — if at all — to the importunings of the Republican party. Members of the Republican National Committee angrily complained that they had accumulated between 10,000 and 12,000 job requests in the opening weeks of the administration but had virtually no success in placing faithful party workers.[143] Those who did receive federal appointments, party leaders observed, did not represent the men and women who had voted for Eisenhower — and whose loyalties they hoped to solidify into a Republican presidential majority. As party chair Len Hall complained, presidential appointments during the opening months of the administration were "economically, geographically, and politically badly out of balance," and there was "next to no recognition of our so-called ethnic or minority groups."[144] Eisenhower supporters throughout the country complained that their service on behalf of the president had earned them no more consideration than the president's foes within the Republican party—and sometimes less.[145] In short, the Eisenhower White House was faced with fierce and sustained criticism from Republicans around the country.

To make matters worse, congressional Republicans joined the fray. Acting in part on behalf of local Republican parties—to which they were still wed—and in part out of a desire to purge the executive branch of bureaucrats who had been open and enthusiastic partisans of the New Deal/Fair Deal agenda, congressional Republicans began to take matters in their own hands. Endowed with control over both chambers of Congress for the first time since 1930, congressional Republicans proposed to sharply increase the number of posts outside the civil service by shifting the line between political appointments and the career service downward—to "unblanket" the thousands of civil servants who had entered during wartime emergencies and were subsequently awarded competitive status, vastly increasing the number of posts available to Republicans on Capitol Hill and at the national committee.

Hemmed in by the claims of other politicians who were too important to ignore, Eisenhower's senior aides capitulated only weeks into the Eisenhower presidency, assuming political responsibilities they had initially sought to shirk, granting Republican party officials (particularly the national committee) a measure of access they had sought to avoid. In short, they established a White House appointments staff that was remarkably similar to that which had served Harry Truman.

On March 31, 1953, Eisenhower issued Executive Order 10440, creating a new category of political appointments, "schedule C" posts: jobs that were "policy determining or confidential in nature."[146] Unfortunately for the administration, the change did little to relieve partisan pressures. Jobs were put into schedule C only after departments made the request—and the Civil Service Commission concluded that the posts were "policy determining or confidential." Republicans alleged that the civil service commissioners in the departments and agencies were Democratic careerists who refused to propose that slots be reclassified, that the Civil Service Commission was unwilling to approve departmental requests, and that the few posts put into schedule C were being filled by Democratic careerists rather than deserving Republicans.

Responding to these complaints, in December 1953 the White House negotiated an agreement with agency heads creating a system of "political personnel officers." Each department, the agreement stipulated, "should have a person at the top policy level to be responsible for matters over and above routine administration ordinarily carried on by [career] Personnel Directors, who should be regarded as technicians."[147] These new jobs, of course, "would be filled by Republicans who are sympathetic towards policies of the administration."[148] At the newly established Department of Health, Education, and Welfare, for example, personnel responsibilities had been the bailiwick of the senior careerist in the department, Assistant Secretary for Administration Rufus Miles. Miles was stripped of responsibility for personnel decisions, and these were entrusted instead to a political appointee, Undersecretary Nelson Rockefeller.[149] Moreover, the White House demanded that the Civil Service Commission regularly inform it of how many posts it had put into schedule C. Even these arrangements alone were not enough, because they offered no assurance that departments and agencies would offer newly vacant posts to the right people: deserving Republicans. Some departments, such as the Department of Defense, had proven stubbornly indifferent to the claims of the party in filling newly created posts.[150]

Moreover, the Eisenhower White House reestablished a close working relationship with the leading spokesperson of the nation's Republican parties, the chair of the Republican National Committee, restoring the sort of access that presidents had extended to their parties in the past. By mid-1953 Eisenhower's assistant for political appointments, Charles Willis, met daily with RNC Chair Len Hall and his staff at the RNC headquarters. Willis recalls, "Every day, invariably, I would walk across the street to the Republican National Committee headquarters at Farragaut Square and sit down with Len Hall and his staff." In the meetings Hall would propose slates of candidates for appointment, inquire about the progress of candidates "in the pipeline,"[151] and learn which posts were about to be reclassified (to schedule C) by the Civil Service Commission.[152] Willis, in turn, would solicit Hall's advice and assistance in resolving conflicts among Republicans on Capitol Hill and in local organizations[153] and submit candidates who needed to be "cleared" by local Republican organizations prior to their nomination.[154]

So consumed was Willis with servicing the needs of party claimants that he devised the "Willis Plan,"[155] which called for the White House to act as a clearinghouse for schedule C jobs (and GS-14 to GS-18 posts *within* the career civil service system as well). Departments were instructed to notify the White House of vacancies in schedule C (or other exempt positions) and to wait sixty days before filling these posts. The White House, in turn, would notify the Republican National Committee (and Capitol Hill Republicans) of job vacancies, thereby permitting them to compete for the openings. Although Willis boasted to Eisenhower and Sherman Adams that "86,665 jobs had been made available to Republicans" through his plan,[156] in fact the plan yielded little fruit. Departments and agencies were loathe to accept candidates referred to them, fearing them to be "party hacks," and public disclosure of the plan — particularly its ambition to fill career posts — elicited a storm of protest and forced Eisenhower to publicly repudiate the plan and its namesake, Willis. Even so, the broad outlines that emerged in the opening months of the Eisenhower administration — of a modest White House staff that "cranked in a much more political side of the consideration" — were sustained until the closing days of Eisenhower's presidency in 1961.[157] In short, the Eisenhower White House had returned to the practices of its predecessor, the Truman presidency, notwithstanding Eisenhower's personal conviction that the Republican party organization didn't "amount to much."

Richard Nixon

Richard Nixon's presidency unmistakably marks the transition from party-centered to candidate-centered election politics and illustrates the extraordinary freedom with which Nixon, free from the claims of party, could organize White House staff work on political appointments. Richard Nixon nurtured his own political organization to pursue his party's nomination and the presidency in 1968, but it was a small and rudimentary organization compared to the candidate organizations that followed it or the Goldwater organization that preceded it. As James Reichley observed, "Nixon conducted a largely traditional campaign for the Republican nomination [in 1968], putting together a coalition of Republican state organizations supplemented by support from some of the conservative nonprofessional activists on the party's right wing."[158] In the general election, too, Nixon relied heavily upon existing Republican organizations. Fundraising for his campaign was carried on largely under the auspices of the Republican National Finance Committee.[159] And Nixon "continued to entrust campaign work at the grass roots level mainly to Republican regulars . . . [and to rely] heavily upon the machinery constructed by [Ray] Bliss [RNC Chair]."[160]

The process of staffing Nixon's presidency was initially a hybrid as well, neither entirely candidate-centered, as his successors' would be, nor party-centered, as was the case for his mid-century predecessors. After eking out a victory in the 1968 presidential election, two sets of Nixon aides set to work staffing the incoming Nixon administration. Ensconced at the elegant Pierre Hotel in Manhattan, the nucleus of the Nixon campaign organization — H. R. Haldeman, John Mitchell, and Peter Flanigan — was charged with overseeing the "top end of the plum book," the senior policymaking positions in the government, while in Washington, D.C., another staffing group, headed by Harry Flemming, was assigned to handle the "bottom end of the plum book," including low-level presidential appointments and nonpresidential appointments.

The Republican National Committee itself played no role in the transition staffing of the Nixon administration. The national committee, leaderless after the departure of Ray Bliss, "was pretty much a nonfactor; they weren't really a part of the thing."[161] However, Flemming's group was closely tied to Republican party organizations: Flemming himself had worked at the national committee during the campaign, and his staff consisted of men who were veterans of Republican party politics, such as Robert Mardian and Dick

Herman.[162] Mardian, for example, had played a leading role in the Arizona Republican party and served as Goldwater's western field director prior to serving as Nixon's western regional political director in 1968. Hence, Mardian "knew who all the people were out there" in Republican organizations, and "[party leaders] sought him out," as they did others on Flemming's staff, as their representative inside the Nixon transition.[163] In short, the working relationship between Republican party organizations and the Nixon organization, although not mediated by the party's national committee, was marked by harmony rather than acrimony. The opposite would be the case in 1972.

Once the Nixon administration was under way, Flemming's personnel work on behalf of the president moved from a temporary to a permanent footing, and the outlines of a thoroughly traditional—and circumscribed—staff emerged.[164] Flemming's staff was dissimilar in magnitude to Truman's or Eisenhower's, but its orientation and methods of operation—and relationship to party organizations—were remarkably similar to theirs. Unfamiliar with the precedents of the Kennedy and Johnson White House staffs and deeply suspicious of seeking their counsel, Flemming relied instead upon the advice of Eisenhower's White House aides to fashion Nixon's appointments staff. Following their advice, Flemming assembled a staff whose members were tied to Republican party politics and organized it to facilitate the servicing of political claimants rather than to exercise policy control over the executive branch. There was no division of labor among the staff members by policy areas or agencies as there had been in the Johnson White House. Rather, the staff was divided into two units, a placement staff and a clearance staff. The placement staff "funneled job requests, resumes, and congressional referrals—the whole thing—down to liaisons in departments,"[165] claiming credit for placing the candidates championed by key politicians and campaign supporters. The clearance staff, in turn, cleared prospective nominees with congressional Republicans and the national committee (and it, in turn, with local Republican organizations). It aimed to mitigate conflict with other politicians and to "touch base" with important allies, that is, to acknowledge their importance to the president.

"We Never Have Any Goddamn Discipline around Here"

Throughout the first eighteen months of his presidency Nixon and his senior aides were bitterly disappointed with the his inability to exercise leadership of the executive branch. Said one Nixon White House aide, the department and agencies of the executive branch "were not marching to the president's drumbeat. I think that it detracts from the long-term credibility of the administration if you have a lot of people who are not marching to the president's drumbeat. I mean it discredits your authority."[166] Nixon and his senior staffers came to the conclusion that the inability of the department to "march to the president's beat" stemmed from the way that they had chosen to staff the administration: with too much attention to the needs of other politicians, including party leaders, and too little direction from the center. By autumn of 1970, persistent criticism of Flemming's staff work on political appointments had turned to action: H. R. Haldeman and Charles Colson asked George Bell, a veteran of Flemming's staff, to evaluate the staff's work. Bell, echoing the conclusions reached by Kennedy and Johnson staffers — now rediscovered by the Nixon White House — argued that the purpose of a presidential staff "is to assist the president to gain and exercise control over the government." The Flemming staff

has failed to achieve this objective because it is burdened with far too many activities of a constituent service nature [e.g. serving Republican party organizations and Capitol Hill Republicans] to make such an achievement possible. Except for [three of its members], the staff is engaged in the processing of boards and commissions, political clearances, and routine paperwork. Of the three named, only a small portion of their time is devoted to initiatives in filling significant positions.[167]

In short, by hewing to the practices of the past — by serving the claims of politicians other than the president — the president's staff had served *the president's* needs badly.

The solution, Nixon's senior aides concluded, was a far larger and more powerful appointments staff, one that surpassed the wildest imaginings of those who planned "Operation Best Brains" or worked for presidents Kennedy and Johnson. The new Nixon appointments staff, as envisioned by Frederic Malek, would subordinate and segregate aides who serviced the claims of Republican politicians to aides who tended to "presidential management," and it would substitute men and women drawn from business management and personnel recruitment for the "hacks" who had peopled the Flemming staff.

Equally important, though, was the way that Malek carried out the reconstruction of the presidential personnel staff, for it showed how completely atrophied were the claims of party: Truman's aides scuttled plans for expanding the staff rather than risk the displeasure of party leaders, and Kennedy's aides trod gingerly as they expanded the reach of the president's staff beyond its traditional bounds; Nixon's aides, by way of contrast, simply confronted party officials with a fait accompli. H. R. Haldeman and Fred Malek neither consulted with party officials at the Republican National Committee as they laid their plans nor even tried to anticipate the response of party leaders, as White House aides before them had. Instead, Malek waited until mid-March 1971 to sort out his relationship with the Republican National Committee — three months after he had taken over as Nixon's appointments chief![168]

What made it possible for Nixon and his staff to show such scant regard for the interests of the Republican party? At the same time that Nixon and his aides were reassessing the relationship of the White House to the executive branch and planning to centralize decisionmaking in a vastly expanded White House Office, they were also reassessing the Republican party's usefulness to Nixon. As Nixon's first term progressed, he and his aides became increasingly certain that successful presidential leadership turned on the use of modern instruments of politics, especially domination of the electronic media.[169] The Republican party, H. R. Haldeman remarked with scorn, "will never amount to anything." Reelection, too, could best be pursued independently of party, Nixon and his aides concluded. Hence, in the opening months of 1972 the Nixon White House poured its energies into the creation of a *personal* political organization for the president, aptly named the Committee to Re-elect the President (CREEP). As the campaign unfolded, it became clear that the president aimed to create his own finance organization, the Finance Committee for the Re-election of the President, displacing the Republican National Finance Committee. He also intended to create his own campaign organization, which would be located in the shadows of the White House at 1701 Pennsylvania Avenue, directed from the White House, and staffed by White House aides whose loyalty to the president was unalloyed.[170] Republican veterans viewed the creation of CREEP with alarm, recognizing that CREEP and Republican organizations were, in part, working "at cross-purposes." One veteran of CREEP described the tension between CREEP and the Republican party this way:

> CREEP had only one mission, which was to win the largest number of votes that had ever been cast for president. County and state parties had another mission: not only to do what they could to help reelect the president, but also county sheriffs, county chairmen, state legislators, and members of Congress, because they also had an organizational responsibility. Most state and county chairs were worried because of CREEP's voter ID and voter turnout efforts [which were aimed at Independents and Nixon-leaning Democrats]. What happens if they stand idly by and let half a dozen Republican state legislators get flushed because the Nixon operation came in and turned out independents and Democrats? County chairs and state chairs — they've got to go back and get elected by their constituents, who are Republicans at the state and county level. They were at cross-purposes.[171]

Republican organizations could acquiesce to CREEP's plans, or they could refuse to accept its demands and risk losing its financial support during the campaign along with the flow of patronage from the Nixon White House afterward. Few Republican leaders chose the latter course. As one veteran of Nixon's 1972 campaign recalled, "1701 [Pennsylvania Avenue, CREEP headquarters] controlled the money . . . and if you were young or you had any ambitions or you wanted to do something in that state, you did [what CREEP ordered]."[172] Those few who openly bridled at CREEP's domination of the campaign were, as they feared, unwelcome at the Nixon White House in 1973. "They [the PPO] knew when a county or state chairman had been helpful to CREEP or not. I remember going over a couple of people for assistant secretary slots. They had the educational and technical backgrounds, and experience. They could have done the job. But because they picked a certain state chairman who hadn't cooperated with CREEP as a godfather, they didn't get to first base. I mean *nothing. Nothing.*"[173]

Having organized a presidential campaign in which it subordinated Republican party organizations to the president's political organization, Nixon's White House staff proposed to organize political appointments for a second term in a like manner. The White House, Fred Malek and Jerry Jones, his successor at the WHPO, urged, "should get out of running the RNC" during Nixon's second term.[174] Instead, the White House should "get the RNC on track" by reorganizing its staff and picking its senior staffers to ensure their fidelity to the president. Once on track, the RNC should be permitted to work as a partner — "a junior partner"[175] — in handling political appointments. Staffers from the Republican National Committee — chosen by the White House Personnel Office — were now invited to attend weekly White House Personnel Office staff meetings, but they keenly felt their limitations and recognized their position as supplicants. Describing his relationship to the Nixon personnel staff in 1973 one RNC aide recalled:

> I sat in on the 7:00 A.M. Monday morning staff meetings. I was at the table when they went through on an agency-by-agency basis, asking "What is open? How close are we to getting this?" And then I had my turn. They all kind of chuckled at me. They would say, "Here is his wish list of the week. Who have you got for us this week that you're trying to pawn off?" They laughed about it, but they and I both knew the relative power of the place. They were being nice to me. They could shut off that White House staff [snaps his fingers] like that.[176]

What was once an obligation for presidents — granting their party's representatives access to vital decisions about political appointments — had become a favor, something bestowed or withheld at the president's discretion. As the Watergate affair began to unfold in the spring of 1973 and the White House became deeply suspicious of all "outsiders," the entree that had been extended to the national committee was quickly revoked — "just like that."

By the end of Nixon's presidency a quarter century had passed since Truman's aides had scuttled "Operation Best Brains." In the years that separated the two presidencies, parties were shorn of their leverage over presidents by changes in electoral technologies and laws; they lost their status as privileged participants in the staffing of the government and their capacity to shape the evolution of the president's White House Personnel staff. After 1974, the president's party, pushed still further to the periphery of presidential elections, disappeared from view altogether, acting neither as a meaningful constraint nor as a claimant on the White House Personnel Office. Nonetheless, presidents still found themselves hamstrung as they tried to turn political appointments into an instrument of executive leadership. Party notables may have been in no position to resist the steady encroachments of presidents, but other leaders in the Washington community were: the leaders of executive departments and the policy networks with which they were allied.

3
Policy Networks and the Evolution of the White House Personnel Office

During the waning months of 1970 and early 1971, Richard Nixon's senior aides moved to purge the Nixon administration of political appointees they deemed to be disloyal to the president, eighty-one in all, and to restaff departments from the White House, filling them with "men and women who are completely devoid of personal political ambition [and] totally loyal to the president."[1] As they set to work, they quickly found themselves stymied — not by the Republican National Committee, as the preceding chapter shows, which was seen to be a politically impotent "junior partner." Rather, the president's staff was hemmed in by the resistance of forceful cabinet secretaries and their allies on Capitol Hill and among organized groups in "policy networks."[2] When, for example, the president's staff made plans to oust Robert Ball, the commissioner of the Social Security Administration and a leading architect of the Social Security system, it ran into the stubborn opposition of HEW Secretary Elliot Richardson, who pledged to Social Security Administration employees that "Bob Ball will remain Commissioner as long as I head this department,"[3] and by the threats of Ways and Means Chair Wilbur Mills, who "vowed that there would be trouble" if his longtime ally Robert Ball was fired.[4] Loathe to take on both the secretary of HEW and the most powerful committee chair in the House of Representatives, Nixon and his aides backed down. This pattern of resistance and frustration was repeated throughout the government, leaving Nixon's aides far short of their aim. "We got part of it [control over appointments] back but not all of it," an appointments staffer acknowledged. Nixon's zeal for rooting out disloyal appointees may have been unprecedented, but the constraints he faced in trying to pull appointment choices into his White House were not. Throughout the postwar years each president has had to reckon with department heads and the leaders of policy networks as they have pursued the aggrandizement of their White House staff.

"NATURAL ENEMIES"? PRESIDENTS, DEPARTMENT HEADS, AND NETWORK LEADERS

> *There is a truth that you have probably uncovered: the natural enemy of the Presidential Personnel Office is the cabinet secretary.*
> —Presidential Personnel Director

> *Get your [own] appointees in place, because the first clash you will have is with the White House Personnel Office. And if you don't get your own people in place, you will end up being a one-armed paper hanger.*
> —Frank Carlucci, secretary DOD, to prospective department heads

What concerns do presidents bring to the selection of political appointees? For presidents, the selection of political appointees is a primary means by which they leave their stamp upon the policies of the government. By selecting a team of men and women who share their policy commitments, presidents may succeed in pushing their beliefs and values into the operating levels of the government.[5] In the Reagan White House, for example, this principle was distilled into a simple and oft-repeated credo, "personnel is policy."[6]

Political appointments, though, are about *more* than policy. They are also a means by which presidents may discharge or create obligations to their electoral and governing coalitions. In short, "personnel is politics," as well as "policy." Political appointments may be used to repay a leading presidential fundraiser, to reward a group that mobilized its membership on the president's behalf, or to consolidate the president's ties to an electoral constituency. "Symbolic appointments of people," argued a Nixon aide, "will do almost more to move groups to you than any issue will. If you name their leader to a key post, suddenly you have access to a whole group that you didn't have before — or you can loosen a group's ties to the opposition."[7] However, presidents are not alone in their concern with political appointments. Rather, they are situated in a political community that includes department heads, members of Congress, and clientele groups, each of whom has its own interest in appointment choices.

For members of Congress, like presidents, appointments are valuable to the pursuit of policy and electoral aims. Members of Congress who secure a prominent constituent or clientele linked to their committee are handsomely rewarded at election time. Hence, members of Congress can be indefatigable in their efforts to lay claim to political appointments.[8] Alternatively, political appointments offer a means by which members of Congress can extend their influence over the policy choices of administrative agencies. Winning the appointment of a trusted staffer, for example, permits members of Congress to exercise an indirect, though profound, influence over administrative policymaking.[9] Thus, members of Congress may be equally relentless in their quest to win appointive posts for their political aides.[10]

For professional and clientele groups, too, political appointments are vital. The "right types" of appointees allow them to sustain privileged access to their department and to uphold the integrity of their programs. Conversely, losing control over appointments choices may result in the redirection of programs in unfamiliar and unwanted directions, the promulgation of hostile regulations, or the loss of access to senior policymakers.[11] Not surprisingly, agency clientele often invest enormous energies in shaping appointment choices,[12] establishing a "right" to participate in proposing and winnowing candidates — and, sometimes, the dominant voice in the staffing of "their" agency.[13]

It is the heads of departments and agencies, however, who are the president's principal agents — and rivals — in the selection of the men and women who will staff the administration. Nonpresidential appointments are vested in the heads of departments by statute, and even appointments that are statutorily presidential appointments (undersecretaries, assistant secretaries) have by necessity been theirs as well. "The typical route to political executive office . . . has been mainly a *departmental system*. Despite their formal status as presidential appointees, most assistant secretaries and the like have been appointed as the result of prior service in the agency, personal acquaintance with departmental officers, and other experience and connections revolving around the agency's substantive program."[14]

Like presidents, department heads make appointments with an eye towards administrative responsiveness and political support. Because department heads are responsible for directing bureaus and agencies far beyond their day-to-day influence, their leadership rests heavily upon their ability to select appointees who are imbued with an ideology that reflects their own priorities and perspectives — or who are bound to them through personal loyalty.

Department heads are far more than administrative leaders. By and large, department heads are judged to be successes (or failures) on the strength of what they do outside their department, particularly on the ability to build coalitions among the clientele groups and congressional committees who control departmental programs. Here, too, political appointments are vital: selecting appointees with close ties to policy networks affords department heads access to network leaders whom they can draw upon to advance their policies. For example, faced with the task of assembling a staff to draft a national health insurance proposal, Joseph Califano, Jimmy Carter's first Secretary of Health and Human Services, strategically chose staffers from the Senate Finance Committee and the House Ways and Means Committee, the committees of jurisdiction, and from organized labor, the leading proponent of national health insurance. "I had under the HEW roof many of the key players of the 1970's in the national health insurance sweepstakes," he crowed.[15]

The concerns that presidents bring to appointment decisions have long been at odds with those of department heads, members of Congress, and clientele.

Seen from the vantage point of department heads and their allies, the president's staff is a potentially disruptive influence, one that threatens to subordinate their interests to the president's. In their estimation, a president's pursuit of responsiveness leads him to be overconcerned with the ideology and personal fealty of appointees and to discount the professional and programmatic consequences of political appointments to their agency. Moreover, presidents and their aides are seen as "too political," willing to subordinate the integrity and competence of their agency to partisan or electoral calculations.[16] As one Carter appointee acidly observed: "We had an absolutely first-class team [at Defense], every one of whom was picked by Harold Brown, Charles Duncan, and me jointly. Had it been done . . . the way Carter would have done it after he got organized, we would have had a lousy team. We would have had a bunch of stooges who represented some constituency that some politico [in the White House] thought important."[17]

This suspicion is reciprocated. Seen from the perspective of the White House Office, department heads and their allies give short shrift to presidential loyalty or fidelity to the president's policies when staffing their departments, favoring instead parochial concerns and personal loyalties. Moreover, department heads are chronically indifferent to the president's political needs — for example, selecting men and women without regard to the factional, racial, or gender makeup of the president's administration. One White House aide put the matter plainly: "Any cabinet secretary within the sound of my voice would like to throttle me for suggesting that there is any difference between the interests of the cabinet secretary and the president, yet that does exist. The natural enemy of the Personnel Office is the cabinet secretary. Throughout time, no matter what the rules are, there will be clashes."[18]

Presidents are not obtuse. They have long recognized that *their* interests in political appointments are dissimilar from those of department heads (and their allies in policy networks). They have repeatedly expressed frustration with the divided loyalties and parochial perspectives of "their" appointees and quietly harbored a desire to build an administration with men and women whose loyalties are solely presidential. Nonetheless, mid-century presidents chose not to act on their frustrations. They did not attempt to pull appointment choices into the White House Office and out of the hands of department heads and network leaders. Instead, they permitted department heads and network leaders to exercise an enormous measure of influence over the staffing of their administrations, turning to them for advice and for candidates — or simply ratifying the choices that others made for them.[19] And, of course, they consciously eschewed the creation of a large and powerful White House appointment staff.

Why did presidents accede to such a system? For the same reason that they permitted party leaders to play a large role in the staffing of their administration: because it was in their interest to do so. To be sure, there were costs to this strategy: permitting politicians outside of the White House to staff their administration resulted in a "diffusion and disintegration of administrative loyalties which in theory belong to the president."[20] But the benefits of permitting others to make choices were still greater: in return, presidents got badly needed political assistance, political assistance grounded in relationships of reciprocity and orchestrated by department heads.

Throughout the middle years of the twentieth century, presidents typically chose seasoned politicians (politicians with their own political base) to head departments. And, they permitted department heads to operate with a good bit of independence. Important decisions — about political appointments or working relationships with the Hill and clientele groups — were made with little direction or supervision from the White House. Presidents did get independent departments that had mixed or weak loyalties. But, they did get something else in return: politicians who could marshal votes on Capitol Hill and deliver the support of their department's clientele.

Consider, for example, the relationship between Richard Nixon and Melvin Laird, Nixon's first Secretary of Defense. Laird, an influential veteran of the House Armed Services Committee, was a notoriously independent operator to whom the White House had ceded control over political staffing and a host of other decisions. John Ehrlichman, Nixon's chief domestic policy aide, recalls the costs of decentralization clearly: "Laird was continually leaking stories to the press" and "actually refused to carry out some of Nixon's instructions regarding the conduct of the war."[21] Nonetheless, in return for his independence, Laird put his considerable reputation and political alliances to work on the president's behalf. "Laird was a creature of Congress who could do the kind of downfield blocking on Capitol Hill that Richard Nixon needed to ensure healthy defense appropriations and a free hand in Vietnam. Laird was so effective with his congressional cronies that everyone realized he was irreplaceable."[22] In this case, reciprocity served Nixon well.

Ultimately, relations of reciprocity remained attractive to presidents only as long the rewards of autonomy (department heads who could "deliver") were greater than its costs (mixed loyalties), and presidents had no alternatives for leadership that cost less or delivered more. By the early 1970s a trio of changes in the institutional setting of the presidency made reciprocity significantly less attractive than it had been at mid century. The dispersion of power within the Congress and the proliferation of organized interests undermined the ability of department heads and their allies to "deliver," while the growing prominence of mass media sharply increased the costs of autonomous departments with mixed loyalties. These changes, coupled with the emergence of an alternative strategy of leadership — "going public" — prompted presidents of the 1960s and 1970s to tentatively expand the size and reach of their White House appointments staffs and to reduce their dependence upon politicians outside of the White House. By the 1980s and 1990s their initiatives were no longer tentative, and the Presidential Personnel Office, which consisted of one professional aide and a few typists in 1960, had mushroomed to an office with scores of aides — a miniature bureaucracy replete with organizational charts, a hierarchy, and a sophisticated division of labor.

TRUMAN, KENNEDY, JOHNSON, AND CARTER

The Truman Administration: "No External Judgments"

Harry Truman's influence over the staffing of his administration was slight. The Truman administration, like those that preceded it, was a "Truman administration" in name only. In reality, Truman and his White House staff played a very modest role in staffing the Truman administration. By one account they played a leading role in only 8 percent of appointments to senior policymaking positions in the executive branch.[23] Most of the men — and the very few women — who served in the policymaking positions were in fact chosen outside of the White House Office by department heads — and they, in turn, were heavily influenced by the claims of congressional committee leaders and clientele groups with which their departments had ongoing relationships. Even posts that did not fall within the purview of a department or agency — regulatory appointments — were heavily shaped by politicians outside the White House Office. Lacking the staff to independently recruit and evaluate its own candidates, Truman's staff, like its contemporaries, leaned heavily upon clientele groups and their congressional allies or departmental executives to furnish it with candidates and political intelligence.[24] In short, politicians outside the White House either selected candidates and Truman and his staff ratified their choices, or they created a "short list" from which the president made his choices.

As I showed in the previous chapter, Truman's aides did recognize the limitations of these arrangements, and they seriously contemplated expanding the capacity of the president's staff to shape appointment choices in their study "Operation Best Brains." "Best Brains" was aborted, in part, because of fears of antagonizing party leaders. However, it was not simply party leaders who hemmed in the president's staff. It was also department heads and network leaders. Dawson and the members of "Best Brains" were also deeply concerned about the controversy their recommendations might arouse among department heads and, indirectly, their network allies. Consider, for example, the talking points for "Best Brains," an inventory of what "the plan . . . does *not* do." After promising not to "circumvent the Democratic National Committee in any way," Dawson next promised not to "substitute external [White House] judgments for those of responsible agency officials."[25]

Assurances notwithstanding, department heads were no more receptive to Dawson's plan than were party officials. As two Brookings scholars reported following an interview with Donald Dawson's assistant, Martin Friedman, "Friedman indicated general agreement with the proposition that there was a kind of undeclared war between Cabinet members and White House staff members on the matter of presidential appointments. Within their fields, Cabinet members tried to control decisions on appointments themselves and to avoid initiative from the White House on such appointments."[26] In this "undeclared war" department heads and their allies consistently won, and they had no intention of ceding their advantage to the White House by permitting it to develop a larger and more powerful staff. "Best Brains," Dawson recollected, was unwise because it was "too ambitious" and because it threatened to create "too much of an intermediary layer [staff] between the president and responsible [departmental] officials"[27] — a judgment with which any cabinet secretary would concur.

Why might the objections of department heads pose such formidable constraints for Truman and his staff? Lacking either the means to routinely "go public" or a Washington community highly susceptible to this strategy of leadership, Truman's leadership in Washington rested heavily upon his ability to forge relationships of reciprocity with other leaders in the Washington community, chief among them the leaders of policy networks or, in Samuel Kernell's terms, "protocoalitions."[28] Relationships of reciprocity were forged out of many currencies, not least of which were political appointments. The president's aides could have converted political appointments from a currency of reciprocity into an instrument of presidential leadership — and slighted the candidates proffered by network leaders and the considerations that these leaders deemed to be important. However, the costs would have been high: congressional committee leaders could easily tie up presidential business in their committees, and the clientele leaders could withhold their groups' support on matters of politics and policy important to Truman as well.

To forge these reciprocal relationships, presidents relied heavily upon departmental executives. Since the White House Office staff was not highly developed,[29] many of the responsibilities of presidential leadership, both substantive and political, fell to the leaders of departments and agencies. It was they who developed the president's program[30] and "cemented alliances with interest groups, drawing them into collaboration with their administration."[31] One veteran of White House politics, Tommy Corcoran, captured Cabinet members' mid-century role nicely: "I have never conceived of the cabinet as fundamentally managers of their departments. I have conceived of them always as political officers, specializing in regional or interest group relationships. They were put in charge of that part of the administration about which they have the most political sensitivity."[32] Hence, presidents typically turned to politicians of some standing to head cabinet departments and permitted them to operate their departments with a good bit of autonomy. In return, the president's independent "political officers" were responsible for providing the president with political assistance, for exercising "political sensitivity," and for using their political alliances on the president's behalf. Pulling decisions about political appointments out of their hands and into the White House Office would undermine the reciprocal relationship that linked the president to department and agency heads (and, indirectly, to their constituencies), evoking their ire or even retaliation, neither of which Truman could afford. Far better, from Truman's perspective, to muddle through with the White House arrangements in place.

The Strengthening of the Presidency: Kennedy and Johnson

I thought that if we could pull this off [the creation of a White House appointment staff] we could make a real contribution to the strengthening of the presidency.
— John Macy, adviser to Lyndon Johnson

Although the resources and sanctions that party leaders could bring to bear had eroded badly between the late 1940s and the mid-1960s, there was remarkably little change in policy networks during these years. The 1960s were halcyon days for the leaders of policy networks. Congressional committee chairs were at the zenith of their power, both inside and outside their committees. Between 1947 and 1964, Smith and Deering write, "House and Senate leadership resembled confederations of committee chairs, each acting as the sovereign over a committee's jurisdiction."[33] Moreover, the organized interests that had dominated the Washington pressure community in the New Deal and postwar years were still unchallenged by the mobilization of new constituencies. Not surprisingly, studies of "iron-triangles" gained their greatest currency among political scientists and journalists during these years, including *Private Power and American Democracy* (1965), *The Political Process* (1965), and *Power in Washington* (1969).

Even so, the environment of presidential leadership changed in important ways during these years. Television, still in its infancy during Truman's presidency, was a widely available and increasingly important medium by the 1960s,[34] and opportunities for presidential travel grew with the introduction of jet aircraft. Thus, opportunities for presidents to "go public" or exercise "plebiscitary leadership"[35] grew significantly between the late 1940s and the mid-1960s. Presidents exploited these opportunities, increasing the frequency with which they "went public."[36]

The years separating Truman's presidency from the Kennedy and Johnson presidencies were marked, too, by the steady accumulation of leadership resources inside the White House Office. As Richard Neustadt observed, by the late 1960s most principal advisors to the president were located in the White House, with department heads becoming, for the most part, second (or third) stringers. As compared with Eisenhower's early years domestic cabinet members in the Sixties seemed far more dependent upon the President's support and services than he upon theirs. This came to pass presumably because in program formulation and in legislative liaison the White House had amassed its own resources.[37]

Able to avail themselves of public leadership strategies with greater ease, presidents became less dependent upon reciprocal relationships with the leaders of policy networks to win support for policies. As presidents accumulated their own resources for policy initiation and legislative leadership, "domestic cabinet members . . . [became] far more dependent upon the President's support and services than he on theirs." Their dependence slowly waning, Kennedy and Johnson found it less costly than Truman to extend their reach over appointment choices by pulling them into an expanded White House staff, gradually undercutting the prerogatives of departmental leaders and their network allies.

John Kennedy

John Kennedy quickly signaled his willingness to break with the highly circumscribed role that his predecessors had played in assembling their administrations. Aiming to assure that "the bureaucracy would be directed in its activities to the president's interests," Kennedy's aides first contemplated "controlling the top three or four hundred jobs in the new administration." To this end, Kennedy's personal aides, the Talent Hunt, supervised the staffing of the administration, working to structure and guide the choices of those who had staffed policymaking positions in preceding administrations, the secretaries-elect.

Working alongside the secretaries-elect, the Talent Hunt aides marshaled their own slates of candidates for the consideration of the secretaries and reviewed the choices of cabinet secretaries, eyeing them for their fitness as "New Frontiersmen." In reality, the success of Kennedy's aides in shaping the administration varied widely. Shriver's staff worked quite closely with some secretaries-designate and very little with others — depending upon the president's interests, the strength of contending claims on the department's posts, and the secretary's political capabilities and predispositions. Robert McNamara, new to Washington, D.C. (and the Defense Department), worked closely with the Shriver staff: "We provided him with lots of suggestions, and he collected suggestions from other places. We worked with him in feeding names to him, checking out people, getting reports on them, and giving them back to him."[38] Another Shriver aide recalls:

McNamara called us. He was fantastic. By the time we finished, all of us, including Shriver, had assignments from McNamara, and we had to meet him either late at night or early in the morning with the net results [of our investigations]. He did this for about three days with us. He got an enormous amount of work out of us. We got behind on all other departments. Finally Shriver said, "I'm afraid its your shop now." He's the only one that worked us like this.[39]

Abe Ribicoff, the Secretary-designate of Health, Education and Welfare, was accustomed to Connecticut politics, in which the claims of party organizations played a prominent role in staffing the government. Hence, he quickly acceded to the claims of both the Talent Hunt and the "Irish Mafia." Eyeing one particular list of departmental positions Ribicoff told one staffer, "I'll take these, and you can have the others."[40] The Interior Department, in contrast, was staffed with little assistance from Kennedy's aides. Neither Larry O'Brien nor Richard Donahue, the senior political operatives in the Talent Hunt met with Interior Secretary Udall to coach him on politics or to lay out the Kennedy program. Udall "already knew the political facts of life," and John Kennedy had no New Frontier program to lay out for Interior. Udall was left largely to his own devices—and to the importunings of western Congressmen and clientele who viewed Interior's appointive posts as their bailiwick. Kennedy and his staff weighed in only when Udall antagonized congressional allies or clientele of the Interior Department loyal to Kennedy, and, occasionally, to request that supporters be rewarded with posts in the department.[41]

To be sure, John Kennedy and his personal entourage did not fully centralize the staffing of his administration during the transition. In fact, they were quite some distance from fully controlling the staffing. As one Kennedy aide acknowledged: "The fact of the matter is, it didn't happen. In terms of looking at 600 or whatever [appointees] and saying, 'Boy, they're all Kennedy loyalists, they're all competent, they're all on the team, they're all dedicated to Jack Kennedy every waking moment.' It never happened."[42] Nonetheless, Kennedy and his aides did succeed in leaving a deeper imprint on his administration than any of his predecessors had. One member of his talent hunt, Harris Wofford, surmised: "I think [the Talent Hunt] meant that Kennedy got down a little further and influenced a few more of the presidential appointments."[43] Mann and Doig's study of presidential appointments, *The Assistant Secretaries*, bears out Wofford's judgment. By their estimate, Kennedy and his staff played a significant role in slightly more than half (54 percent) of the presidential appointments made during the first year of the administration—a figure nearly three times that of Eisenhower's first year.[44]

The Administration Under Way

After a hiatus of a few months, during which time the president's appointments staff receded to a highly traditional and circumscribed role, the president's senior aides decided to reconstitute the Talent Hunt in the White House Office, opting for a White House staff remarkably similar to that outlined — and aborted — a decade earlier in the Truman administration's "Operation Best Brains."

Although Kennedy's aides did not shrink from expanding the president's staff, as Truman's aides had done, they were keenly aware that they were viewed with suspicion. They understood that previous administrations had established a powerful tradition among departments that the president's staff intervened in appointment choices only to introduce narrowly political considerations. "The White House has not operated a recruiting staff long enough to overcome the immediate reaction of a lot of people around the government: that when you say "Can we help you with your recruiting problem?" you really are saying, "Can we shove these people down your throat?"[45] Moreover, the aides recognized that regardless of their reputation, department and agency heads would be reluctant to cede control over staffing decisions — control they wished to use to further their working relationships with the Hill and their clientele, and to press their own policy agendas. Hence, Dan Fenn, summoned from Cambridge to oversee a reconstituted Talent Hunt, got off to a cautious start. He added only one professional staffer during his first year in the White House, an aide chosen from the staff of the Civil Service Commission, and two additional staffers the following year.[46] Fenn confined his staff's energies to a small proportion of vacant posts, one-third by his reckoning, recruiting perhaps thirty-five to forty appointees in all.[47]

Moreover, Fenn was especially circumspect and careful in approaching department heads. Describing his staff in 1962, Fenn offered this characterization of their role: "By and large we have moved into this on the basis of 'Can we help you out?' We have established a staff service to departments and agencies and . . . to the President."[48] When approaching Secretary of State Dean Rusk about a position at the Agency for International Development (AID), Fenn's boss Ralph Dungan was careful to provide a reference to vouch for his integrity and to describe his role in remarkably circumspect terms:

As you know, Dan Fenn was recently brought into the White House to work on the problem of establishing a systematic procedure here so that we can assist in the recruitment of top quality people for selected high level appointments. Essentially what we do is generate a large number of names from many contacts throughout the country, screen them, and suggest a selected group to the officer filling the vacancy.

Attached is a booklet recently prepared for Eugene Zuckert [Secretary of the Air Force] to help him in his effort to find an assistant secretary. You and I have talked about the post of Inspector General for AID. It occurs to me that a booklet similar to the one prepared for Zuckert might be helpful in making that choice. If you wish, we will work on putting one together in the next two weeks.[49]

Breaking with precedent — but carefully — Dungan and Fenn avoided arousing the suspicions or antipathy of those who might otherwise find their customary claims on political appointments jeopardized. Dungan and Fenn may have been the president's men, but they pressed the president's cause with sufficient discretion to win the respect and confidence of executives outside the White House. Discussing regulatory appointments one commissioner volunteered, "While I have the floor may I pay special tribute to Ralph Dungan. I don't know anybody who is more surefooted in dealing with these problems, or has shown more consideration, who manages the discharge of the irons that are entrusted to him by the President with such a high regard for the objectives of the agency. This plug is entirely unsolicited."[50] Five other regulatory commissioners joined in praising Dungan's integrity and judgment — strong praise indeed from men and women who are normally suspicious of presidential aides "meddling in their affairs" and jealous of their autonomy.

Its staff and reputation established, Dungan's staff did play a significant role when the president had an especially strong interest in a post or when a cabinet secretary had proven that he was unable to manage his department without White House guidance.[51] At HEW's Office of Education, for example, both of these conditions were true. Within the White House, HEW Secretaries Abe Ribicoff (1961–1962) and Tony Celebrezze (1962–1964) were seen to be "the weakest, the least competent in managing their bureaucracy. Theirs was a tough bureaucracy to manage, and they had neither the talent nor the desire to manage it."[52]

Moreover, education policy "was an area of great concern" for the president.[53] Hence, when Sterling McMurrin, the first Commissioner of Education, wished to leave his post and return to Utah, Kennedy's appointments staff began a concerted search for his replacement, hoping to find an appointee who would revitalize the moribund Office of Education and carry Kennedy's ambitious program for secondary education.[54]

Former Cleveland Mayor Tony Celebrezze voiced no opposition to an extensive White House staff role. Instead, he eagerly surrendered selection of the ommissioner to the president's staff: "Tony didn't know the Office of Education from Cleveland City Hall, and as far as he was concerned, whatever Ralph [Dungan] wanted was all right with him. He didn't have any ideas at all [about the post]."[55] Hence, the appointments staff assumed responsibility for the post. The search took months, beginning with discussions with the Budget Bureau's career staffers, trusted figures within the Office of Education, and "people with whom the president was acquainted at Harvard."[56] Over the next few months Fenn's aide spoke to more than a hundred people "in the educational field, at the university level, the local level, and around the federal government" trying to "get a fix on the job," that is, to "find out what had been missing in terms of leadership in the job, and what the federal role will be."[57] All the while, the staff was gathering a pool of potential candidates and trying to fend off the attempts of education interest groups to control the choice.[58] John Clinton, Fenn's aide responsible for the post, was detailed from the BOB, and reflecting his training as a budget examiner, he "put this little spreadsheet together, with about 12 or 15 candidates, and maybe 15 evaluators," finally settling on Francis Keppel, dean of the Harvard School of Education.[59]

Often, though, the White House appointments staff played a more modest role or no role at all in the selection of Kennedy appointees, most often where the president's stakes in a choice were small, and the claims of those outside the White House were strong. As Fenn recounts, the personnel staff was sometimes the last to learn of an impending appointment.

> I'll never forget the night I was at some party and somebody said, "What do you do?" And I said, "I work at the White House." And she said, "What do you do over there?" I said, "Well, I'm involved in the talent search." She said, "What jobs are you trying to fill at the moment?" And I said, "Well, the Assistant Secretary of State . . . and an Assistant Secretary of Commerce." She said, "Well, that Assistant Secretary of Commerce, you don't have to worry about that any more do you?" And I said, "What?" She said, "I heard on the news tonight that Franklin Roosevelt [Jr.] has been appointed." I said, "What! You mean he has been suggested as a possibility?" "No, [she replied] the White House announced the thing today." I had no idea the thing was in the wind at all. We would run into this kind of problem very, very frequently.[60]

What limited the reach and influence of the White House appointments staff? It was not the leverage of party officials outside of the White House, as it had been in earlier administrations. Rather, Fenn was "hemmed in" by another set of powerful rivals inside the administration: cabinet and agency heads and their allies on Capitol Hill and in the Washington pressure community. Though there were cases like the Office of Education, in which the appointments staff could take the lead without resistance from a department, this was not the norm. After listening to his colleagues describing the staffing of HEW's Office of Education, another Fenn aide interrupted: "If you will pardon a note of envy, I think the key element here is that you had a free hand . . . simply because the head of the agency wasn't pushing somebody

else and it wasn't a highly visible position into which half of Congress was trying to shove its man."[61] Indeed, many department leaders were so jealous of
their autonomy that Fenn and Dungan learned about vacancies after the fact.[62]

Though Dungan and Fenn instituted bimonthly reporting requirements for
vacancies, not all departments were eager to disclose their vacancies. Fenn's
staff recalled the reticence of the Defense Department with mocking humor:

> *Scanlon:* We would call [all departments] on a bimonthly basis . . . and
> ask what positions were vacant at the GS-16 level or above. Many agen-
> cies did their best to help us out. On the other hand, in the case of
> [Defense] this was not the case.
> *Sherman:* He [Yarmolinksy] was working for somebody else.
> *Fenn:* The Secretary.
> *Sherman:* That's right, the other President of the United States.
> [Laughter] This was the only guy who could sit there over — you know,
> they must have had five million people there — and say, "Well, I don't
> know whether we have anything open this week." [Much laughter]
> *Clinton:* "I think they are all filled." [Continued laughter]

Even when Dungan and Fenn learned about vacancies at the Defense Department, their offers of assistance were rebuffed: "Of all the people in the
cabinet, McNamara was the one you couldn't touch. We tried to help him
after the inauguration, but he dismissed us — he had his own files and his
own sources he wanted to rely on. We never touched DOD, we didn't even
make one recommendation about an appointment.[63] Another aide recalled,
"the Secretary of Defense and the Attorney General both did it [staffing]
far better than we could do it. So, that was acknowledged" — and their independence was countenanced.[64]

In sum, Kennedy's personnel staff expanded the reach of the president
where the personal interest of the president was keen, and where the claims
or capabilities of others, particularly department and agency heads, were
weak. Conversely, it ceded choices to those outside of the White House under
the opposite circumstances. The skills and size of Kennedy's staff rendered
it far more capable of pursuing policy leadership through political appointments than the Truman or Eisenhower staffs, but its size and ambitions were
far more modest than what would soon follow during the Johnson and Nixon presidencies.

The Johnson Presidency

Building upon the precedents forged during the presidency of John Kennedy,
Lyndon Johnson aggressively expanded the size, competence, and reach of
the president's appointments staff. At Johnson's direction, *all* departmental

recommendations on appointments were to flow through his personnel office, headed by John Macy,[65] and department heads were instructed by Johnson to collaborate with Macy in "seeing candidates for presidential appointments." Moreover, Johnson admonished Macy, all senior appointees were to be "the president's people." The president "is the appointing officer, and they are part of *his* administration," Johnson instructed. Macy responded by trebling the size of the personnel staff (from six to seventeen), and by establishing a rudimentary specialization among his staff, paralleling that of the BOB.

In the main, department and agency heads, particularly those new to Washington or eager to avoid staffing blunders, worked remarkably closely with Macy. John Gardner had been at the helm of HEW for only a few weeks when he had to fill fourteen PAS posts (presidentially appointed and Senate confirmed), among them the newly created post of Commissioner of Aging. Gardner solicited candidates from his assistants in HEW, from acquaintances outside of the government, and from Macy, who supplied over a dozen candidates for the post and met with Gardner to discuss them. When Gardner tentatively selected a candidate for the position, he wrote Macy: "Since Kahn was not on your original list, I don't want to take another step until you have had an opportunity to make whatever independent checks you wish."[66] Macy's relationship with departments was not only close, but marked by harmony and trust. "Macy was a gem," volunteered one cabinet secretary.[67] In fact, some cabinet secretaries regularly solicited his staff's assistance. "I did all my searches in collaboration with John Macy. It was a wonderful arrangement," commented another secretary.[68] Seen from the perspective of department heads, Macy was a useful collaborator. Departments found it fruitful to consult with Macy because it gave them "access to his network and his staff — they'd dig out resumes and read the damn things, and check out things, you know. He was bound to do his staff work more thoroughly than I did."[69] And, because Macy enjoyed the respect of Johnson, his imprimatur on a department's recommendation would virtually guarantee its acceptance by Johnson.[70]

To be sure, Macy's staff did not work equally closely or harmoniously with all departments. Some cabinet secretaries, such as HEW's Wilbur Cohen, were especially confident about the adequacy of their own networks and the caliber of their staff work. They had little use for Macy. "Cohen thought he knew all the answers," and was reluctant to "go through the system," one appointments aide recalls.[71] Other department heads, such as Robert McNamara, were prickly about their independence and were permitted a good bit of autonomy by the president — and therefore by Macy as well. Still others, such as Interior Secretary Stewart Udall, were closely tied to constituencies outside the White House, and made few attempts to make positive use of Macy's staff.[72] "In some cases we offered a service to the department, but in *that* case [the Interior Department] our role was to look out for the president's interests."[73] As Macy understood, a capable personnel staff inside the White House Office did mitigate Johnson's dependence upon traditional sources of candidates outside of the White House—if he chose to use it.

> [Our staff] preserved the president's options. Without this kind of [staff] service he was likely to be buffeted by the press for individual candidates. Now this didn't eliminate the pressures. But for the most part this system gave him names before the pressures could mobilize. . . . We were a couple of steps ahead. And the president, consequently, was in a position to control the appointment process to the benefit of strengthening the presidency rather than reacting to the National Committee or reacting to a powerful Senator, or reacting to a pressure group or reacting to friends. He had an orderly process to rely upon *if he wished to rely upon it.*[74]

Ultimately, of course, Johnson was under no obligation to opt for candidates proffered by Macy. Johnson often chose instead to "react to pressures" outside of the White House, particularly when selecting regulatory commissioners championed by industry groups. Macy's steadfast opposition to the maritime industry's candidate for the Federal Maritime Commission, for example, fell on deaf ears at the White House,[75] as did his candidates for posts at the Federal Communication Commission and Federal Trade Commission.[76]

By and large, Macy's staff was remarkably successful in bringing presidential perspectives and candidates to bear on choices that were once little influenced by the White House. In roughly eight out of ten cases, Macy's staff either proposed candidates for vacancies or offered the president its *own* evaluation of candidates that had been proposed by departments and agencies, evaluations that it solicited from a network of contacts across the nation and throughout the EOP (especially the BOB).[77] In the estimation of HEW Secretary Wilbur Cohen, a handful of White House staffers were equivalent in stature to Johnson's cabinet members, including John Macy: "I rank him with them [cabinet heads], because when you come to the personnel side, John Macy . . . is extremely important."[78]

How did Macy's staff come to occupy such an important role yet elicit little conflict and rivalry? Why, despite its ambitious reach, did Johnson's staff not run headlong into antagonism and resistance from departments and their allies, as they had from party politicians? Two reasons stand out. First, Macy was the beneficiary of an unprecedented harmony of interests between the Johnson White House and domestic agencies. Johnson wanted appointees who could carry forward his Great Society program—men and women who were familiar with and "committed to the programs they administered," largely the same thing that the departments themselves wanted. As Macy recounted: "There was a desire on [Johnson's] part to select strong appointees . . . who could give leadership to the bureaucracy, could focus the bureaucracy in the direction of his programs. He was very admiring of Wilbur Cohen for his capacity to do this. Cohen's identity with the [career] service made him tremendously effective in bringing them along, in making changes, in pushing programs forward."[79]

Moreover, Macy's personal reputation and his staff's orientation acted to dampen suspicion and hostility. Macy, a longtime veteran of the Civil Service Commission, was seen by department heads to be "fairly insulated from the political process," unlike his White House colleagues. As one cabinet secretary recalled:

> The risk you have with the White House is that there are always political interests seeking jobs at the White House. At any given time you've got 23 Senators and 145 major corporate executives and 92 members of the House . . . saying, "Appoint this person." So you've got all of these names — and some of them are real bums, I mean they're just awful. Now, the people working at the White House are working on legislation, [or] they were worried about the next election. . . . So they look around, and they're busy as all get out, and they're fighting fires . . . so they picked up what they've got there, and it tends to be a highly politicized, pressure-boiler sort of thing. Whereas John [Macy] — I don't know how he did this — but he seemed to remain fairly insulated from the political process. When you looked at John's list you could tell these weren't from political sources; [the names appeared to have been chosen by] experts in their fields. He was a jewel.[80]

Macy's staff, which was drawn from the Foreign Service and BOB, was imbued with a strong sense of "neutral competence."[81] A former budget examiner (and State Department official) recalled his training: "There was a strong grounding in the Budget Bureau; they'd say you got to represent the agency to the White House and the White House to the agency — and you've got to do it while maintaining your integrity."[82] Another volunteered that they were "honest brokers between the agencies we were dealing with and the White House."[83] Hence, the appointments staff could even be a valuable ally within the White House, protecting departments from the depredations of patronage-minded aides elsewhere in the White House:

> By and large, I think most agencies appreciated the way in which we handled it. There was always somebody they could deal with when they had a problem. And they used us in that regard, too. [For example] there is always a concern that the president will push political candidates onto them [the State Department]. I met with State to work out a procedure [for selecting ambassadors]. We allowed all of the political names to

get judged through the State Department process — what we called the "technical evaluation" — as to whether they were capable of doing an ambassadorial job. We always told State who was recommending people. State, on the other hand, would say, "We don't have an opening in country X, or we have diplomatic problems in country Y." And we would represent that back to the president. And a lot of these agencies came to feel that we were not antagonistic towards the agency — indeed, that we were pretty friendly towards them.[84]

In the end, though, even Macy and his staff were unable to bridge the deeply rooted conflict separating the political interests of the White House and those of departments and their allies. Unlike his successors, Macy did not become embroiled in conflict with departments as he pursued the president's interests. Rather, Macy's staff came under attack from within the White House — from the president and his political aides — for being too "neutrally competent": too concerned with professional competence and programmatic commitment of prospective appointees and too little concerned with their fidelity to Lyndon Baines Johnson.

The first sign of discord came in March 1965, when HEW Secretary Celebrezze and Commissioner of Education Francis Keppel decided to appoint Henry Loomis to serve in a departmental (schedule C) post: deputy commissioner of Education. Loomis, head of Voice of America (VOA) had the temerity to blast Johnson for politicizing the VOA. The press "immediately jumped on this and in no time at all Johnson found out about it — and was furious."[85] The next day John Macy, attending a meeting at the Brookings Institution, was summoned from the meeting with the message, "The President is on the phone." Macy was "reamed out by Johnson" for his lack of political sensitivity and directed to "fire the son of a bitch" before he took his post.[86] The Loomis episode, Macy acknowledged, badly shook Johnson's confidence in the adequacy of his staff work.[87]

In itself, the incident might not have led Johnson to revise his thinking about the responsiveness of his administration and the adequacy of Macy's staff work. However, events in the following year proved the incident to be the part of a larger pattern of untoward events for Lyndon Johnson. The remainder of Johnson's administration would be marked by growing criticism of Johnson's war policies in Southeast Asia,[88] growing public disapproval of Johnson's performance,[89] increasingly unfavorable news coverage of the Johnson presidency,[90] and continued speculation within the Democratic party about the presidential ambitions of Robert F. Kennedy — all of which led Johnson to the conclusion that his administration was increasingly unresponsive to his political fortunes.

Johnson's solution was to turn to fellow Texan Marvin Watson, his de facto political affairs officer and "an absolute LBJ loyalist, a man with no other political agenda or base."[91] In 1966 Watson's involvement in political appointments — and his staff — began to grow, beginning with his designation as the recipient of FBI field reports on prospective nominees and "principal point of contact with the Bureau [FBI]."[92] Prior to 1966, Macy had received FBI reports, which in his estimation "gave you a lot of garbage" and "weren't worth a damn."[93] Watson — and Johnson — thought otherwise, and in a "vote of no confidence of our review [of FBI field investigations]," Watson and his aides began to scrutinize FBI reports for information that marked prospective appointees as potentially disloyal to the president. In 1966 Watson also brought on an assistant, Doug Nobles, and assigned him to place candidates of unquestionable *personal* loyalty to Johnson — chiefly Texans — throughout the government and to provide a "preliminary political screening" of Macy's candidates.[94] Watson also concluded that "he personally had to deal with departments and agencies, or he couldn't tell Johnson what was going on, or protect his interests."[95] Hence, he began to "cultivate people in the departments," establishing his own channels to loyal Texans scattered in the departments and agencies, channels which competed with and sometimes superseded Macy's "systematic channel."[96] Watson often insisted on meeting personally with candidates prior to their nomination, trying to discern whether they were likely to be loyal to their president.[97] Finally, Watson sought out agency heads to inquire whether their appointees were loyal and offered his help in establishing loyalty. Predictably, most agency heads reacted with barely concealed scorn. Said one agency head, "Marvin Watson asked me, 'Are these people that you're appointing to supergrade jobs, are they politically right?' I said, 'I have no idea.' He said, 'Are they responsive?' I said, 'They will do what I want them to do.' He said, 'What can I do to help you?' and I said, 'I don't want any political clearances. You can leave me alone.' "[98]

In the main, Watson's efforts were amateurish and remarkably similar to services provided by the Eisenhower and Truman staffs. Though Watson came to "dominate the final aperture" of the appointment process,[99] his staff lacked the resources, the expertise, and the network of contacts that Macy's staff possessed. Lacking a national network of ties to professional communities, Watson and his aides could supply "Johnson loyalists" for only a handful of lower-level posts. "He [Johnson] didn't rely on us to supply upper-level managers like assistant secretaries," a Watson aide recalled.[100] Instead, Macy and the departments set the agenda and supplied the candidates; Watson scrutinized what had percolated up through the systematic channels. Because Watson's staff was small and unspecialized, the scrutiny it added was based upon brief face-to-face meetings with the candidates shortly before their nomination,[101] or a hurried phone call to a member of Johnson's inner circle — Clark Clifford, Abe Fortas, Ed Weisl, or Jake Jacobsen — soliciting their judgments about the proposed nominee.[102]

Macy struggled to do the president's bidding while at the same time protecting the autonomy of department heads and insulating them from the crudest political demands. In the autumn of 1965 Macy strengthened what had been a perfunctory review of departmental appointees at the senior policymaking level (those in "supergrade" positions, the high-level schedule C posts).[103] Agency heads were notified that "in addition to the usual bio data and last known legal or voting address [for a party registration check] we will need evidence of loyalty, sympathy and/or understanding concerning the aims and programs of the Administration—this should be delved into by a Presidential appointee within the agency."[104] Macy's staff also tried to nurture Johnson's confidence in their work by leavening their network of professional and academic contacts with Johnson's longstanding political allies in Texas and Washington, D.C. Each aide "kept a copy of the list on his desk," asking himself "Who can we call that might have a connection [to Johnson] that we can use to keep [LBJ] in the loop [using Macy's advice and candidates]?"[105] At the same time, hoping to protect the interests of departments, Macy directed his staff to bring Watson's aides inside his staff, and to "coopt them."[106]

Macy's knife-edged balancing act was something that his successors would not—and could not—emulate. The underlying political conflict between the White House and departments, quietly resolved in favor of departmental autonomy during the Truman presidency, was bridged, precariously, by a harmony of substantive aims and an ethos of "neutral competence" during the Kennedy and Johnson presidencies. Macy's successors, inhabiting a different institutional setting, would choose otherwise. The conflict between the White House and the departments (and their allies) would soon be exacerbated, and it would henceforth be resolved in favor of pressing the president's interests through an expanded White House staff and circumscribing the autonomy of executive departments.

The Carter Presidency: The Institutional Setting Transformed

Separated by a time span of only eight years, the presidencies of Lyndon Johnson and Jimmy Carter were widely separated in another, more meaningful sense: the institutional setting for presidential leadership changed substantially between the mid-1960s and second half of the 1970s, significantly altering the costs and benefits of centralization. Beginning in the late 1960s a wave of changes in national politics significantly diminished the political standing of department heads and the policy networks with which they were aligned.

The relationships of reciprocity that linked presidents to department heads were undermined by a host of changes in the Washington community. First, the ability of department heads to "deliver" on behalf of presidents was sharply

eroded by the dispersion of power within Congress and the expansion of the
Washington pressure community. By the 1970s the U.S. Congress was a far
more open institution than ever before, and the "sovereign" committee chairs
of the 1950s and 1960s found their power curtailed by reforms that dispersed
power inside committees and sharply increased the frequency of floor challenges to their work.[107] Described as an institution led by "a few whales"
in the 1960s, by the late 1970s Congress consisted instead of "lots of min-
nows."[108] The Washington pressure community changed dramatically between
the mid-1960s and mid-1970s, too. The number of groups represented in
Washington grew rapidly, and the composition of the pressure community
changed as well, substantially diminishing the preeminence of long-standing
Washington-based groups.[109] As Salisbury observed: "The growth in the
number, variety, and sophistication of interest groups represented in
Washington DC has . . . helped to bring about a transformation in the way
that much public policy is made . . . [creating] a process not dominated so
often by a relatively small number of powerful interest groups as it may have
been."[110] Even the venerable American Farm Bureau Federation, the
apotheosis of group power and the dominant force in agricultural policy,
began to lose its grip on policy to a host of newly formed groups in the late
1960s.[111] Presidents might still choose politicians of independent standing
to head cabinet departments, but as legislation spilled onto the floor of
Congress[112] and newly mobilized interests weighed in on policy, even skilled
politicians could deliver less and less for presidents.

At the same time that the rewards of reciprocity were diminishing, the costs
of permitting departments to operate with a great deal of autonomy were
growing. Washington became a far more permeable, more open governing
community during the late 1960s and 1970s. News about the performance
of presidents and their administrations changed substantially. By the 1970s
there was much more news flowing from Washington to the public,[113] and
the public, now only weakly bound to political parties, seemed to be increasingly influenced in its judgments by news about presidents. Increasingly
dependent upon public strategies of leadership, presidents became convinced
that "news matters," that unfavorable information about presidents and their
policies, if amplified by national news media, would cause serious damage
to the president's standing with the public. For presidents and their aides,
it became increasingly important that unfavorable news not emerge from the
executive branch, that their administration speak in one voice — a favorable
voice.[114] In the media age, departments that operated with a great deal of
autonomy resulted in an administration that "spoke in many voices," raising
questions among the public about the president's mastery of Washington
politics and the "blurring of his message." Beginning with Johnson's presidency and continuing thereafter, White House aides voiced a criticism of
departmental autonomy that was unknown to their predecessors: independent

departments jeopardized presidential leadership by permitting criticism of the president and his policies.[115] A Nixon aide explained that centralized control over appointments was necessary because "at HEW and State you had a lot of people who were really not marching to the president's drumbeat. I think that it detracts from the long-term credibility of the administration if you have a lot of people who are not marching to the president's drumbeat. I mean it discredits your authority."[116] A veteran of the Reagan White House observed: "The White House should have a large role in staffing departments because the first person who gets blamed when an appointees goes off the reservation or does something goofy is . . . the president. It is the *president's* name that gets in the paper. The article doesn't read, "This Is Louis Sullivan's Appointee at HHS." It reads, "Bush Appointees Does Stupid Thing." Presidents get the heat, so they ought to be the one choosing that person."[117] From a White House staffer serving a sharply dissimilar leader, George Bush, one hears the same concern:

> What happens . . . when no one does truly owe his or her loyalty to the President? When things start getting difficult, when the president starts getting hit by the press, if he starts dropping in the polls . . . what appears are various anonymous quotations from high-ranking administration officials who said, "The president gave a stupid speech last night." Or, "I can't believe that crowd over there at the White House is saying and doing the things that they are." Or, "Who do they think they are taking money away from my program and the little children of America." You see those kind of quotations, and the reason is that those people weren't chosen by the president and don't owe their loyalty to the president.[118]

At the same time that autonomous departments were becoming less attractive to presidents, alternative avenues of presidential leadership were emerging — reliance upon an expanded Executive Office of the President to formulate policy and offer in-house political assistance, and the use of public relations to build support for the president and his program. In the estimation of presidents and their aides, these alternatives promised fewer political costs and greater returns. Thus, by the 1970s, the mid-century view of department heads — that they were "political officers specializing in regional or interest group relations" to whom the president had to accord autonomy — had fallen into disfavor. In its place, a new view of the relationship between presidents and cabinet departments was being forged.

Nowhere was the reassessment more sweeping than in the Nixon White House. In a series of memos to President Nixon just days after his reelection victory in 1972, presidential aide Peter Flanigan captured just how thoroughly the transformation of the presidency's setting had altered the political calculations of presidents and their aides. The "problem with the cabinet system," Flanigan argued, was that cabinet members have been chosen to act as emissaries from the White House to key constituencies, and, once chosen, they were far removed from the White House, and subject to the importunings of clientele and Capitol Hill. The result, Flanigan lamented, was that "instead of being an Executive Committee under the president, the secretaries tend to become a group of semi-independent barons with whom the president deals at arms length through his White House staff."[119] The solution to this problem, he wrote, was to vastly strengthen the centripetal forces within the executive branch: to expand and politicize the Executive Office of the President (especially the Office of Management and Budget); to flood the executive branch with proven presidential loyalists (veterans of the Nixon White House staff); and to draw department heads into the White House Office — physically — severing them from the centrifugal forces at work in their departments. Once these steps were taken, the "cabinet system would operate as does the management of a large conglomerate," and the president would have "much tighter management control of the executive branch, a greater degree of management support, and a reduction in Executive Branch friction."[120]

What, though, were the costs of these changes? Might the president lose valuable political assistance by abandoning reciprocity in favor of a tightly centralized executive branch? Endowed with a extensive White House apparatus for policy development and the orchestration of public support, Nixon's aides saw little need for the political services that departments could offer. To be sure, Flanigan acknowledged, a strategy of centralization "excludes the experienced politician who makes a good spokesman for the administration." But, he argued, since "White House spokesmen have in many cases become at least as effective as Cabinet officers," the president has little to lose.

In short, the anticipated benefits of increased centralization were far greater than its expected costs. Richard Nixon and his aides never fully carried through their designs. Instead, these plans were swiftly abandoned as the Watergate affair engulfed Nixon's presidency. Peter Flanigan was neither eccentric nor unusually power-hungry. Rather, he was prescient: each of the presidents who followed Nixon came to similar conclusions about the desirability of centralization, even — eventually — Jimmy Carter.

Remembrance of Things Past: Cabinet Government
and the Carter Presidency

In the wake of the Watergate affair, journalists, scholars, and politicians concluded that a large and powerful White House staff was a dangerous excrescence on the national political system. A large and centralized White

House staff, in their estimation, had usurped the traditional prerogatives of the president's cabinet, insulated the president from the judgments of other leaders and ordinary citizens, concentrated far too much power in the White House, and created an unwieldy bureaucracy within the White House. The Watergate affair, they argued, was not an aberration, but rather a logical culmination of an imperial presidency centered in the modern White House Office. Responsibilities that had become vested in the White House Office, they proposed, should be located elsewhere, thereby permitting presidents to personally preside over a smaller, more open, more accountable White House Office as their mid-century predecessors had.[121]

Presidential aspirant Jimmy Carter, who campaigned in 1976 as the candidate who least resembled Richard Nixon, eagerly embraced this analysis of the White House Office. Throughout the campaign of 1976 Carter pledged that there would be "no all-powerful palace guard in my White House, no anonymous aides, unelected, unknown to the public, and unconfirmed by the Senate, wielding vast power from the White House basement."[122] If elected, Carter promised, he would by reduce the size of the White House staff by 30 percent, eliminate the White House chief of staff, bar his aides from interposing themselves between the president and cabinet secretaries, and reinstitute "cabinet government"—in other words, permit cabinet departments to enjoy their customary prerogatives in formulating policy and advising the president. And what of the costs of decentralization? So powerful were the lessons of the Nixon presidency that neither Carter nor his senior aides paid any heed to the costs that might accompany decentralization. Within two years, however, their thinking would change dramatically.

The Carter Presidency Under Way

> Matt Coffey [director of Carter's transition talent hunt] tells an amusing story about seeing Jim King [first director of Presidential Personnel] at President Carter's inauguration. After Carter was sworn in, Coffey said, "I can see that the pecking order has changed already; you're four rows in front of me. King responded, "Yeah, but look how far back both of us are. That tells you something about being director of personnel."[123]

Throughout the fall of 1976 Carter's transition staff, located in Atlanta and directed by Jack Watson, planned for a possible Carter presidency. It labored to devise a budget and a legislative program and prepared to staff a Carter administration. Carter's personnel staff, known as the "Talent Inventory Program" (TIP), prepared for a Carter presidency by updating the "plum book" for Carter's use, devising job descriptions of thirty-two key executive branch positions and assembling a national network of contacts to whom they could turn for names and evaluations of job candidates after the November election. Two days after the election the TIP staff rented a truck and drove its massive collection of resumes from Atlanta to Washington, D.C. Considering the disappointment they would soon face, they would have been well advised to drive to another city.

As Carter's planning staff delivered its work to the president-elect it collided with two forces that were immeasurably more powerful than it was: the president's campaign organization and cabinet secretaries. When Hamilton Jordan and other political aides to the president turned their attention to the work of TIP, they were immediately dissatisfied. In their estimation, TIP's work was politically naive: TIP had simply inventoried all recommendations sent its way without regard to the political loyalties or campaign commitments of job candidates.[124] Just days after TIP delivered its massive resume files, the president's political advisers, led by Hamilton Jordan, elbowed Jack Watson and his TIP staff aside and "set up a parallel operation immediately," dragooning his campaign staff into duty as a makeshift appointments staff.[125] As Carter's political aides would soon discover, the struggle for control was pointless.

In keeping with his pledge to reduce the size and responsibilities of the White House, Carter told his cabinet secretaries that they would be staffing their own departments, provided that they give serious consideration to women and racial minorities. Joseph Califano, Carter's secretary of Health and Human Services (HHS) recalls that his first query of Carter was "Will I have the ability to pick my own people?" And, by his recollection, Carter replied: "Yes. Barring a crime or some serious embarrassment in an FBI check, you can select your own people. I intend to keep my promise of Cabinet government to the American people."[126] By design, then, the president's aides could make their lists of candidates available to those cabinet secretaries who called, but they would have no presidential mandate to press their services upon department and uninterested agency heads. As one aide ruefully recalled, "cabinet government" meant that "we gave away 90 percent of all the jobs."[127] Carter's personal aides were left fighting over the crumbs.

Like their predecessors from other administrations, Carter's cabinet secretaries strongly preferred to staff their departments by relying on the assistance of longstanding allies whose judgment they could trust rather than the counsel of people who were unknown to them — and least of all young men and women who were members of Carter's "Peanut Brigade." HEW Secretary Joseph Califano, Lyndon Johnson's senior domestic policy aide and a powerful Washington lawyer, never phoned the White House to request that the TIP files be sent to his office.[128] Instead, he relied upon two assistants who had worked for him on Johnson's domestic policy staff, Jim Gaither and Larry Levinson, as well as a host of other acquaintances from academia and journalism, to assist him in staffing HEW.[129] Unlike the Carter transition staff, they were men and women in whose judgment Califano could repose trust, people who were personally loyal to Califano, and seasoned in HEW's programs and politics.

Demurring to accept the assistance of the transition staff made sense for a second reason: it permitted cabinet secretaries latitude to make appointments that served their own political concerns, such as building alliances among congressional and clientele constituencies whose cooperation they would soon need. As Califano recalled, in staffing HEW he was continually concerned to "check individual qualifications against required skills and against the access I would need to various interest groups. If an appointee in one post had excellent contacts in the labor movement, then an appointee to another might be preferred if he or she had an understanding of the civil rights community or the women's movement."[130] The political concerns of Jimmy Carter—his obligations to the National Education Association, African-Americans, and feminists—were, by way of contrast, far less compelling to cabinet secretaries. As Califano sneered, these were simply efforts to "appease constituencies" with which he had no intention of complying.[131] Other cabinet secretaries, equally free to accept or reject candidates recommended by the president's political aides, chose likewise.[132]

"No Direction from Us": The Carter Personnel Office

The administration under way, Carter and his senior aides hewed to their promise of cabinet government. With responsibility for staffing a Carter administration vested in departments and agency heads, the White House appointments staff would simply review candidates proposed by the departments to ensure that they passed the necessary hurdles—FBI, IRS, conflict-of-interest, and party clearances—and veto the rare candidate who failed to meet these tests. Beyond this, the White House staff would monitor the composition of appointive ranks, ensuring that politically appropriate numbers of women, African-Americans, and Hispanics were represented in the Carter administration.

In light of this modest role, only a small staff was required—one for which familiarity with federal agencies and programs was not a prerequisite. During the first few months of the administration Carter's appointments staff, burdened by a heavy load of paperwork, swelled to twenty-eight permanent and fourteen temporary staffers.[133] Though fairly large, it was less than half the size of the staff assembled by the Reagan administration in 1981, and after the initial round of appointments was made, the staff diminished to a size consistent with Carter's call for cabinet government. It consisted of Jim King, its director, and three other professional staffers, one of whom handled all boards and commissions, and two others who divide the twelve cabinet departments between them.[134] Unmistakably a return to the past, the Carter staff was smaller than the one that had served Lyndon Johnson a dozen years earlier.[135]

Responsible for tending to the political complexion of the Carter administration — but not to its substance — the staff brought no prior executive branch experience to the White House. Instead, it brought campaign experience: Jim King, director of the PPO, was a veteran longtime Democratic activist who had served as the coordinator of travel arrangements for the Carter campaign,[136] and King's deputies had served as junior staffers in the Carter field organization. With uncommon candor one PPO staffer acknowledged: "I had no real background for the job I got. I had no recruiting background, and I didn't know what a lot of the agencies did. I never should have had the job I got. I should have been hired as my assistant. I was 29 years old and had no prior governmental experience. I even drove a moped to work. The guards at the White House gate just laughed at me when I came to work."[137] As a result, the aide continued: "Califano found the White House staff, including us, to be unprofessional, unskilled, laughable, and so forth. He had deep contacts in Washington, and he wanted no direction from us. He thought he knew much better than us — and in many ways he did."[138]

The appointments staff, used neither as a resource by departments nor as an investigative staff by Hamilton Jordan, struggled simply to achieve control over the "mounds of paper that accompany presidential appointment" — to ensure that each nominee had passed through FBI, IRS, conflict-of-interest, and party clearances. One White House aide recalls just how insignificant their role was in filling departmental posts:

> I had formal responsibility for the Department of Labor, State, HEW, and other departments, but it really meant that when they had a presidential appointment, they selected the presidential appointee and sent me the FBI form and conflict of interest form and I gave them to the Counsel's Office and I monitored the movement of it. When press calls came in, I would take them. We'd call congressional liaison and say, "we're going to announce, do you want to notify the home state Senators?" Then when the checks were done I did the letter from the president saying "I'm nominating this person." That really was all we did for cabinet departments.[139]

Frustrated by the PPO's inability to protect the president's political interests, Carter's senior political aide, Hamilton Jordan, began to ignore the appointments staff, drawing instead upon his senior campaign aides and other staff units inside the White House to review departmental recommendations and propose candidates for presidential posts outside cabinet departments.[140] However, lacking the institutional assistance and presidential authorization, Jordan was unable to carefully review candidates proposed by departments, let alone systematically recruit his own candidates. Though the Carter staff had reserved the right to veto unacceptable candidates, in the opening months of the administration—when the bulk of staffing decisions were made— "no one could cite an instance of a candidate being vetoed."[141] In the rare instance when Jordan lodged a serious objection to a departmental candidate, as he did to Joseph Califano's deputy commissioner of Education, he was reproached by cabinet secretaries and told that "Carter cherished his differences from Nixon, and a grossly political move on Ellis [the deputy commissioner of Education] looked more like Nixon and his political hatchet man Fred Malek than Carter and his strong Cabinet."[142]

The Fruits of Decentralization

What were the consequences of decentralization? Department heads, as always, championed these arrangements, believing that their needs were best served by decentralization. Their commitment to decentralization was shaped by their conviction that the president's appointments staff lacked the capability to intelligently advance the president's interests. White House appointments aides, Joseph Califano complained, only "delayed and embellished the process."[143]

However, Carter's senior political advisers—Hamilton Jordan, Tim Kraft, and others—gradually became convinced that decentralization served the president's needs badly. Decentralized staffing, they argued, had resulted in department heads staffing the government with men and women who were loyal to them—or other politicians—and not to the president. As one Carter loyalist complained, decentralization produced "a government [staffed] with McGovern people, Kennedy people—people with no loyalty to him and, more important, with different views of government."[144] Lacking strong personal, programmatic, or ideological ties to their erstwhile leader, Carter's appointees, in the estimation of the president's aides, "pursued their own agendas, cut their own deals on the Hill, and worked against the president."[145] As one assistant secretary acknowledged: "There is a belief that some assistant secretaries are in business for themselves. Officially, when they testify on the Hill, they say the right thing with respect to the president's budget and legislative program. But privately, they tell committee staff members, 'I really don't think that.' "[146] In short, Carter and his aides believed they were losing control over policymaking within their own administration.

Equally important, from their perspective, were the political costs of decentralization. In their view, permitting staffing choices to rest in the hands of departmental executives, who recruited their appointees from the ranks of their personal or programmatic allies, meant that the president's appointees were remarkably unconcerned with the political repercussions of their actions for "their" president. Jack Watson, Carter's cabinet secretary, recalled a typical incident: Joseph Califano launched an antismoking campaign just on the heels of efforts by Carter to resuscitate his support among southern

Democrats: "[Califano] had a tendency to say something about tobacco and how it was the weed of the devil when we were trying to make some gain in North Carolina."[147]

Most costly of all, in the estimation of the president's aides, were the repercussions of decentralization that spilled into the national news media. Decentralized staffing produced an administration whose appointees "didn't feel that they work for Jimmy Carter" and within whose ranks dissension was commonplace.[148] This "multiplicity of voices . . . embarrassed the administration" and "put the administration in an unfavorable light and contributed to doubts about the president's leadership ability."[149]

Had the costs of decentralization been offset somehow — by the political support that the president's cabinet officers mustered — Carter's aides might have sustained their commitment to "cabinet government." Instead, the institutional foundations of reciprocity were crumbling. The dispersion of power on Capitol Hill had significantly reduced the opportunities for department heads to enter into alliances with congressional leaders on the president's behalf. "The dissipation of power in Congress meant that department heads had less opportunity to wheel and deal"[150] than did their predecessors in the Truman or Kennedy presidencies, one Carter aide opined. Returning to the federal government in 1977 after serving in the Johnson White House, Joseph Califano was stunned by the transformation of Congress. Writes Califano: "The Secretary of HEW worked in world of molecular [i.e., atomized] politics. More than forty committees and subcommittees claimed jurisdiction over one or another part of HEW each month and demanded hundreds of hours of testimony and thousands of documents from top departmental appointees. Power has been fragmented in Washington, not just within the executive branch . . . [but] within Congress itself."[151]

The dispersion of power in the Washington pressure community had the same effect, eroding the capacity of the president's traditional emissaries, department heads, to forge relationships of reciprocity with organized interests. More estranged from organized labor than any Democratic president since Grover Cleveland, Carter had hoped to solidify its support by appointing John Dunlop — whom George Meany had described as "my first, second, and third choice for Secretary of Labor" — as the Secretary of Labor. In the Washington community of 1961, only the concerns of organized labor would have been articulated (or taken seriously) and the president's solicitude for organized labor would have established a partnership — mediated by Labor Secretary John Dunlop — that Carter badly needed. However, Carter inhabited a substantially different political community than had John Kennedy, and Dunlop's candidacy came under attack by organized interests that were virtually invisible in 1961: feminists and African-Americans. Leaders from both groups alleged that Dunlop was unsympathetic to their interests while a dean at Harvard, and they succeeded in forcing Carter to scuttle the nomination. Carter began his presidency as he ended his campaign: still estranged from his party's core constituency.[152] Leaders in a political community vastly more open and decentralized than during the presidencies of Kennedy and Johnson, the president's "chief political officers" could provide him with little assistance, regardless of the president's efforts to restore department heads to their mid-century status.

As 1978 opened Hamilton Jordan had become convinced that Carter's commitment to a scaled back White House staff cost him dearly, and that "cabinet government" ought to be abandoned.[153] In the coming months Jordan was joined by members of Carter's inner circle and "elders" of the Democratic party, such as Clark Clifford and Robert Strauss, who urged Carter to "tighten his operation and show the public he was in charge and leading the way."[154] By the spring of 1978 Carter himself was beginning to suspect that the costs of decentralization, including decentralized staffing, outweighed its benefits. At an April 1978 "summit meeting" of his cabinet, Carter "lectured his subordinates on the need to improve their performance and work in harmony" [with his White House staff].[155] Carter wanted to "continue giving [cabinet secretaries] autonomy in carrying out his policies, but he expected more political and substantive cooperation from them than he had received."[156]

By the autumn of 1978 — his fortunes continuing to ebb — Carter had reassessed his initial embrace of decentralization, and rejected it. As he publicly acknowledged: "I think that I went through a year or more where I was not sure about what the authority of the president was or the influence. And I think at the end of that 15 months or so, I was quite disappointed. Now I am beginning to see that there is a proper, stronger role for the president to play than I had thought maybe six months ago."[157] Carter's once-halting moves to recentralize authority in his White House staff were now more aggressive, and throughout the Washington community it was clearly understood that "cabinet government" had passed. As the *National Journal* reported in November 1978: "Discreetly yet forcefully, the Carter White House is increasing its centralization of executive authority and tightening its control over the Cabinet departments. Carter has taken concerted action to strengthen the White House role in the pursuit of his goals."[158]

Others in Washington, most notably, department heads and the clientele allied with them, were displeased by Carter's decision to expand the size and influence of his White House staff. However risky "interposing a layer between the president and responsible [departmental] officials" might have been in 1950 — or even the early 1960s — this choice posed no serious political problems for Carter. By 1978 others in the Washington community had grown to expect and even need an expansive White House Office. Cabinet secretaries, now "far more dependent upon the president's support and services than he upon theirs," could do nothing to prevent the move.

Changing Horses in the Middle of a Stream: Rebuilding an Appointments Staff

One of the most significant moves towards recentralization of authority in the White House Office came in the handling of political appointments. In response to the political problems caused by the decentralization of staffing, Carter's field coordinator for the 1976 election, Tim Kraft, was designated Assistant to the President for Political Affairs and Personnel in April 1978.[159] Shortly after obtaining his post Kraft directed the cabinet secretaries to "make personal and professional evaluations of all presidential appointees under their purview" and instructed departments to clear all schedule C appointments with the White House.[160] Kraft and two aides "quietly eased out of office or transferred . . . at least 20 officials at the assistant secretary level."[161] Even so, as the "principal envoy of the Carter White House to the political community,"[162] Kraft was overburdened with purely political responsibilities, and his initiatives faltered.[163] Carter's White House aides concluded—as Nixon's had in 1970— that an ephemeral purge was no substitute for an ongoing, institutionalized White House presence in the staffing of the government. Thus, by the summer of 1978 Kraft brought Arnie Miller, a veteran Democratic operative and manager of Carter's 1976 campaign in Maryland, to the White House and deputized him to enlarge and strengthen the White House Personnel Office.

Miller's arrival at the helm of the PPO commenced a period of sustained growth in the staff, and by late 1979 the personnel staff was more than twice the size it had been in late 1977, expanding from fourteen to thirty-three.[164] Miller also made concerted efforts to bolster the competence of the staff, the caliber of which its new leaders acknowledged to be "very poor."[165] Miller brought in aides who had prior experience in the executive branch and directed his staff to draw upon the policy staffs within the Executive Office of the President, such as the Domestic Policy Office, the OMB, the cabinet secretary's office, and the vice-president's staff.[166] Finally, armed with Carter's commitment to a strengthened White House staff, Miller made the rounds from one department to the next to inform departments that "the game has changed a little bit. The White House is going to take a much more aggressive role in appointments, both presidential appointments and schedule C jobs."[167]

What were the consequences of Carter's attempts to reestablish a significant White House role in the staffing of his administration? The staff did manage to exercise considerable influence over the staffing of a handful of posts. When new positions were being filled—posts over which no customary claims had been established—such as the recently created inspector general positions, the staff was able to take a leading role.[168] In general, though, if asked whether the Carter staff managed to "take back control" of appointments, staffers offered cautious judgments: "It's too much to say that we 'took control back.' Instead, we became players. Our predecessors weren't players; they didn't know how the federal government worked, they just didn't play a role. But we did."[169] Another aide observed, "We became part of the information flow. And if information is power, then we had power. You could say we became a player."[170]

Nevertheless, Carter's staff fell well short of consolidating control over political appointments in the Presidential Personnel Office: their efforts were too modest and too tardy. Carter's efforts didn't come until well into his administration, and "there weren't all that many appointments to be made at that point."[171] Moreover, Carter continued to provide weak backing for his staff. "They didn't give him a lot of resources to do that. No letter went out to the cabinet saying 'You are now directed to cooperate with Arnie Miller.'"[172] Lacking orders compelling them to rely upon the PPO staff, many departments struggled to confine the staff's role,[173] while others simply avoided making use of Miller's staff. Restaffing his department in early 1979—after a revitalized appointments staff was in place—HHS Secretary Joe Califano nonetheless once again relied upon his personal confidants who had assisted in first staffing the department, rather than Miller's staff, and confronted him with a fait accompli.[174]

In July 1979 Carter cleaned house dramatically, ousting four secretaries "who had failed to be team players" (Califano, Schlesinger, Adams, and Blumenthal) and Hamilton Jordan followed up by directing cabinet members again to evaluate the loyalty and competence of their subcabinet appointees.[175] Not surprisingly, in the remaining months of Carter's administration, Carter's cabinet secretaries proved to be more solicitous of the White House staff's concerns, in part because the president turned to politically seasoned cabinet members such as Neil Goldschmidt and "Moon" Landrieux, who "knew how to be team players."[176] But by the second half of 1979 most of the appointments staff were turning their energies to pulling Carter's irons out of the fire. Many staffers returned to the Carter campaign organization whence they had come and struggled to rescue the Democratic nomination for Jimmy Carter.[177] The others remained at the White House and began to plan for a second Carter administration, hoping to profit from the hard-won lessons of the first four years.[178] In the end, of course, Carter's aides had no opportunity to put their hard-won experience to use: Carter was soundly defeated in his bid for reelection.

Carter's successors, though, did not take two years to discover that the foundations of reciprocity had been irretrievably eroded by changes in the institutional setting of the presidency. Rather, they "went to school" on the experience of the Carter presidency and found in it incontrovertible evidence that the practices that had served Truman, Eisenhower, and Kennedy could not be resuscitated in the 1970s and 1980s—at least not without serious damage to the president's fortunes. Indeed, as Carter's own aides later acknowledged, "in order to countervail all that out there, you've got to build your own [staff] in the White House."[179]

4

Plus ça Change? The Emergence of New Constraints, 1974–1994

The declining strength of party organizations has . . . freed presidents to use appointments for other ends [presidential control of the bureaucracy].
— Terry Moe

The Presidential Personnel Office is a political organization, and it has to be. That's what it was designed for, and that's what it has always been, and you must make it that.
— John Herrington, Director, Presidential Personnel Office, 1982–1985

According to rational choice accounts of the institutional presidency, the evolution of the presidency's setting has yielded a White House Personnel Office that is marked by sustained growth and by a commitment to use appointments to "control the bureaucracy." Since "the gap between [public] expectations and capacity will continue," centralization will continue to be attractive to presidents. And, because the "strength of party organizations" has declined, presidents will use their enhanced control over appointments "for other ends"—not for meeting the claims of presidential supporters, but for presidential "control of the bureaucracy."

The reality of the Presidential Personnel Office's evolution has been far different. The Presidential Personnel Office has not grown inexorably in recent years. Rather, it is roughly the same size in the early 1990s as it was two decades earlier. And, even though it has been freed from the claims of party, the Personnel Office in the 1990s is not simply an instrument of administrative leadership; rather, it is deeply engaged in meeting the claims of the organizations that dominate contemporary, postparty electoral politics in the United States.

The transformation of American electoral politics during the past quarter century has consisted of far more than the destruction of party organizations.

77

Rather, the collapse of parties has been accompanied by—indeed, precipitated by—the creation of a new constellation of organizations that now dominate electoral politics: candidate organizations, ideological groups newly mobilized for politics, such as feminists and the Christian right, and, "at one remove from electoral politics," foundations and think-tanks.[1] This new electoral politics has profoundly shaped the evolution of the modern Presidential Personnel Office: Jimmy Carter, Ronald Reagan, and Bill Clinton may have been freed from the fetters of party in fashioning their White House Personnel Office, but they were *not* from claims rooted in electoral politics. Instead, the new organizations that came to electoral prominence in the 1970s, 1980s, and 1990s proved themselves formidable claimants, shaping and constraining the Presidential Personnel Office in much the same way that party organizations once did.

Not only have electoral constraints persisted, but a new constraint—the costs of managing the modern White House Office—has also emerged. Nowhere have the organizational costs of centralization been more apparent than at the Presidential Personnel Office, the largest specialized staff within the White House Office. As the PPO has expanded, it has become more costly to monitor the performance of its members and to coordinate its work and reconcile its conflicts with other staff units. Those responsible for running the White House Office have slowly come to the conclusion that the costs of its continued growth are greater than its contributions to presidential leadership.

Taken together, these new constraints pose formidable limits to the further aggrandizement of the Presidential Personnel Office. For the foreseeable future—that is, as long as the institutional setting of the presidency remains the same—the Presidential Personnel Office will be neither "less political" nor appreciably larger than it was from the early 1980s to the mid-1990s.

THE DECLINE OF PARTY AND THE RISE OF CANDIDATE-CENTERED ELECTIONS

The Decline of Party

Only sixteen years separated Jimmy Carter's first bid for the presidency from John Kennedy's—and Ronald Reagan's first successful bid for the presidency from Richard Nixon's. Even so, their campaigns for the presidency were vastly dissimilar: the parties that Carter and Reagan inherited in the 1970s and 1980s had been greatly weakened by the continued proliferation of new campaign technologies and by the adoption of new rules governing the financing of elections and the selection of delegates to national party conventions.

Throughout the 1950s and 1960s, fewer than half of the delegates to the national conventions of the Democratic and Republican parties had been selected in party primaries. Following the tumultuous Democratic convention of 1968, party leaders adopted a host of reforms drawn up by the McGovern-Fraser Commission,[2] resulting in a surge in the proportion of delegates chosen through primaries. By 1976 three-quarters of the delegates to the Democratic National Convention were chosen through presidential primaries and roughly two-thirds of all delegates were committed to presidential candidates by state primary procedures.[3] Presidential primaries were no longer "eyewash," as Truman had contemptuously dismissed them in 1952; rather, they were an avenue through which candidates from outside the ranks of party establishment, such as Jimmy Carter, could capture their party's nomination, even over the opposition of the party's putative leaders. By 1976, party elites, once in control of nominating conventions, were relegated to the role of bystanders. Control over presidential nominations had passed into the hands of candidates, voters, and the mass media.

In general elections, too, the fortunes of party leaders had waned. Again, institutional and legal changes significantly diminished the role of party organizations. The Federal Election Campaign Act of 1974 created a system of public subsidy (and spending limits) that left candidates substantially independent of their party's fundraising apparatus. In 1976 Jimmy Carter received a public subsidy of $21.8 million, while his party's National Committee contributed a mere $2.8 million to his general election campaign.[4] In 1968 the Republican National Finance Committee remained the primary fundraising instrument for the Nixon-Agnew campaign;[5] by 1980 the once-powerful committee had lost its place as financial intermediary in presidential elections. In 1980 the Reagan-Bush campaign raised $64.1 million — only $4.6 million of which came from the Republican party.[6]

Party organizations became less important as a source of organizational assistance, as well. As communication through the mass media, especially television, was substituted for party-based "non-media activities to contact voters" (campaign rallies, door-to-door canvassing), the relevance of party organizations ebbed.[7] Republican party organizations, especially the national ones, adapted to the changing technologies and demands of electoral politics in the 1970s far more rapidly and successfully than did Democratic organizations, developing an array of campaign services for Republican office-seekers that the Democratic party could not.[8] But, as John Aldrich notes, these changes did *not* permit the organizations of either party to command or even fetter their officeholders. "Extant party organizations can be of service to candidates — presidential contenders have discovered, for example, that state or local party-run voter registration and voter turnout drives can be of assistance and are exempt from mandated campaign expenditure limits — but they cannot command. The candidate is ultimately responsible for his or her own success, unfettered to a large degree by party."[9]

Largely displaced from presidential campaign politics by a host of institutional and technological changes, party organizations found themselves displaced *between* elections as well. The new technologies of politics that Kennedy and Johnson had cautiously installed in the White House Office—public opinion polling and professional public relations—had grown sharply in significance as presidents increasingly resorted to "going public" in order to govern. Their institutionalization in the White House Office continued apace during the late 1960s and 1970s, leaving the national committee ill-suited to meet the needs of presidents. Moreover, the national committee lost its usefulness as an intermediary to party politicians. For Kennedy and Johnson, for example, local party organizations remained significant allies; the strongest among them exercised tight control over the nomination of congressional candidates—and consequently, over blocs of congressional votes.[10] Discussing Bill Green, the leader of Philadelphia's Democratic party, John Kennedy's chief congressional aide recalled: "Now there is a fellow that had an open door to us. Ken [O'Donnell] and I would often have lunch with him. He had the final say so on the five or six Congressmen up there [in Philadelphia]."[11] By the 1970s and 1980s congressional office-seekers had been liberated from local party organizations by "candidate organizations and capital-intensive campaigns"[12]—and no local party organization could boast a "say-so over five or six Congressmen." Thus, the Democratic and Republican national committees were intermediaries to local party organizations that had been stripped of their control over members of Congress and party nominations—which is to say, the national committees were intermediaries to nowhere.

However, the evolution of presidential politics in the 1970s and 1980s consisted of far more than the simple deterioration of parties. Seizing the opportunities afforded by the deterioration of parties, presidential aspirants drew together activists, money, and campaign technologies in a new kind of electoral organization: candidate campaign organizations. Few politicians understood or exploited the emerging opportunities better than Jimmy Carter and Ronald Reagan.

The Rise of Candidate-Centered Elections

> *I completed my* own *election process, which lasted almost two years, without have made any commitment in private to anyone about an appointment. . . . I'm completely at liberty to make my decisions about the Cabinet membership on the basis of merit and who can do the best job in working with me harmoniously to lead our country. There are no other commitments.*
> —President-elect Jimmy Carter, December 1976[13]

Jimmy Carter's claim that he had completed his "own election process" was only partly accurate. True, Carter owed little to the men and women who made up the traditional infrastructure of the Democratic party. However, Carter's campaign for the presidency, like Reagan's, was not "his own," but the work of a complex, national political organization: a *presidential* campaign organization.

Consider, for example, Carter's bid for the presidency. As Carter began his quest for the Democratic nomination in 1974, he successfully sought appointment as the chair of the DNC's Campaign '74 Committee. The experience, one Carter intimate suggested, led Carter and his senior political adviser, Hamilton Jordan, to conclude that "the National Committee consisted of 363 of the least influential political figures in the country. They decided that the Committee itself had little use for them, and they would have to build their own organization [to win the Democratic nomination and the presidency]."[14]

And build they did. Carter's pursuit of the Democratic nomination did not rely upon cultivating the support of traditional party leaders. Carter was far from their favorite candidate, and, in any event, their support was no longer necessary—they no longer controlled the bulk of delegates to the party's nominating convention. Instead, Carter and Jordan planned to campaign *around* the party's putative leaders, amassing delegates by making appeals directly to Democratic voters in now-decisive primary elections. The work of the nomination campaign would be performed by Carter's *own* political organization, an amalgam of youthful volunteers (dubbed "the Peanut Brigade"), professional campaign consultants, and Democrats drawn to Carter as he gained momentum through victories in early primaries.

The campaign went as planned: Carter won the Democratic nomination with precious little support from Democratic party elites. Reflecting on Carter's victory and his relationship to the party's erstwhile centers of power, Carter aide Mark Siegal observed: "State chairmen were generally opposed to Carter throughout the primary process. Governors were a real problem. Jimmy . . . ran against Congress and did not have a Congressional background so there was no relationship there."[15] Confronted with big-city mayors who opposed his candidacy, such as Philadelphia's Frank Rizzo, "We just ran right around him—and won [the Pennsylvania primary]," one Carter aide proudly recounted.[16]

As Carter began his general election campaign, he could organize his bid for the presidency in two ways: he could campaign with the organization that he had assembled to win his party's nomination, expanding it to meet the needs of a general election. Or, Carter could rely heavily upon local Democratic party organizations. Suspicious of the loyalties and capabilities of Democratic organizations,[17] Carter chose to draw upon the campaign organization that had assisted him in his presidential nomination contests.[18] The campaign organization, now subsidized by the federal treasury, swelled to a staff of roughly five hundred paid workers and another thousand volunteers[19] and assumed responsibility for the work of campaigning that was once the province of Democratic party organizations.[20]

Although Ronald Reagan was not as estranged from his party's leaders as Carter had been in 1976, he, like Carter, won his party's nomination by building a national political organization.[21] And, like Carter, Reagan constructed a personal political organization with which to campaign during the general election. To be sure, the Reagan campaign did rely upon a handful of officeholders who led political organizations. "Jim Thompson in Illinois, Dick Thornburgh in Pennsylvania, Bill Milliken in Michigan. . . . In those states there was quite close coordination, and many of the governor's people wound up on the Reagan campaign."[22] In the main, though, there were far fewer party organizations with which collaboration was fruitful in 1980 than there had been in 1968. "In 1968 we selected for chairman of the state [Nixon campaign organization] some who had an organization—probably an elected officeholder, a senator or a governor. He became the Nixon chairman, and then you inherited his organization and tried to meld in with it. But by 1980 Ronald Reagan had a lot less to rely on."[23] With "a lot less to rely on," the president's aides found it wise to build their own campaign organization, an expanded and subsidized version of the organization that had won the Republican nomination for Ronald Reagan. Having put their own campaign organization in the field—and supplied its money—Reagan's political aides found themselves in full control of the campaign. As one Reagan regional political director boasted, "We [the Reagan campaign organization] had complete authority over the conduct of the campaign in those states within our region. That included everything from the development of the [campaign] plan to its implementation."[24]

The rise of presidential campaign organizations was not the only change that marked presidential politics in the late 1960s and late 1980s. The late 1960s and 1970s was an extraordinarily fertile period for the formation of interest groups and the mobilization of social movements. At the same time, presidential nominations were becoming increasingly open and increasingly amenable to the exercise of group power. As James Caesar observed, during the 1970s and 1980s "interest groups and temporary currents and movements, such as the nuclear freeze movement or the evangelical movement . . . have gained at the expense of parties. Candidates seek support from groups and movements to help build their organizations, to secure funds, and to win a base of support. The new system brings the candidates into direct contact with groups, compelling them to court group support with a promiscuity that often appears excessive, even by modern standards."[25] Taken together, the rise of candidate-centered campaigns and the mobilization of groups and movements into presidential politics reshaped not only presidential elections, but the face of the White House Office as well.

The White House Personnel Office in a New Electoral Order

The imprint of the new electoral order was immediate and obvious: the president's party, once feeble, became altogether inconsequential. Among veterans of mid-century presidencies, the president's party was seen to be both a constraint *and* a useful ally. As Clark Clifford advised President-elect John Kennedy in 1960: "Before the inauguration the National Committee should be the locus of an office to deal with requests for patronage and recommendations for appointments to office in the federal bureaucracy, particularly below the level of assistant secretary and agency heads. The flood . . . will be enormous . . . [and the national committee] will give the president-elect a place to divert the pressure."[26]

Carter and his aides, in contrast, saw the Democratic party neither as a meaningful constraint nor as a useful ally, and they never contemplated using the party's national committee to assist them in building an administration. Instead, as Carter's aides planned for a possible Carter administration during the summer of 1976, they solicited the advice of John Macy—anathema to Democratic party politicians for his work during the Johnson presidency.[27] And, once the election was over, Carter's transition staff did not move into the offices of the Democratic National Committee—or even work alongside the party's representatives, as Kennedy's staff had. Veterans of Democratic party organizations, including the national committee, were conspicuously absent from Carter's transition. "[The transition] was not a textbook operation of the National Committee funneling the names of key state operatives to some White House transition team. They were nowhere to be found."[28] Another senior Carter aide recalled that "they weren't in the loop."[29] Carter's transition, like his campaign for the presidency, was not organized and directed by the veteran Democratic leaders, but rather by the staff of Carter's own political organization.

Like the campaign that preceded it, the Carter transition was a federally subsidized[30] and president-centered affair. After a brief intramural struggle within the Carter organization that pitted Carter's Atlanta-based transition planners, headed by Jack Watson, against his senior political aides, led by Hamilton Jordan, Carter's political aides quickly took control of the transition. Hamilton Jordan and "his operatives," his senior political aides, set up shop in the upper floors of HEW's headquarters on Constitution Avenue. Having won the presidency by constructing an independent political organization, the leaders of the Carter organization now reaped the fruits of their strategy. "We were besieged from dawn until midnight with names and demands and requests from *our* network—our state campaign directors," a senior Carter political aide recalled.[31] Arnie Miller, Carter's PPO director, observed: "You used to have the National Committee, but now the president picks up support by building his *own* political organization—and the White House subsequently has to take care of it."[32]

That was not all Carter's aides had to care for. Within the Democratic party, a host of new blocs and movements — feminists, environmentalists, and racial/ethnic groups — rose to prominence during the late 1960s and 1970s. "Blocs and movements," James Sundquist noted, "have *replaced* party organizations as the elements of electoral coalitions."[33] Having elbowed the Democratic party aside, Carter found that no one else was "out in front to divert the pressure," as the national committee had been during Clark Clifford's days in the White House Office. Rather, the demands of the Democratic party's new constituencies were now the president's to handle — without intermediation. "They were not going to work through the party; the party was not their vessel."[34]

Consider, for example, the case of women's organizations. No bloc or movement rose more swiftly than the women's movement. The early 1970s witnessed an extraordinary resurgence of organized feminism, and by 1976 the women's movement had established an important place in presidential politics, particularly within the Democratic party. Faced with a confrontation with feminists over the composition of state delegations to the Democratic National Convention, Carter met with women's groups prior to the convention and established an advisory committee. The "Committee of 51.3%" was an appendage to his campaign organization that was to "advise him on issues, support his campaign, and assist him in seeking 'qualified' women to serve in his administration."[35] If elected, Carter pledged, he would appoint women to "jobs of importance throughout [his] administration."[36] To follow up on Carter's pledge, Carter aides Mary King and Joan Tobin headed up "Talent Bank '77," an effort to assemble the resumes of women for a prospective Carter administration.[37] Women's organizations saw no point to working through the Democratic National Committee and were reluctant to let the initiative lie in the hands of Carter's *own* political organization. Instead they responded to Carter's commitments by launching their own efforts: more than fifty women's organizations, led by the National Women's Political Caucus, formed the Coalition for Women's Appointments (CWA), which marked the first independent effort of women's organizations to collect resumes and lobby for the appointment of women.

For White House aides who handled political appointments in the Truman and Kennedy administrations, the claims of women's organizations were unknown. Women's organizations, nonexistent in presidential politics at mid century, were altogether absent from appointment politics. To the extent that women's concerns were represented at all, they were voiced by women who held the few posts set aside for them — and to which they were confined — within the staff of the national committee: usually vice-chair of the National Committee or director of the Women's Division of the National Committee.[38] Political parties were intermediaries, organizing and channeling the claims of women (and others) within the party's coalition.[39]

By the 1970s, the rise of candidate-centered elections had stripped parties of their capacity to act as intermediaries, and demands once handled by the president's party were now placed directly at the president's doorstep. It was not the Democratic party, but rather Carter's political aides who were responsible for propitiating the claims of women's organizations as well as other blocs and movements. As the transition got under way, the files of Talent Bank '77 and its staff were assimilated into Carter's transition organization.[40] And, in the opening days of January, Carter and his senior aides met with representatives of the coalition,[41] receiving the slate of candidates they had assembled. Moreover, Carter instructed members of his cabinet to whom appointment choices had been delegated to meet with representatives from the Coalition on Women's Appointments. Senior women with the Carter campaign, most importantly Barbara Blum and Anne Wexler, also pressed from inside the Carter transition for the appointment of women, preparing slates of candidates for the consideration of Carter and his closest aides.[42]

The Administration Under Way

As the White House took shape in early 1977, the Personnel Office that Carter and his senior aides created was profoundly shaped by the new electoral politics outside the White House Office, just as its forerunners had been by the demands of mid-century electoral politics. Barred from imposing the president's policy preferences on appointment decisions by Carter's pledge of "cabinet government" and besieged by the demands of new electoral constituencies, the White House Personnel Office that emerged in 1977 and 1978 was engaged solely in propitiating the claims of the president's political supporters. This state of affairs is altogether at odds with what rational choice accounts lead us to expect.[43]

One constituency, the Democratic party, received little solicitude from the Carter White House. The Carter White House made no provision for meeting with the Democratic National Committee to solicit its participation in political appointments, nor did it solicit recommendations from state and local party organizations. Even the leaders of the Cook County Democratic organization, the sine qua non of local Democratic organizations in the postwar years, complained that they had not been consulted about local appointments. Instead of notifying local Democratic party leaders of pending appointments, Georgia State Chair Marjorie Thurman complained, the Carter White House chose to "deal with 'Peanut Brigaders.'"[44]

Its leverage over the president gone, the Democratic National Committee feebly protested Carter's slights by adopting a resolution of censure. On April 1, 1977, appropriately enough, the party's national committee unanimously adopted a resolution pleading with the Carter White House to allow the "full and meaningful" participation of party leaders in appointment decisions — a plea for access.[45] Carter's senior aides paid no heed to the resolution. One year later, Democratic National Committee officials complained that the Carter White House continued to ignore even the smallest of traditional courtesies: notifying state and local party figures of federal appointments prior to their public announcement.[46] "We've raised the problem again and again," lamented Ann Campbell, president of the Democratic State Chairs, "and nothing happens."[47] Little wonder that nothing happened: in the estimation of Carter's senior political aides, "the party just didn't amount to much. The party was absolutely irrelevant. [Therefore] they just weren't part of the personnel process."[48] Freed from dependence upon the Democratic party in his quest for the presidency—and expecting that Democratic party organizations would play little role in the adoption of his program or his reelection campaign in 1980—Carter could ignore the claims of party with an impunity that his predecessors might have envied. The sanctions of party organizations, eroding for the past thirty years, were now entirely gone, and with them the party's access to appointment choices.

Carter aides did not, however, find themselves freed from the demands of electoral politics by the disintegration of party organizations. Rather, they continued to struggle, as they had during the transition, with the participants that had recently come to prominence in presidential election politics: the presidential campaign organization and ideological groups newly mobilized for politics. Many leaders of women's organizations were displeased with the consideration they had been accorded during the transition to a Carter administration. In their estimation, most of the 1,500 names compiled by the Coalition for Women's Appointments "were never considered," and the jobs awarded women "are less senior than those given to loyal male workers of this and previous administrations."[49] Veterans of the president's own political organization were equally disappointed. In their estimation, their work on behalf of Carter was a "kiss of death" in many departments and agencies.[50] In contrast to the indifference with which it met the importunings of Democratic party politicians, the Carter White House scrambled to give succor to these new, and more compelling constituencies.

Stung by feminists' charges and the critical news media coverage they elicited,[51] Carter's aides struggled to blunt their criticism. In late January, Arvonne Fraser, head of the Women's Equity Action League (WEAL) was brought into the Carter personnel office for a sixty-day stint,[52] and in early March, President Carter met with representatives of the Coalition for Women's Appointments at the White House. Meanwhile his aides publicly trumpeted a presidential memo directing department heads to report on their hiring of "women and minorities above the GS-15 level."[53]

As the administration progressed, the Carter PPO staff was deeply engaged in monitoring the composition of appointive ranks to ensure that politically appropriate numbers of women, African-Americans, and Hispanics were appointed. Although Carter pledged to his cabinet secretaries that "you can select your own people," he repeatedly directed them to appoint women and blacks whenever possible. As one feminist within the administration proudly recalled, Carter "was never ambiguous [about the appointment of women and African-Americans]. They [cabinet secretaries] all got the message."[54] Indeed, they did get the message. As Joe Califano recalled: "Carter and Johnson did share one important personnel objective. They both pressed affirmative action in federal appointments. Carter pressed me with notes to appoint more blacks, Hispanics, and women, and fewer white males."[55] In fact, it was the president's personnel staff that monitored the composition of appointive ranks and enforced Carter's commitment to "diversity" — thereby earning the enmity of many agency and department heads. One PPO head recalled his struggle with Califano over the appointment of a general counsel.

We came to blows about this over his appointment of the general counsel — we got in a real pissing match over this. When he sent his general counsel candidate up I wrote a memo for the president telling Califano that there would be no more white males. I sent a list of the real policy jobs and the kinds of people holding them. Joe and Hale Champion [his undersecretary] fired back a similar memo on the White House staff, pointing out that it was virtually all white males — and they eventually won their point.[56]

However, the job of nurturing presidential constituencies consisted of far more than pressing for the appointment of women — and blacks and Hispanics — to posts in the Carter administration. Most important of all to the Carter White House were the claims of the president's core constituency, the "Carter network, a coast-to-coast . . . group of local officials, campaign volunteers, and ordinary Democrats" who had supported Carter in 1976 — loyalists whom "the White House looked to for political support and fieldwork rather than the formal structure of the Democratic party."[57] Carter's predecessors had sometimes assembled personal followings in pursuit of the presidency. What was distinctive about post-party presidential politics was that the *maintenance* of a presidential campaign organization was seen to be central to the president's political fortunes. As one journalist noted, "The maintenance of a [personal] campaign organization seems a risk worth taking. The Carter network could provide a reliable support group across the nation that could be employed both as a pressure group in support of the president's policies and the hub of his reelection effort in 1980."[58] In the opening year of Carter's presidency responsibility for giving succor to the "Carter Network" rested largely in the hands of Carter's personnel staff.[59] The Carter personnel staff — each of whom was a veteran of the Carter campaign — presided over the

"Political Inventory of Talent," or "PIT," a retort to the transition staff's politically inept "Talent Inventory Project," TIP.[60] By February 1977 the staff had assembled a slate of five hundred candidates to recommend for temporary "schedule C" posts[61] and other departmental appointments.[62]

"Half My Time Was Spent on This Stuff": Politics and Policy at the PPO

I really looked forward to coming back [for a second Carter term] but I used to shudder at the thought of the other half of this job. The other half is servicing all of that stuff [political demands].
—Arnie Miller, Carter PPO Director, 1978–1980

As the Carter administration progressed, doling out low-level appointments to the president's supporters proved to be far from sufficient to establish the leadership and direction of the executive branch. By 1978 Carter and his senior aides came to the conclusion that effective leadership of the executive branch could be achieved only by creating a White House Personnel Office that was larger, more professional, more respected within the administration —and far more capable of gaining control over appointment choices on the president's behalf.[63] By 1979 the staff was more than twice the size it had been in 1977. And, as the PPO grew, many of the new staffers who were added were men and women who had *not* served in the Carter campaign but in the executive branch—at the Office of Management and Budget, State Department, and elsewhere.[64] Brought on to strengthen the staff's reputation and expertise, these staffers found an office that was, they recalled, "too small and too weak to do the job. Many of them had never been in government, and working in the White House is no place to gain seasoning."[65]

In spite of the changes, the Carter Personnel Office fell far short of becoming a professionalized instrument of policy leadership. In part the staff was simply unable to shake the (well-founded) reputation that it had acquired during the first two years of the Carter presidency: that "its main function was to refer people who had been involved in the campaign for several years and were looking for a way to serve."[66] As Arnie Miller recalled,

I had a struggle with the Deputy Secretary of Defense, Charles Duncan, about a year after I came, over one word in a memo that would somehow outline the responsibilities between our office and the Defense Department. He thought that our office was appropriately the place to provide the *political* screening. I added one word, where we would review the political credentials and *competence* of presidential appointees. This resulted because the office's main function was to refer people who had been involved in the campaign for several years and were looking for a way to serve.[67]

More important, though, were the effects of the new electoral environment of the presidency. No longer willing or able to rely upon the assistance of the president's party, the Presidential Personnel Office found itself burdened with political chores that were the province of the party during the presidencies of Truman and Kennedy. For example, 1980 was a census year, and the Presidential Personnel Office was responsible for deciding how the 800,000 temporary jobs created by the census—minor patronage plums once handled at the national committee—would be allocated among claimants.[68] Regardless of its commitment to "professionalize" and establish policy control through appointments, the PPO was still needed to tend to the needs of the "Carter network." Thus, a host of political operatives from the Carter organization remained active in the Presidential Personnel Office[69]—working directly under the supervision of Tim Kraft, assistant to the president for personnel *and* political affairs. These aides monitored schedule C vacancies, championing well-connected candidates who "brought something extra to the table . . . people who could be helpful to us back home in their state, helpful to us in getting legislation passed on the Hill, in building support among minorities or women, or in winning the [1980] nomination."[70]

Like his predecessors, PPO head Arnie Miller struggled with "trying to separate . . . the political operation from the [professional] recruiters."[71] As he acknowledged, "My problem . . . was that the political operation sometimes hurt our reputation. They would often call in with people who really didn't fit lower-level positions. Those inappropriate recommendations sometimes jeopardized our credibility with the Cabinet."[72] Predictably, the departments and agencies did not view the staff as a "neutral broker." Rather, they continued to view the staff with suspicion and sought to circumscribe Miller's role to narrowly "political" supervision of their recommendations. In short, the atrophying of parties had an ironic twist to it: it expanded the political responsibilities of the White House staff, compelling presidents to "politicize" their Personnel Office staff in ways that were unknown during the Kennedy and Johnson presidencies. Told of the Carter PPO's responsibility for handling census appointments, Dan Fenn (of the Kennedy PPO) exclaimed: "I can't underline too strongly that this little enclave of ours didn't do those things. We just didn't respond to those proposals."[73] By the 1970s and 1980s, presidents had no choice but to "respond to those proposals"—as the experience of the Reagan presidency confirms.

THE REAGAN PRESIDENCY: "PERSONNEL IS POLICY"

How far can presidents pursue the centralization of appointments in the White House—and the use of appointments as a "policy instrument"—given the new electoral environment of the presidency? No president was more committed to the centralization of appointments and to their exploitation as an instrument of presidential leadership than was Reagan; hence, his presidency offers us an opportunity to explore the outer bounds of the modern Presidential Personnel Office. The answer to the question, "How far?" is, "not as far as Ronald Reagan's staff had hoped or anticipated — and, not as far as rational choice accounts suggest." The commitment to act on the credo "personnel is policy" collided with the reality of modern presidential politics: "personnel is *politics*," albeit, not party politics.

That Reagan's entourage was deeply committed to a strategy of centralization, including the centralization of political appointments, was evident long before Reagan's inauguration — and even before Reagan's 1980 bid for the presidency. The efforts of Reagan's senior staff to control staffing of the administration were more prolonged, more elaborate, more expensive, and drew upon more people than ever before. Reagan's aides, hoping to centralize control over budgeting, policy, and appointments, built a transition organization of five hundred paid staff and six hundred to seven hundred volunteers. The transition staff, housed in a ten-story office building only a few blocks from the White House, spent more than $2 million of federal funds and $2 million of private contributions assembling the pieces of a "Reagan Revolution."[74]

Even in 1976, during Reagan's unsuccessful bid for the presidency, the Reagan entourage was convinced of the need to devote considerable resources to planning the staffing of a Reagan administration.[75] By November 1979 — the same month that Ronald Reagan formally declared his candidacy — the first efforts to plan for the staffing of the Reagan administration were under way. That month Reagan's most trusted policy adviser, Ed Meese, met with Pendleton James, a close personal friend and former assistant to Fred Malek, to lay out his thoughts on the staffing of a Reagan administration.[76] Like Anderson and others in the Reagan entourage, Meese shared three basic assumptions about political appointments:[77] "Appointments were absolutely critical to the success of the administration; careful, thorough personnel organization was necessary; control of appointments had to be centralized and controlled tightly by President Reagan and a few others on the White House staff."[78] The aim of centralization, Meese instructed James, was to populate the government with men and women whose first loyalties were to Ronald Reagan. "Ed [Meese] laid out the five criteria that we were to follow [in staffing the administration]. We were to choose people who will carry out this man's [Reagan's] philosophical commitment — people who will help move programs in the directions he wants. Then you have to find people who are team players — who will work in a team effort to get things done. And I forget what the other three are."[79]

Without question, the dominant value would be loyalty: "Loyalty, goddamn it, you can't knock it. Jimmy Carter appointed Califano Secretary [of HHS] and that guy wasn't loyal at all; he had his own agenda. Nixon appointed Wally Hickel and he had his own agenda. You have to recognize that you have to bring in people who are committed to carrying out the programs the president was elected to see through, and not to do what they think is best."[80] As this lapse of memory—"I forget what the other three are"—suggests, the other criteria, described by Meese as "integrity, competence, and toughness," figured far less prominently in Meese's hierarchy of values or in the design of an appointments staff for the Reagan administration.

By April 1980 Reagan was assured of receiving his party's nomination, and Meese returned to James, requesting that he draft plans for staffing an administration. Three months later, in July 1980, James had been brought into the Reagan campaign organization, given a separate budget, and had begun to build a staff organization in the former Bush presidential campaign headquarters, in Alexandria, Virginia.[81] James quickly sought the assistance of McKinsey and Company, a collaborator with Republican White House aides since 1952; architects of Nixon's "administrative presidency," including Roy Ash and Caspar Weinberger; and veterans of the Nixon Personnel Office, including Fred Malek, his former boss.[82]

On the basis of these discussions James devised three ground rules to ensure that appointments would be "centralized and tightly controlled" by a presidential staff. First, as the experience of the Nixon and Carter presidencies demonstrated, the president could not give away his prerogatives at the outset of his administration and hope to retrieve them.[83] Instead, the president's prerogatives would have to be carefully guarded from the first moment: Reagan's secretaries-designate would be offered their posts upon the condition that each recognized that "the White House is going to control the appointment process. All of them [appointees] are going to be controlled right here by Pen James."[84]

Second, because "you can't beat something with nothing," the president would have his own cadre of candidates from the moment his cabinet was chosen. This, in turn, meant that a good deal of staff work would have to be done prior to the selection of cabinet secretaries. When these secretaries arrived at their desks, they would be greeted by a large, specialized, and powerful presidential appointments staff that had already assembled notebooks filled with a slate of candidates. Reagan's cabinet secretaries would not be left to their own devices, as Nixon's and Carter's had been.[85] Instead, Reagan's cabinet would be directed to choose from among a slate of candidates whose "commitment to the president's agenda" had been certified by James's staff.[86] Finally, the influence of the president's staff would depend upon its ability to establish its "clout and access within the administration."[87] "Clout" and "access" would be ensured, James anticipated, if the president's senior assistant for political appointments was given the trappings of power keenly watched by Washingtonians: title (Assistant to the President); propinquity to the president (an office in the West Wing of the White House); and a firm commitment that all appointments recommendations would pass through his office.[88]

As the summer of 1980 drew to a close, James drew up a transition appointments organization and recruited its members. The staff would consist of fifty aides and be organized along the line of Richard Nixon's Personnel Office. The office would be divided into five "issue clusters," each of which would be staffed by an "associate director" who was a seasoned hand from the Nixon or Ford administrations.[89] These associate directors would begin by searching for candidates to fill the top eighty-seven policymaking positions in the executive branch — undersecretaries and deputy secretaries — and proceed to the next tier of posts, one hundred assistant secretary slots, by inauguration day.[90] By January 20, James anticipated, the senior policymaking posts in the government would be filled — by cabinet secretaries whose choices had been structured and carefully monitored by a presidential appointments staff.

In spite of their elaborate and ambitious plans, James and Meese failed to anticipate two things. First, there would be important repercussions from claiming such centralized control over appointments. With a highly decentralized system of political appointments, job seekers and their allies disperse their importunings through the new administration. Attempts to thoroughly centralize appointments, by way of contrast, lead virtually the entire Washington community to focus its importunings on the president's staff.

Second, appointments are a means of establishing policy control throughout the executive branch, but they are much more, too. Meese and James, neither of whom had "rung a doorbell or made a phone call on behalf of a candidate in their lives,"[91] ignored the fact that presidents are political leaders — leaders who incur debts to the women and men who assist them in gaining office and obligations to other politicians who inhabit separate institutions and share in governing. Though James spent months canvassing experts about the creation of appointments staff, not once did he speak with the leaders of Reagan's campaign organization, and the organization chart that he drew up before the November election had no boxes representing a staff to service political claims!

Not surprisingly, during the opening year of the Reagan administration James would become the target of bitter and sustained criticism from the president's campaign organization and their allies in the "new right" of the Republican party, and his staff would undergo a metamorphosis, ballooning to more than twice the size that James had planned, as he struggled to cope with the demands of electoral politics in the postparty era. In the struggle between "policy" and "politics," policy would give ground.

Describing his tenure as director of the Reagan PPO, Pen James recalled, "I was blind-sided by all those [political] demands." Who "blind-sided" him? Like the Carter PPO staff, the Reagan PPO aides found that the claims of their party organizations were inconsequential. Accorded no role in the handling of personnel during the transition, the Republican National Committee was viewed by the president's aides with disdain. For Reagan's personnel aides, "they [the RNC] were not a big headache. They were not even a small headache. They were just no headache at all. They played a *very small* role."[92] Seen from the perspective of the president's political aides, the party's national committee was an appendage of the White House staff, to be used or ignored as convenient. Asked about his relationship with the RNC, one of Reagan's senior political advisers replied: "They were really not big players. I mean they pretty much were an appendix [*sic*] of mine. . . . Appendix is not the word, but it was sort of my operation. They basically did what I told them to do."[93] In the estimation of the national committee's staff, the White House staff served only the president's political needs and the president's political organization while neglecting the needs of the national committee and the Republican organizations that it represented, that is, by denying it opportunities to obtain sinecures for donors to the Republican party—"the people who pay our salaries." The RNC's patronage staffer described the problem she faced in these terms:

> The White House [personnel staff] looks to see whether you've had Reagan/Bush experience—*whether you've done your duty to that campaign.* And it has made my job very difficult. For instance I had a person who we wanted to get on a board or a commission. He had an extensive political background, working for governors, lieutenant governors, Ford, Nixon, you name it, it goes way back. I was on the phone [with the PPO] for 30 minutes listing all the things he had done and how much money he had raised. And after I had finished she [the PPO staffer] said, "Gee, I don't see any Reagan/Bush on there." And that man to this day has not gotten a board or commission.[94]

Bereft of leverage over the president and his White House staff, there was simply nothing the RNC could do—short of publicly censuring its president, as the Democratic National Committee had fruitlessly done in 1977.

Although the Republican party may not have been "even a small headache," the PPO found itself besieged by a new set participants that had risen to prominence in electoral politics. As David Mayhew noted, the "structural components" of the Republican party of the 1980s consisted of "aggressive self-propelled candidate organizations, . . . a Christian [and secular] right newly mobilized for politics . . . [and] at one remove from electoral politics, corporate-funded foundations and think-tanks."[95] Each of them—the Reagan campaign organization, and new right journalists, fundraisers, think tanks and "policy entrepreneurs"—presented extraordinary problems for Pen James and his staff throughout the opening years of the Reagan presidency, reshaping the Reagan Personnel Office in ways that were unforeseen by Ed Meese and Pen James.

Having displaced the Republican party as the president's campaign vehicle, Ronald Reagan's *own* political organization found itself saddled with the responsibilities of party. It was besieged by job-seekers from around the country who had supported Reagan throughout his career. Like the Carter staff, James and his staff assiduously sought to remain invisible. But, like the Carter staff, James and his aides were "out in front," and months before the November election his staff began to receive a steady flow of mail from job-seekers.[96]

In the days following the election—before the "plum book" was even published—the staff received over 600 unsolicited resumes in the mail each day.[97] James drafted Helene Von Damm, Ronald Reagan's longtime personal secretary and financial director for the northeastern United States in the 1980 campaign, and her campaign aides to handle the flood of resumes and phone calls. One veteran of this effort rolled his eyes as he recalled their efforts: "Thousands and thousands of resumes came with every day's mail. It was chaos. There were duplicates [resumes], and people were coming from all directions, and we were trying to figure out where they should be slotted. There were tens of thousands of resumes, it was unbelievable. Just unbelievable."[98] Many of the unsolicited resumes came from "worker bees in the campaign organization,"[99] while others—the solicited resumes—were being channeled to James's staff by senior members of the Reagan campaign organization. "The regional political directors [from the Reagan organization] were taking care of the people in the areas where they had worked. They kept coming in and saying, 'Here is a good guy, he has contributed to us since day one.'"[100] Still other resumes came from job-seekers who had no special claims on the attention of James's staff, save for their creativity and boldness: "One lady sent one hundred identical resumes, each applying for a different job; an acquaintance shipped him [James] a whole frozen turkey . . . with a resume stuffed in its neck."[101]

Though Von Damm began with only a handful of aides, soon "there were a couple dozen of us who sorted through the resumes."[102] And, even though the staff was expanded, it simply could not keep up with the flood of resumes.[103] "It's not easy. It was a losing proposition for us," one aide recalled.[104] The administrative problem of handling this deluge of job-seekers was exacerbated by a strategic decision that James had made during the summer of 1980: his staff should focus its efforts on the senior policymaking posts in the government and proceed to staff lower-level posts, such as schedule C jobs, much later. James and his advisers failed to anticipate, however, that the president's campaign organization would be most keenly interested in these jobs and unable to wait six or eight months for their sinecures.[105]

Hence, James rapidly found himself in a head-to-head confrontation with the president's political organization. Just a few weeks into the transition

James summoned a gathering of the campaign organizers, including Nofziger, Rollins, and the regional political directors from the Reagan-Bush campaign organization, hoping to quell their anger at not having received appointments. James recounts:

> They all expected an appointment, and deservedly so — and they expected an appointment the next day [after the election]. Hell, we hadn't gotten the cabinet done yet. . . . But they kept saying "When are we getting our jobs?" They were beating the shit out of me. So, I called up Paul Laxalt and I said "Paul, there is only one way I can handle this, let's call them all together and explain to them the process — but I need you with me." So, we called a meeting at a conference room on M Street [the transition headquarters]. And all of them were there. . . . [I explained the process to them, but] that just didn't cut any ice with these guys. These are the type of people who say "I want to go there" and then they go through the wall, they don't take time to go through a door. Paul [Laxalt] tried to defend me, and he couldn't even handle them.[106]

After Reagan took office, the problem persisted. With the president's own political organization now ensconced in the Office of Political Affairs, the struggle became an intramural one. One aide to Lyn Nofziger, head of the White House Office of Political Affairs, recalls the first months of 1981: "He [Nofziger] had people burning down his door. He was getting 300 calls per week. People were calling and saying 'What is this? I can't even get my letters answered.'"[107] Another observed: "The political office became the wailing wall. Everybody who wanted jobs came to us, and in turn we were trying to get our [campaign organization] people placed."[108] In the estimation of the president's political aides, "our personnel operation was so screwed up; it was one of the great debacles of this administration."[109] The appointments staff simply had no sensitivity to the realities of electoral politics:

> There was no political sensitivity whatsoever. And there was not any desire to acquire any. . . . The people that put him in office were ignored. The Comptroller General of the United States, Charles Bowsher, was an Assistant Secretary of the Navy under Lyndon Johnson, and he won out his political appointment — a fifteen year political appointment — over the Reagan finance chairman from Arizona, who was a highly experienced guy. One was a registered Democrat, anti-administration, and he was chosen by Pen James over the Republican finance chairman for Reagan![110]

Thus, one staffer from Reagan's Political Affairs Office observed, "I would say that we [the Political Affairs Office] spent about 90 percent of our time on this in the first year. I often said that what we should have done for the first six months was let Pen James run the political office and let Lyn Nofziger run the appointment office."[111]

Worse still for James, the protests of the president's campaign organization were joined by the men who had bankrolled Ronald Reagan's rise to political power and served as his intellectual mentors: the Kitchen Cabinet.[112] Reagan's Kitchen Cabinet played a large role in the selection of his cabinet,[113] and its members were eager to ensure that Reagan loyalists and ideological fidelity were rewarded in subcabinet appointments as well.[114] The president's campaign aides, recognizing a valuable ally, set up an office for the Kitchen Cabinet adjacent to Lyn Nofziger's office, from which they, too, joined the fray. Kitchen Cabinet members demanded—over Pen James's opposition—to meet with James's associate directors and review the slates of candidates they had assembled for presentation to the cabinet members. Seen from James's vantage point, the Kitchen Cabinet was an "untenable and uncomfortable" presence:

> They were on the phone every ten minutes with me: Joe Coors, Bill Wilson, Charlie Wick. These were guys with nothing else to do, who felt left out. But, they were friends of the president—and you listen to friends of the president. They felt that they should have control of appointments, and I felt that they shouldn't. I was really dealing with a very strong political force. They moved into the EOB and were calling in the cabinet officers and interrogating them; they were calling in my staff and telling them what to do.[115]

One associate director recalled the "grilling" that she received from the Kitchen Cabinet:

> I was the first person to put together "the book" to present to the secretary-designate. . . . And right before or right after [completing it], I had to go over that book with the Kitchen Cabinet, in the whole sense of being a Reaganite. A lot of the people I knew [and recruited] were Nixon and Ford Republicans. And there I am at this huge conference table with the Kitchen Cabinet, and I'll never forget Charlie Wick standing up and saying, "Let's not forget why we are here for. We've got to keep our eye on the ball." It was somebody that they were all tearing their hair out about. And so I slinked away—I don't remember the job.[116]

The campaign organization and the Kitchen Cabinet were joined by yet another kind of claimant: "new right" politicians, publicists, and think tanks. Like the Kitchen Cabinet, the new right feared that "movement conservatives" were being given short shrift in favor of "Nixon-Ford retreads." In fact, the new right had been shown considerable solicitude in the creation of the Reagan administration. During the summer of 1980 Ed Meese, a board member of the Heritage Foundation, had solicited the help of Heritage in drafting a conservative blueprint for policymaking (*A Mandate for Leadership*), and he invited Heritage to assist Pen James in devising plans for staffing a Reagan administration.[117] Before election day Heritage had assembled a "talent bank" for James to draw on; throughout the transition it carted the resumes of thousands of certified conservatives to the transition office on M Street; and some of its staffers joined the Kitchen Cabinet in reviewing the cabinet members' presentation of their staffing decisions.[118]

Nonetheless, as the transition drew to a close, the new right had grown deeply suspicious of political allegiances of James and others in his personnel operation. Many of James's staff — including James himself — were "Nixon-Ford retreads" who had shown no deep commitment to new right causes, or worse still, had locked horns with the new right in the 1970s.[119] Moreover, the new right believed that James and his staffers, many of whom were "corporate headhunters" by vocation, had a pecuniary and intellectual bias in favor of "proven managers" drawn from the traditional Republican business constituency, rather than men and women who "could supply conservative intellectual leadership to the bureaucracy, like Don Devine."[120] Hence, as the administration got under way the new right began to push, both quietly and publicly, for changes in Reagan's appointments staff. James Lofton, editor of the *Conservative Digest*, devoted the February 1981 edition of his magazine to cataloging the shortcoming of James's staff and exhorted his magazine's most prominent reader, Ronald Reagan, "You must fire Pen James."[121] Others in the new right enlisted their allies on Capitol Hill, such as Senator Jesse Helms (R-N.C.) to press their case. Ronald Reagan joked that "sometimes our right hand doesn't know what our far right hand is doing." In late 1981 Pendleton James, wearied by his political clashes with his party's far right, had an answer: "I know what our far right hand is doing. It is beating the shit out of me."[122]

Often the Reagan campaign organization, the Kitchen Cabinet, and new right groups made common cause, joining together to press for their candidates and changes in the appointments staff. In early February 1981, for example, Lyn Nofziger, Reagan's longstanding political adviser and assistant for political affairs, convened a meeting of twenty-eight conservative organizations, at which a slate of loyal but overlooked "Reaganauts" was assembled and strategy to secure their appointment was planned.[123]

Prodded by these pressures — and by people in the White House who were eager to dampen these conflicts — James scrambled to propitiate his critics. James sought to soothe new right organizations by permitting some of "their own" to join his staff. James encouraged the Heritage Foundation to send the Reagan PPO one of its staffers, Willa Johnson, to "ride herd on us and watch over us. I thought it was a good idea, that it would help us put out fires: send her [Willa] over and then she can watch what we're doing and make sure we're bringing in Reaganauts."[124] James hired a set of Reagan campaign aides to assist his staff in handling relations with women's groups, ethnic minorities (especially Hispanics), and to service the claims of the Reagan field organization. One of these aides described his role this way:

> We had constituency groups . . . Jews, Hispanics, Blacks. Our job was to make sure they were being consulted on appointments during the transition. They [the appointments aides] were getting bombarded with resumes and requests for political favors and they needed someone to organize that process. The first weeks my job was to answer telephone calls from Hispanics around the country, to organize a resume process, and to put together a filing system. I had a staff of about 7–8 people. . . . [Later] my job was to put forward the names of qualified Hispanic candidates for PAS, boards and commissions, and schedule C jobs, but mainly schedule C jobs.[125]

Still dissatisfied, Ronald Reagan's chief of staff, James Baker, authorized a major shake-up in the appointments staff: James was "kicked upstairs," and day-to-day direction of the PPO was taken over briefly by William Draper, a Baker ally and major Republican fundraiser, and subsequently by John Herrington and his assistant, Becky Norton Dunlop.[126] Herrington, a proven loyalist who had worked in Reagan campaigns since 1966, quickly set about reducing the size of the personnel office, pruning its staff and, more important, rebuilding the PPO, making it an organization that was unabashedly devoted to serving the president's new political claimants. It was Herrington's credo that "the PPO is a political organization, and it has to be. That's what it was designed for, and that is what it has always been, and you must make it that" — which is precisely what he did.[127] Herrington fortified the political capabilities of the staff by deputizing Becky Norton Dunlop, an aggressive, far-right aide who was "completely networked into the conservative movement in Washington," to administer political litmus tests and act as a conduit for candidates from the new right, and by hiring Bob Tuttle, son of Reagan Kitchen Cabinet member Holmes Tuttle, "to act as a sop to the Kitchen Cabinet" and "represent long-time Reaganites within the White House on personnel."[128] Leaving no stone unturned, Herrington moved to please even disgruntled state Republican party officials who had been ignored in the opening round of appointments: Herrington and his aides negotiated an agreement with Republican state chairmen promising them five "must-hire" recommendations for honorary posts.[129]

As the Reagan Personnel Office adapted itself to the exigencies of the presidency's electoral setting in 1982, 1983, and 1984, it found that its ties to department and agencies were fraying. To an HHS assistant secretary with years of experience in his field (and no political experience whatsoever) the PPO's demands made the selection of his deputy secretaries "a bizarre process."

> I recruited one candidate who was extraordinarily distinguished in her field. Her father had been a finance chairman of a major U.S. Senator who was defeated — and clearly not a Reagan Republican. And, she was rejected, even though she had good ties and was an independent. The people they sent to me were not very good. They either weren't too bright, or didn't have professional credentials. Their major claim to fame was that they had spent some time on the campaign.[130]

Another assistant secretary complained:

> I had quite a fight getting him [a conservative social policy expert] in because he hadn't voted in 1984. Actually, on election day, what he was doing was developing a proposal for the administration. There is a certain mentality there [in the PPO] that sort of says, "the first thing you want is someone who has put in their duty to the campaign." I used to joke that it was better to have handed out leaflets in front of the local Safeway than it was to have written a book about something.[131]

Within the White House Office some aides who worked with the PPO came to view the staff that Herrington had assembled as consisting of "low caliber people with no substantive expertise or meaningful Washington experience," for whom electoral considerations loomed too large in their judgments.[132] Worse still, some aides within the PPO itself thought likewise:

> To serve the interests of the president, you need to discount whether somebody has been a card-carrying Reaganite for the past 150 years, and find someone who philosophically supports the program of the president and who is expert — who is smart enough to carry it out. You just can't take somebody from the campaign and expect them to serve the president's interests. I had constant problems, constant conflict, with the political clearance people. And I would argue with them, "political checks are an important piece of information, but they shouldn't drive the process."[133]

Even with Herrington's departure, the PPO changed little. As Washington journalists noted, the PPO's staff was one that was "as a group, . . . light on personnel experience, strong on Reagan campaign experience, and largely from California."[134] Saddled with a reputation as narrowly political — and faced with an erosion of leadership and initiative in the Reagan White House, the PPO staff gradually lost its ability to control appointment choices.

BILL CLINTON AND THE POLITICS OF DIVERSITY

Taking a page from Ronald Reagan's presidency, Bill Clinton and his senior aides aimed to exploit political appointments as an instrument of presidential leadership in the executive branch. The Reagan administration mantra of "personnel is policy" was resuscitated and revised—but only slightly—into "people make policy." According to one aide, "We wanted this president [Clinton] to have the benefit of having *his* people in place to push *his* programs and *his* plans."[135] But, for Bill Clinton, as for his predecessors, personnel was much more than policy. Personnel was in large part *politics*—albeit a modern, postparty politics dominated by the mass media, ideological groups, candidate organizations, and foundations and think tanks—and the Clinton Personnel Office thoroughly bore its stamp.

Bereft of the assistance that the president's party once provided, the Clinton transition personnel operation, federally subsidized and swollen by volunteers, burgeoned to nearly 300 and commandeered the entire eleventh story of a downtown Washington, D.C., office building.[136] While one-third of Clinton's personnel staffers performed policy chores (such as preparing job descriptions and slates of candidates for department heads), the bulk of the staffers tended to have political responsibilities that were once the province of the president's party: receiving, cataloging, and responding to the entreaties of job-seekers; and fielding the claims of the campaign organization, campaign contributors, and the organized constituencies that had brought Clinton to office.

To cope with a swarm of job-seekers and 3,000 pieces of mail each day,[137] roughly 40 percent of the transition personnel aides—most often young volunteers who had been low-level campaign workers—worked around the clock entering resumes into the "resumex," the computerized resume filing system, and replying to job-seekers.[138] A second group of twelve to fifteen personnel aides were organized into a "priority placement staff." The staff, headed by the field director of the Clinton-Gore campaign organization, Michael Whouley, tended to the claims of the 800 men and women who had worked for the Clinton-Gore campaign organization,[139] major campaign contributors, and "key people in the states [in state party organizations]."[140] And, in a bow to the politics of blocs and movements, a third group of aides within the personnel organization labored as "points of contact" for "important constituencies."[141] Clinton's personnel team put together a staff that was finely calibrated to the demands of contemporary Democratic constituency politics, recruiting staffers to serve as liaisons to feminist, African-American, Hispanic, gay, and disability groups.

> In the beginning we brought on Bob Nash, he was an African-American from Arkansas, and Maria Haley, who handled Asian-American outreach

during the campaign, and Maria Echeveste, who handled Hispanic outreach during the campaign. And, later we brought Carol Tucker Foreman to work specifically as a liaison to women's groups [and Bob Hattoy as a liaison to the gay and lesbian community]. In the middle of the transition, when we realized we had a problem, we brought on somebody to work with disability groups.[142]

Describing their role, another aide observed: "We had people, 'search managers,' whose job it was to comb each of those communities. The imperative from the election was you had to do that. If the cabinet and subcabinet is going to look like America, you're not going to come up with the best Latino candidate for these positions unless you go look for them. You meet with LULAC [League of United Latin American Citizens] and you meet with La Raza and you meet with all of them."[143]

And, in yet another bow to the demands of sharply ideological and media-centered politics, Clinton's personnel organization broke new ground by creating a "vetting staff." Recounted one senior staffer, "we had upwards of 30 lawyers and researchers " who performed a "public records vet — a NEXIS vet and did financials [financial disclosure forms]" as well,[144] in preparation for "a potent [conservative] borking machine" consisting of "Republican Senate aides who compile negative dossiers on nominees; like-minded outside groups that seek to stir up 'grass-roots opposition'; and conservative columnists, whose simultaneous alarms can create an echo effect."[145]

As the Clinton administration began, the transition personnel organization metamorphosed into a Presidential Personnel Office, its size diminishing to just over a hundred in early March 1993, and to half that number by early summer.[146] By and large, Clinton's enthusiastic embrace of the blocs and movements that constituted his coalition bore fruit.[147] For example, after a rocky start[148] the Clinton administration earned the praise — and support — of feminist groups for its efforts, and by the spring and summer of 1993 print and television journalists reported kudos from feminists for Clinton's diversity efforts.[149] By the beginning of Clinton's second year in office, Martha Richie lauded the search for diversity in the *Washington Post*, announcing "The Bean Count Is In! A Promise Fulfilled: Clinton's Appointees Really Are as Diverse As America."[150] One month later hundreds of women from the Clinton administration — including Hillary Clinton and Jan Piercy, her Wellesley roommate and deputy director of the Clinton PPO — joined together at the Mayflower Hotel for a fete hosted by the National Women's Political Caucus (NWPC). Harriet Woods, head of the NWPC, offered this benediction: "One year after President Clinton took office, there is indeed a government that looks a lot more like America."[151]

Yet, the success of the Clinton PPO as a political organization — as a "bean counter" — strained its capacities and reputation as an instrument of policy leadership. To be sure, Clinton's aides struggled to protect the PPO's "substantive expertise and credibility with the departments"[152] by introducing a division of labor and specialization at the PPO. The staff's work was organized into six policy portfolios, similar to those of the Office of Management and Budget.[153] Yet the demands of constituency politics were inescapable: each of the men and women who held a "policy portfolio" was also responsible for "serving as a point of contact" for important constituencies.[154] And, having recruited men and women to the PPO to act as emissaries to constituencies, the Clinton PPO sometimes found itself saddled with aides whose loyalties to the president were alloyed — and sometimes superseded — by their allegiance to causes and constituencies outside of the White House. The Clinton presidency's most prominent liaison to the gay and lesbian community, PPO associate director Bob Hattoy, for example, garnered extraordinary attention (and the ire of senior White House aides) for his outspoken attacks on Jesse Helms and other antigay politicians — and Bill Clinton's temporizing on the appointment of an "AIDS czar."[155]

Moreover, the Clinton PPO, as the enforcer of the president's diversity standards[156] and the champion of the Clinton campaign organization, came to be seen by departments and their allies as an inexpert and meddlesome presence that badly slowed the filling of appointive posts. As one PPO aide acknowledged:

> When [an associate director] did an audit and realized there were few noncareer SES appointments left at the State Department, Bruce Lindsey began holding up whole tiers of assistant secretaries, and saying "I'm just not going to move on these because you have no diversity in these, and you have none of our people. None of the people who are [politically] important to us were even interviewed. And I'm not going to be slam-dunked like this. So, yeah, we *are* bottlenecks in the process.[157]

The slowness with which posts were filled generated anger inside the Clinton cabinet,[158] criticism from Capitol Hill,[159] and a torrent of critical new stories and commentary from Washington journalists. "High-Level Grumbling over Pace of Appointments," typical of the genre, trumpeted that "after four months in office Clinton has filled fewer than a quarter of upper-level positions, making work in all sectors of the executive branch nearly impossible." As a result, "much day-to-day management is in the hands of civil servants and Bush Administration holdovers."[160] Long into Clinton's presidency journalists continued their criticism, noting that "in areas where the administration wants to change course, its progress has often been painfully slow, hindered particularly by the delay in filling jobs."[161]

In short, Clinton's PPO staff, like its predecessors, found it extraordinarily difficult to meet the demands arising from contemporary electoral politics *and* to ensure that "people are policy"—in other words, that political appointments were used to achieve presidential control of the bureaucracy. There is no escaping the pressures that lead presidents to search for political responsiveness in the men and women who serve them, but there is no escaping the pressures of the modern electoral order, either. As the past quarter-century shows, presidents must win elections by dint of their own efforts, and they must do so in the face of blocs and movements that have grown only more numerous, formidable,[162] and legitimate.[163] Regardless of their dispositions,[164] presidents must make their personnel staff into "a political organization"—and by doing so they must simultaneously jeopardize its capacity to act as an instrument of policy leadership.

INTERNAL CONSTRAINTS

Among the constraints facing presidents as they pull decisions and resources into an expanded White House Office are organizational constraints—the costs of managing a large and complex bureaucracy. As the White House Office has expanded in size and complexity, it becomes increasingly difficult for presidents to monitor the performance of its members, to reconcile conflicts among its specialized units, and to coordinate the staff's activities. Presidents have adapted to this burden by shifting responsibility for managing the White House Office from themselves to members of their staff, notably, the "chief of staff."[165] Nonetheless, the risks of an expanded White House Office, including free-lancing subordinates and intrastaff conflicts, remain, as the Iran-Contra affair suggested. Nowhere has this problem been more keenly felt than in the Presidential Personnel Office, which has become the largest of the specialized staff units within the White House Office.[166]

When the Presidential Personnel Office first emerged at mid century, it neither received nor deserved the appellation "Personnel Office." Rather, appointment responsibilities were handled by a single aide—or perhaps two—supported by a handful of typists and clerks. Problems of supervision were nonexistent. With little real authority over political appointments, few other aides in the White House Office took a keen and ongoing interest in the work of the Personnel Office; hence, problems of coordination were negligible.

During the Kennedy and Johnson presidencies both the White House Office and the Presidential Personnel Office grew far more rapidly than they had in the preceding decades. Even so, the Presidential Personnel Office was a rather intimate staff; no more than seven or eight aides had a hand in the substantive business of the office. The heads of the PPO were in daily contact with their aides, and monitoring the work of the staff was simple and informal. Moreover, the PPO staffers had little difficulty coordinating their work with that of other staffers inside the White House Office: the White

House staff was so small that aides could coordinate their work through face-to-face contact. Asked about the problems of coordination with Ralph Dungan's appointments staff, one Kennedy policy adviser reminisced: "One of the advantages [of a small White House staff] was that you could get in touch with somebody by walking into the men's room. There was no need for [formal] coordination and all that crap. It was all informal. I knew who Ralph was and what he was doing, and vice versa."[167]

However, as the size and influence of the PPO grew, like that of the larger White House Office, the first signs of conflict with other specialized staff units—each with its *own* responsibilities and constituencies—began to emerge. Mike Manatos, Larry O'Brien's chief liaison with the Senate, endured a tense relationship with John Macy's office. In Manatos's estimation, Macy's staff "produced eggheads" who were "qualified but [didn't] have a lick of sense. I had no questions about their qualifications for the slots . . . but I thought that a lot of them—and we all thought that down here [in Congressional liaison]—that a lot of them were just not very practical people . . . they weren't politically involved; they'd had ideas and theories, but they hadn't had this association with members of Congress."[168]

Lyndon Johnson's special assistants with substantive portfolios, such as Lee White, Douglass Cater, and Joseph Califano—Johnson's ad hoc White House policy development staff—were new and sometimes aggressive rivals for control over political appointments. "Each one of these power-seekers really feels he's in charge of getting the people in his particular program area," Macy recalled. "They would try to race me to it [a job opening]." And, Johnson's nascent "political affairs staff," headed by Marvin Watson, created persistent problems of conflict and coordination with Macy's staff. Suspicious of Macy's personal loyalty to Lyndon Johnson, Marvin Watson and his aides attempted, with some success, to build their own lines of access to departments and to add a "politically sensitive" layer of review beyond Macy's.[169] Even so, the organizational costs of sustaining—and expanding—a presidential personnel office remained modest.

In the dozen years after Macy's tenure, the Presidential Personnel Office became an "office" in name as well as fact. As the staff increased tenfold between the mid-1960s and early 1980s, the organizational costs of aggrandizement became readily apparent. Because they had set such ambitious aims for centralizing control over appointments and acquired political obligations once handled outside of the White House Office, Reagan's aides found that they needed a massive staff to sift resumes, interview candidates, and check on ideological credentials—a staff of over a hundred during the opening days of the Reagan administration.

The sheer size of the staff made it remarkably difficult for the PPO's head to monitor its work. The vastly increased power of the PPO exacerbated the problem, making the PPO "the best stepping stone" in the government. "If you're a young buck and you want to do something else in the Reagan administration, the Presidential Personnel Office is the best stepping stone. [Another PPO aide] saw this as a . . . proven bankshot, so he moved down to Presidential Personnel and took my portfolio and then used that in the same way that I did to become the Executive Assistant to [a cabinet secretary]."[170]

Hence, in the opening year of the administration, Reagan's PPO head Pendleton James found it difficult to keep track of who was on his staff,[171] let alone monitor the performance of its members or ensure that its staffers were pursuing the interests of the president they served rather than their own pecuniary or ideological aims. One staff veteran acknowledged: "People were coming in there, finding their own jobs, and leaving. There was one man, for instance, that was solely positioning the minority small business interest people all over the government. He built his own network, so that when it came time to get 8A contracts for minority contractors, he could simply call on this man or that man in this department."[172] Other staffers discovered they were free to use their posts to pursue their own political agendas. Another personnel aide recalled: "There were people in the Personnel Office who thought they were the certified true believers. If they were upset with an appointment decision, they would access their constituency of true believers outside of the White House—maybe at the Kitchen Cabinet or the Heritage Foundation."[173]

In an effort to ensure that the Personnel Office was not only large and powerful, but capable, Reagan's aides had the staff draw upon the acumen of other specialized units within the White House. The PPO routed candidates for appointment through the Political Affairs Office (for political clearance), to the Domestic Policy Office (for tests of policy fidelity), to the Legislative Affairs staff (for Capitol Hill clearance), and the White House Counsel's Office (for legal scrutiny).[174] Other staffs responded eagerly to the invitation, hoping to remedy what they saw as the inadequacies of the PPO's staff work. Seen from the vantage point of the Domestic Policy staff, the PPO was staffed with "low caliber people" who were drawn largely from the president's campaign organization and lacking in either Washington experience or substantive expertise. And, since even the best PPO staffers were "buried in importunings, in paper, and in interviews," they had few opportunities to become knowledgeable. Seen from the perspective of the Political Affairs staff, "the PPO was so screwed up; it was one of the great debacles of this administration." But involving other staffs proved to be unworkable: "after inviting everybody else in the White House to weigh in on appointments, the PPO found that it lost control of the process—that everybody else was holding them up to get what they wanted out of the process."[175]

Persistently criticized as bloated, badly administered, and politically inept, the Personnel Office came in for sharp criticism from those responsible for running the Reagan White House Office: the chief of staff and his aides.

As the first year of the Reagan administration came to an end, the staff was pruned to from eighty-eight to a more manageable sixty-five, and as the administration progressed the staff was reduced still further, to roughly fifty aides. The staff's formal prerogatives were pruned, too. The PPO head was no longer an "assistant to the president," but rather a "deputy assistant to the president." And, the staff's leverage over department and agencies waned significantly. Members of the president's cabinet increasingly resisted its efforts, and journalists announced that the "White House Personnel Office Struggles with More Vacancies, Less Influence."[176] In short, the aggrandizement of the Presidential Personnel Office was not simply hemmed in by the resistance of political leaders outside the White House Office; it was also constricted by the managers of the White House Office itself, who had concluded that the PPO's contributions to presidential leadership were outweighed by the organizational burdens it was imposing on the presidency.

5

Do Presidents Make a Difference?

By the waning years of the Eisenhower presidency journalists, scholars, and political professionals alike sensed that basic changes were occurring in party politics: issue activists, nonparty groups, and professional consultants[1] began to assume a significant role in election campaigns while party organizations exercised progressively less control over election campaigns (and became less dependent upon job patronage for their maintenance than was once the case). Presidents (and other politicians), it was argued, were freer than ever before to ignore the dictates of party.[2] Moreover, there were short-term forces that reinforced the weakened hold of party leaders: Dwight Eisenhower had campaigned in 1956 as he had governed earlier — as a politician above party — and he began his second term with relatively few obligations to his party's organizations. For the Eisenhower administration, these changes meant that the party constraints that had initially hemmed in the White House appointments staff were eroding and that costs of enlarging the personnel staff and increasing its capabilities to act as an instrument of administrative leadership were diminishing.

These opportunities for an expanded White House staff were accompanied by a powerful intellectual rationale: the public administration community, good government groups, and civil service leaders urged Eisenhower — as they had urged his predecessors — to bolster the presidential role in the appointment process, arguing that the centralization of political appointments in an expanded White House staff would diminish the play of centrifugal, parochial, and narrowly political forces at work in the selection of political executives.[3]

Nonetheless, these opportunities were unexploited. The White House appointments staff of 1961 was indistinguishable from the staff of 1953; only the faces had changed. It would take a different president — one far more eager to exert policy and political leadership over the executive branch — to exploit the opportunities that were emerging at the end of the 1950s. As it happened, two such presidents followed Dwight Eisenhower: John F. Kennedy and Lyndon Johnson. Between them they sharply altered the size and capabilities of the president's appointments staff. Only seven years after the conclusion of Eisenhower's presidency the White House appointments staff had grown to seventeen aides, and its aggrandizement was hailed as a "change of permanent significance for the power position and the institutional apparatus of the presidency."[4]

Kennedy's and Johnson's actions — and Eisenhower's inaction — remind us that the decision to pursue additional control in an expanded White House staff ultimately rests in the hands of one individual: the president. And, because presidents differ from one another in important ways, they may make sharply dissimilar evaluations of the costs and benefits of expanding the size and reach of their White House staff.

LEADERS AND INSTITUTIONS

As the preceding chapters have shown, the evolution of the White House Office is rooted in systemic forces: its evolution is "structurally induced," as rational choice accounts propose. But, as the contrast between the Eisenhower White House and the Kennedy White House suggests, the evolution of the White House Office is not a steady and regular response to "systemic forces." Rather, presidents may make a difference. Some may aggressively propel the aggrandizement of the White House Office, while others retard or even pare back the size and responsibilities of their staff — enough of a difference to raise serious questions about explanations of the presidency's evolution that argue that the PPO's evolution is institutionally induced.

Why might some presidents aim to accelerate the aggrandizement of the White House Office while others aim to retard — or reverse — it? Because presidents bring dissimilar policy ambitions, political resources, and party affiliations to the Oval Office, they assess the costs of their actions differently. Republican presidents, for example, have seen far larger political and policy costs than Democrats to permitting Washington-based professional groups and program advocates to influence political appointments; thus they may be more eager to centralize control over political appointments in the White House Office than Democrats. Although law and custom may push all presidents to lead, some presidents — presidents with ambitious policy aims — go far beyond what they are required to do, while others do what they must and little else. Lyndon Johnson and Ronald Reagan, both eager to reshape domestic policy during their presidencies, went far beyond what they were compelled to do; George Bush, by way of contrast, was content to pursue a remarkably limited agenda. Centralization may be far more attractive to presidents like Johnson and Reagan than those like Bush. Ambitious presidents are eager to garner control over policy choices, rather than cede them to others in the political system. And, of course, some presidents may be far better endowed to pursue centralization than others: Lyndon Johnson, for example, began his presidency with far greater "political capital" to invest in centralizing appointment choices in his White House staff than Richard Nixon did.

How *much* difference do leaders make? In the end, leaders do make a difference, I believe, but institutions matter, and matter far more. Presidents may be driven by their own dispositions to bring changes to the White House Office, but they make changes within boundaries — boundaries that are rooted in the needs, demands, and expectations of other leaders and backed by the sanctions other leaders can bring to bear. As Hugh Heclo observed, "On the surface the new president seems to inherit an empty house. In fact, he enters an office already shaped and crowded by other people's desires." The White House has a "deep structure" that is a "web of other people's expectations and needs," a structure that presidents "can change slowly if at all."[5] Presidents may try to follow their own dispositions and move the White House Office beyond the institutionally defined boundaries, but as they do, they will be met with resistance, criticism, and retaliation. In other words, trespassing institutionally established boundaries is costly. The further presidents try to move the White House Office beyond these bounds, the costlier they find their choices.[6] Two presidents who ventured beyond the upper and lower bounds of the modern White House Office and then retreated from their choices are Richard Nixon and Jimmy Carter.

CROSSING THE LIMITS:
NIXON AND THE WHITE HOUSE STAFF

Life can only be understood backwards; but it must be lived forwards.
— Soren Kierkegaard

When Richard Nixon won the presidency in November 1968, he had no intention of sharply accelerating the aggrandizement of the White House Office. Rather, Richard Nixon condemned the over-ambitious reach of Lyndon Johnson's White House staff and set about building his administration almost exactly as Dwight Eisenhower had sixteen years earlier.

In keeping with tradition, Nixon's 1968 transition was headquartered in not in Washington, D.C., but in New York City, at the Hotel Pierre. Although President-elect Nixon personally attended to the selection of his cabinet members, the remainder of the government, just over 2,000 positions, was staffed by Nixon's secretaries-designate with virtually no guidance from Nixon or his aides. Although Nixon did have a set of personal aides housed in the Pierre Hotel,[7] they never undertook the work necessary to establish centralized control over the staffing of the nascent administration, nor were they authorized to do so.[8] After kibitzing and "throwing out names of people we knew,"[9] Nixon's aides submitted lists of candidates for cabinet secretaries to consider, and the secretaries, free to employ or ignore the books of candidates as they saw fit, promptly assembled their own teams of appointees. A member of the Pierre Group recalls: "George Schultz looked at our book and he took a few ideas, but not so many. Mel Laird . . . [sigh]. . . . He said, 'I don't need your damn book.' "[10] In short, Richard Nixon and his senior staff left precious little imprint on the senior levels of the nascent Nixon administration.

The Administration Under Way

As the administration got under way, Nixon and Haldeman chose Harry Flemming, in charge of "the bottom end of the plum book" during the transition, to assemble a White House appointments staff. Flemming, guided by the advice of "the old gang from the Eisenhower administration,"[11] created a personnel office of modest size and prerogatives — and a reputation to match. Flemming's choice met with the approval of Nixon and other senior staffers in the White House, and it was ratified by Nixon himself, who announced at the outset of his administration that cabinet members had the prerogative to staff their own departments as they saw fit.[12]

During the opening weeks of the administration, as Flemming struggled to handle the heavy volume of job-seekers, his staff briefly swelled to fifty-five aides. Soon, however, the staff diminished to a more modest seventeen aides, roughly the same size as the Macy staff under Johnson.[13] More important, the aims and capabilities of the staff were far more modest than they had been a few years earlier: Flemming aimed to serve the needs of politicians who were important to the president, not to exploit the political appointments in such a way as to establish policy control over the executive branch. In keeping with this role, Flemming hired aides who were long on campaign experience rather than government experience or programmatic expertise,[14] and he made no attempt to bolster the staff through specialization. Staffers were not assigned a portfolio of departments to handle on an ongoing basis, as Johnson's aides had been. Instead, the staff was divided into two units, a placement staff, which "funneled job requests, resumes, and congressional referrals — the whole thing — down to liaisons in departments,"[15] and a clearance staff, which "cleared" candidates with Senate Republicans and key Republican constituencies, as circumstances dictated.[16] Flemming's office aspired to play a third role as well: assisting departments in filling posts. But, departments were loathe to use Flemming's computerized list of job seekers — the "Executive Personnel Biographical Index" — suspecting that it was little more than a list of party hacks.[17] Thus, "the search for particular positions," one Flemming aide observed, "is conducted by departments and agencies, who use the talent bank as a last resort and to a limited extent. This set up . . . *leaves all initiative elsewhere*."[18] Left to their own devices — and to the importunings of constituencies outside the White House — department heads assembled teams of appointees that had few ties to their putative master, Richard Nixon.

By the middle of 1970 a new consensus had emerged within the White House Office, the lineaments of which were captured by George Bell, a WHPO veteran: other politicians had been well served by decentralization, but the president was badly served by these arrangements. The purpose of a White House personnel staff, Bell argued, "is to assist the President to gain and exercise control of the government." The Flemming staff had "failed to achieve this objective" because it was burdened with "far too many activities of a constituent service nature [serving Republican politicians on Capitol Hill and in state parties] to make such an achievement possible." In the absence of a guiding White House presence, there had been "a build-up of provincial hierarchies having major allegiances to department and agency heads, rather than to the president."[19] This would soon change: Richard Nixon and his senior aides had come to the conclusion that they were going to build an institutionalized means of "getting control of key personnel decisions."[20]

Testing the Limits of Centralization: 1971

When Richard Nixon embraced a strategy of centralization in late 1970, he did not simply return to the modestly centralized arrangements that his Democratic predecessors Kennedy and Johnson had instituted. In searching for an alternative to the appointments practices of the first two years, Nixon's aides met with John Macy and asked him to describe how the Johnson White House had handled political appointments. Macy's White House staff, Fred Malek told H. R. Haldeman, "was not a very impressive operation," — that is, it did not provide the president with sufficient control over appointment decisions. The handiwork of Fenn and Macy may have permitted sufficient centralization for Democratic presidents, but the staffs they devised did not offer enough control to suit the needs of a Republican president who suspected that the loyalties of program executives lay with the programs they administered, the professional communities with which they routinely dealt, congressional committee chairs, and — only *lastly* — with Richard Nixon.[21] These executives, Nixon and his inner circle surmised, put their political resources to work on behalf of their programs and constituencies. Where the protection of programs and clientele conflicted with the president's political needs or policy priorities, executives often sided with the president's rivals — those with whom they shared programmatic, ideological, or partisan affinities — rather than with the president. When, for example, Richard Nixon sought to claim credit for a 20 percent increase in social security benefits during the 1972 campaign (by including notices along with monthly checks) Social Security Commissioner Robert Ball, a program executive with a formidable reputation, political ties to Capitol Hill,[22] and mastery of his organization,[23] reacted predictably. Fearing that the integrity of his program might be jeopardized, Ball threatened to resign and go public with his criticism of Nixon.[24]

If Richard Nixon could not compete with policy networks for the loyalties of the men and women who were serving him, then he and his appointments staff would pull appointment decisions into the White House Office and find other kinds of appointees: appointees who were endowed with few political ties or modest political skills, but "men and women who are completely devoid of personal political ambition, totally loyal to the president, politically sensitive, highly objective and analytical, and capable, result-oriented managers."[25]

From Idea to Reality: Building a White House Staff

Although the centralization of appointments was clearly the way to proceed, a practical question faced the senior White House staff: *how* should the president centralize control over appointments? After briefly toying with the idea of assigning the staffing of departments to a newly reconstituted Office of Management and Budget, Bob Haldeman decided instead to expand the White House staff to handle this responsibility. To build up White House capabilities, Haldeman drew upon the services of Frederic Malek, then a thirty-year-old deputy undersecretary at HEW. Malek had joined HEW in April 1969 "armed with a mandate to sharpen the Republican Secretary's ability to control the largely Democratic HEW bureaucracy."[26] Malek was a political novice, but a man whose ambition and discipline were palpable: a West Point graduate, he had served with the Special Forces in Vietnam, acquired a Harvard M.B.A., worked for the nation's premier management consulting firm, McKinsey and Company, and earned his first million — all by the age of thirty. Within a year he had established himself as Finch's chief assistant on the organization and staffing of HEW.

The chief impediment to policy control over HEW — and departments more generally — Malek observed, was that program executives were "disinclined to accept new leadership willingly," because their "loyalties were divided" between the president and other claimants outside the executive branch. The cause of the problem, he suggested, was not so much personal or ideological as it was institutional: program executives are not managerial generalists, but rather subject-matter specialists. Worse still, Malek wrote:

they spend their careers within a single bureau or narrow specialty area. As the specialist progresses, he becomes increasingly involved with the relevant outside interest groups and congressional staffs. These external groups determine his standing and prestige in the field, represent the major source of employment outside of the government, and are long-lived compared to political leadership. Consequently many of the top career officials direct their loyalty more towards these groups than to the administration in power.[27]

Malek's solution to this problem at HEW was "the removal and Siberian placement of officials felt to be a problem for the new administration" and the recruitment of new, managerial men — men who were willing to follow the lead of their hierarchical superiors in the secretary's office and the White House, and to discount the competing claims of Capitol Hill, professional groups, or careerists.[28] Where could these people with the right orientation be found? Certainly Malek could not turn to Washington-based policy networks — they were dominated by the very types of people that he was seeking to avoid.[29] Instead, Malek chose to reach out to the business management community whence he had come. He brought in assistants who were professional business consultants,[30] and even let contracts to consulting firms such as Peat, Marwick, Mitchell for the recruitment of business managers.[31]

Malek's tenure at HEW was not always marked by political perspicacity.[32] Nonetheless, his single-minded devotion to Nixon's agenda for HEW and his "can do" orientation earned him the attention and admiration of H. R. Haldeman, and in the summer of 1970 Haldeman requested that Malek describe how a similar operation, directed from the White House, could permit the president to establish managerial control over the executive branch. Malek's response, titled "Strengthening the President's Ability to Manage the Government," noted that:

in the first year and a half of the Nixon administration, the difficulty in truly managing the Federal Government has become an increasingly serious and perplexing problem. The relative lack of control at the top and the non-responsiveness of many parts of the bureaucracy have resulted in presidential directives not being carried out, counterproductive efforts taking place inside a number of agencies, and a general failure to carry out initiatives and achieve planned results.[33]

Malek proposed to weed out "weak spots" among existing political executives, to "require that a certain percentage of [senior] career employees . . . be rotated every few years . . . to break those ties that produce mixed loyalties,"[34] and to form "a small, mobile strike force at the White House that can move into trouble spots . . . [such as] severe outbreaks of employee dissent" or "agencies that have been generally unresponsive and caused substantial political embarrassment at the White House," such as the IRS and Bureau of Labor Statistics.[35] Most important, Malek proposed to establish White House control over the staffing of key posts throughout the executive branch. By late autumn of 1970, Malek and two assistants completed a forty-five-page study of the White House role in the staffing of the executive branch, laying out in painstaking detail the failures of the first two years, and Malek's plans for the second half of the Nixon administration: a highly centralized process of staffing the administration directed by a large White House staff.

Malek's study called for substantial changes in the aims, staff, and procedures of the White House Personnel Office. It would continue to serve the needs of leaders who were important to the president, such as campaign contributors, because this obligation could not be avoided. However, the new Personnel Office would go much farther: it would extend the president's influence throughout the executive branch by finding men and women who were attuned to the president's political needs and policy concerns. These men and women would not be found in think tanks, universities, or nonprofit groups; nor could people whose loyalties to Nixon were unalloyed be located among the retinues of Republicans in Congress.[36] Rather, they would be found by "reaching out to the power centers in the largest cities, like the First National Bank in Chicago"—recruiting from a "pool of people who were uncontaminated by deep program commitments."[37]

Given the dual aims of his staff, Malek proposed to organize the Personnel Office into two units. One unit would handle the traditional "political" responsibilities (placements and clearances). The other unit, staffed by men and women borrowed from the nation's largest executive search firms, would handle the recruitment of presidential loyalists.[38] Given the desire of the president to emphasize bureaucratic control rather than traditional political service, those who were charged with establishing "management control" over the executive branch would be freed from traditional political responsibilities (such as the placement of campaign contributors) and be permitted to recruit solely for senior policymaking posts in the executive branch (subcabinet posts).

Finally, the new White House personnel office would be linked to the remainder of the White House Office—now a highly specialized bureaucracy—by means of an elaborate system of clearances. This system of clearances, like the Personnel Office itself, would serve a dual purpose. Clearances with the OMB and newly created Domestic Council were introduced to ensure that job descriptions and candidate searches were harnessed to the president's policy agenda—thereby extending his influence throughout the government.[39] Clearances with the Political Affairs staff and congressional liaison aides, in contrast, were intended to ensure that Nixon's executives were acceptable to the constituencies they represented: Republican notables in state and local politics (Political Affairs) and Republicans on Capitol Hill (Congressional Liaison).

Implementing Centralization: Half a Loaf

The opening months of 1971 were a time of opportunity and change for the White House. With the mid-term elections over, Nixon and his aides were "willing to take the political heat" that would accompany an attempt to take back their prerogatives.[40] Establishing control over the staffing of the government would come in two pieces. First, the personnel office would have to direct a "housecleaning," ridding the administration of those who were disloyal and creating vacancies to be filled. At the same time, a vastly expanded White House staff would have to be created to ensure that the White House would play a significant role in filling the vacancies it had created.

The opening move in the shift towards centralization was a very public bloodletting: on Thanksgiving eve in 1970, Interior Secretary Hickel was fired, and two days later Fred Malek was sent to Interior to fire Hickel's entire staff. The Interior "housecleaning" captured a great deal of attention, catapulting Malek onto the front pages of the *Washington Post* and establishing his reputation within the Washington community as Nixon's "hatchet-man."[41] In fact, this was only a small part of a much larger — and less visible — purge of the "weak spots" in the administration.

In the months before the mid-term election, H. R. Haldeman charged Harry Flemming — and subsequently Fred Malek — with drawing up a confidential list of appointees who were incompetent, unresponsive to the president, or both. In mid-November of 1970, after soliciting the opinions of White House staff and agency officials, Malek presented Haldeman with list of sixty-two appointees who had served the president poorly. Malek's list, like Flemming's, took particular aim at HEW: of the sixty-two appointees he identified for removal, seventeen (27 percent) were from HEW.[42] Among the domestic agencies, only the Justice Department (no removals), Commerce (2), and Labor (1) fared well. Agriculture (8) and Interior (11), by way of contrast, were targeted for sweeping changes. For the next four months Malek, sometimes assisted by John Ehrlichman, cajoled and pressured department heads to remove targeted appointees — while trying to "minimize conflict and use up a minimum of the President's equity with Department Heads."[43]

At the same time, Malek also put his plans for the new WHPO into action.[44] Malek began by purging Harry Flemming's staff, whom he regarded as "a group of political hacks," and recruiting a new staff of his own. In keeping with his proposal, Malek established two relatively independent sets of aides: "politicos" and executive recruiters.[45] The nation's largest "headhunting" firms eagerly assisted Malek in assembling a staff of executive recruiters, loaning him men and women who would serve for a year or so on the personnel staff—and return to their firms with links to the nation's largest law firms, banks, and industrial corporations.[46] And, as Malek had planned, his executive recruiters went directly to the business community for candidates, eschewing professional communities that were closely linked to Democratic programs and politicians. When Malek's staff assembled a slate of candidates for HEW in the second Nixon administration, for example, they compiled a list of forty candidates for thirteen slots. Of these forty candidates, twenty-three (58 percent) were business executives, corporate lawyers, or management consultants, while another ten (25 percent) were veterans of the Nixon White House or CREEP. Only six of the forty were drawn from the educational and health communities tied to HEW, and they were college presidents (2) and physicians (4)—hardly professional groups that were tightly linked to Democratic program executives in the bureaucracy or Democratic politicians on Capitol Hill.[47] The "political unit" of the new personnel office operated much as it had under its predecessor, Harry Flemming: it devoted assiduous attention to the needs of defeated congressional allies, campaign contributors, and other claims relayed to it at biweekly meetings of the "political coordinating group": Robert Timmons (congressional liaison), Charles Colson (organizational liaison), Harry Dent (Political Affairs), and Tom Evans (RNC vice-chairman).[48]

In March of 1971 Malek could claim to H. R. Haldeman that forty-nine out of sixty-two of those slated for removal had been ousted "for a total success ratio of 79 percent throughout the government," including fourteen of the seventeen targeted at HEW.[49] Moreover, he could point to a personnel staff of thirty-three, twice the size of his predecessor's and far more influential vis-à-vis executive departments and other offices within the White House.[50] Nonetheless, Richard Nixon believed that the housecleaning had not gone far enough—that "we were not getting as much control of key personnel decisions as we should."[51] The problem, as Nixon and his staff saw it, was that cabinet secretaries and their people were already in place when the drive towards centralization began. Removing political appointees who are already in place, as Malek pointed out in a memo to H. R. Haldeman, is costly: "Major changes are needed at State but are unlikely to be achieved without strong intervention by the President and the use of considerable equity. The strategy, therefore, should be to try to persuade Secretary Rogers to move on a minimum number of the best documented cases, keeping the remainder under close evaluation."[52] A senior aide to the president described the constraints they faced this way:

> You face the obvious limitation of having to deal with the reason the person is there to begin with. Each of those people . . . was there because someone wanted him in there, or because someone was afraid to put

him out, like Robert Ball, or Hershey over at the Selective Service, or [J. Edgar] Hoover. You've got the problem in making the change of dealing with the person's sponsors, which might be internal administration, external political, external congressional, or just the guy's own sheer weight, like Hoover's.[53]

In addition, Malek's staff also discovered that departing from the decentralized staffing arrangements to which departments and their allies had become accustomed also provoked resistance. Hence, in the judgment of the appointments staffers, "we got part of it [control over staffing] back, but not all of it." To "get it all back" — to make radical changes — the president needed to start with a clean slate.

Although the president and his staff were frustrated with the small measure of control they had recaptured in 1971 and 1972, they were also hopeful. Richard Nixon was keenly aware that the constraints faced by presidents are at their low ebb immediately after their reelection. If Nixon could win an overwhelming victory in the 1972 election *and* move immediately to capitalize on this opportunity, he could realize his ambition: to staff (and organize) the executive branch with little regard for the traditional prerogatives of others in Washington — be they congressmen, clientele, or careerists.[54] They would "have Washington by the balls."[55] As Nixon instructed his staff in 1972: "You've got to do it [firing and restaffing the executive branch] fast because after the first year it's too late. You've got to do that right after the election. You've got one week, and that's the time to get all those resignations in and say, 'Look, you're out . . . you're finished, you're done.' Knock them the hell out of there."[56] Hence, in the spring and summer of 1972 elaborate plans were laid for the second Nixon transition. The president would request that *all* members of his administration submit their resignations immediately after the election; this would "clear the decks for a whole new start."[57] His appointments staff, having evaluated each member of the administration in the preceding months, would apprise him of which resignations to accept.[58] Finally, the appointments staff would provide him with a slate of candidates drawn from the business world to fill the posts of those who had been removed.[59] These candidates, like the carefully winnowed veterans of the first administration, would be "objective managers" who would make "departments and agencies truly responsive arms of the presidency."[60]

In the weeks following the election of 1972, Nixon retreated to Camp David with Bob Haldeman and John Ehrlichman to follow through on their plans to reorganize and restaff the executive branch.[61] The day after the election Nixon shocked official Washington by demanding resignations from the cabinet and all other political appointees within two days — and by making it clear that he would be accepting many of them. This time around Richard Nixon would have no unwanted holdovers in his administration, and he would move quickly enough—completing his restaffing by January 12, 1973, he hoped—that others inside and outside the executive branch would be unable to assert their traditional prerogatives.[62]

To ensure that the White House would sustain its tight grip on the staffing of departments and agencies beyond the transition, the second-term White House Personnel Office was going to be still larger and more aggressive than that of the previous two years. By the start of 1973 the White House Personnel Office had grown to fifty-two, and it aimed to extend presidential influence throughout the government by ignoring the boundaries between the political appointees and the career civil service. "To extend the president's policy control over the departments and agencies," the new WHPO director Jerry Jones wrote to H. R. Haldeman, we will "weed out individuals in key program and policy positions, both career and noncareer, who are not responsive to the President's policy objectives and replace them with individuals who are."[63]

Washington "By the Throat"?

Could Nixon and his aides, acting under the cover of the "mandate" they had received in the 1972 presidential election, finally establish the measure of control they yearned for? Although the Watergate scandal brought their experiment to a premature conclusion, the preliminary evidence—the response of others in the Washington community—suggests that the costs of their aggressive centralization would have been extraordinarily high—too high to sustain.

Although the size, prerogatives, and specialization of the president's staff were far greater in 1973 than ever before, it still encountered serious problems in dealing with its traditional rivals: cabinet departments and their allies. The president's appointments staff, though vastly expanded, was hard pressed to match the political and policy acumen that departmental officials could bring to staffing decisions. "Weinberger and Carlucci were a fast team," an appointments staffer acknowledged. "They were as quick and competent and as good at coming up with options [for appointments] as the WHPO was. He continues: "They had both been in government for some time—Carlucci all his life. That is a real asset. Someone like that can come up with people off the top of his head. I mean, I think Frank Carlucci could probably staff a government just out of the people he knows."[64] Moreover, the president's appointments staff still found it very difficult to deal with agencies that had power bases independent of the White House or legitimate claims to professional autonomy. Some departments resisted the postelection flood of Nixon loyalists by appealing to norms of expertise and professionalism. "The strategy was to control the people and the dollars in the agencies—the Assistant Secretaries for Administration, Assistant Administrators, the political shop, and so forth. And that system was to go into every agency. Well, in the State Department they said 'Screw that. We're professionals over here, we're not politicians.' And the Justice Department was another one that didn't want any of it. 'We're lawyers and prosecutors and all that. We don't do that.' "[65]

Although the president's personnel staff had broken free of the Republican party,[66] it was confronted with a new and unanticipated challenge to its control over appointments from *inside* the White House Office itself: the president's *own* political organization — led by White House aide Charles Colson — was emerging as a powerful new rival for control over political appointments. Colson was not opposed to centralization, as cabinet secretaries were. Rather, he wished to use White House control over appointments in a very different way than Fred Malek did. Colson wanted to convert the president's 1972 electoral coalition into the "New Majority," and in his judgment, doling out political appointments to representatives of the New Majority was a particularly valuable tool for solidifying the president's coalition. A Colson sympathizer observed: "Symbolic appointments of people will do almost more to move the groups to you than any issue will. If you name their leader to a key post, suddenly you have a whole group that you didn't have before — or that is loosened from the fold of the opposition."[67]

Malek and his business recruiters, by way of contrast, were preoccupied with finding "managerial types" who would carry out the president's aims with fidelity. They gave "no attention to the mix of people being appointed." They did not have "any women or any Spanish people. No Italians, no Catholics. All guys from Greenwich, Connecticut, who went to Princeton and Harvard Business School. They're white-shoe, country-club, Westchester-Fairfield County types from Fortune 500 firms."[68] "We began to be attacked," a personnel staffer recalls, "from within the White House."[69] Nixon sided with Colson and directed Haldeman and Malek to balance policy control against "politics" — representing the president's new constituencies.[70] In addition to the normal struggles for control, though, the Nixon staff faced new and unprecedented resistance, which was a response to its unprecedented efforts to centralize appointments in the White House Office and use them to presidentialize the bureaucracy. Nixon's attempts to punish the Bureau of Labor Statistics were opposed by a host of professional associations (such as the American Statistical Association, the Federal Statistics Users Group) which banded together into the "Committee on the Integrity of Federal Statistics" and sharply criticized the White House for exerting "political influence on the development and interpretation of statistical programs."[71] Former HEW executives, such as Wilbur Cohen,[72] leaders in the scientific community linked to HEW,[73] and newspaper editorial writers[74] expressed criticism and alarm that "virtually the entire leadership of HEW is leaving." Other agencies, such as the Department of Agriculture, drew upon their clientele and congressional ties for protection from the depredations of the

White House appointments staff. Even though the White House often succeeded in placing loyalists in key posts, its people were persistently challenged: "Joe Wright [undersecretary] was our guy at Agriculture. He would call [the White House] each week and say, 'I don't think I can take any more of this.' They ostracized the hell out of him. They leaked stuff."[75]

Under politically favorable circumstances Richard Nixon and his aides might have had the political capital to invest in a costly and protracted struggle of radical centralization that evoked the retaliation of other Washingtonians, but as the Watergate affair engulfed the Nixon administration in the spring of 1973, Nixon had no surplus political support to invest in centralization — or any other of his political projects. His painstaking plans for the centralization of appointments were swept away in a matter of weeks. On April 30, 1973, Haldeman and Ehrlichman, the architects of centralization, resigned, and they were quickly replaced by Alexander Haig.[76] On May 10, 1973, the White House issued a press release indicating that it was restoring a "direct line of communication with the cabinet" — abandoning its organizational plans for the second administration.[77] Later that month, Haig met with the cabinet to consider *abolishing* the presidential personnel office. With 260 of the 555 presidentially appointed positions (47 percent) still unfilled, the president's senior aides decided to keep the staff, but to sharply reduce its size and prerogatives,[78] ensuring that the remaining posts would be filled with far less White House influence than the first 53 percent.[79]

By the summer of 1973 those who were only recently under attack by the White House suddenly found themselves free to reassert their traditional prerogatives. Cabinet secretaries soon discovered that "the departments have become more autonomous regarding appointments and internal operations."[80] Caspar Weinberger publicly boasted, "We're in charge of this department [now]. One area in which there had been some difficulty . . . was in getting presidential appointments. But that problem is not with us now."[81] In dealing with congressmen, members of the White House Personnel Office were suddenly compelled to be "responsive to just about anybody who wasn't against us [in favor of impeachment]."[82] The Republican National Committee, once scorned by the president's senior aides, was now treated with solicitude.[83] As impeachment votes threatened, "everything was expendable" in the quest for support, and the White House "lost control of the [appointment] process altogether."[84] Even the Civil Service Commission, long cowed by the Nixon White House, screwed up its courage and began an investigation into widespread violations of civil service laws by Nixon's White House staff and their agency liaisons. Throughout the last year of Nixon's presidency, his large and aggressive White House personnel staff, once feared and reviled throughout the executive branch, returned to a more modest role than any time since the presidency of Dwight Eisenhower.

Ironically, Richard Nixon's first popularly elected successor, Jimmy Carter, would have a chance to prove what Nixon's presidency tentatively demonstrated: institutionalized boundaries exist, and they are costly to trespass. Jimmy Carter, however, would prove the power of institutional constraints on presidential choice in the opposite way: by aggressively attempting to diminish the size and responsibilities of his White House Personnel Office.

TRESPASSING THE LOWER BOUNDARIES: THE CARTER PRESIDENCY

> *Kennedy aide Dan Fenn:* "You've got to say, 'I just can't run the whole bloody thing'" [control all appointments].
> *Ford aide Bill Walker:* "But you can't do that. I don't think that you can do that anymore."[85]

Campaigning for the presidency in the shadow of the Watergate affair, Jimmy Carter fashioned himself as the mirror image of the discredited Nixon: Carter would be the outsider to Nixon the consummate insider; Carter would bring trustworthiness rooted in evangelical Christianity to the White House in place of Nixon's rootless shrewdness; Carter would disperse power that Nixon had illegitimately accumulated in the institutional manifestation of the "imperial presidency," the White House Office. If elected, Carter pledged, he would reverse the aggrandizement of the White House Office that had been fueled by Lyndon Johnson and Richard Nixon.

Carter kept his promise. As the administration began Carter did, in fact, return to a pattern of decentralization—in political appointments and other decisions—that was typical of the Truman and Eisenhower presidencies. One year into the Carter administration the president's appointments staff was smaller than any since Johnson's, and it exercised less influence over appointment decisions than any staff since Dwight Eisenhower's.[86] Having spurned the experience of his predecessors, Carter could not know that he had diminished the size and influence of his appointments staff well beyond its lower boundaries, defying the "web of other people's expectations and needs" that structure the White House Office. Before long, however, he would learn.

Predictably, Carter's embrace of cabinet government met with the approbation of department heads and the clientele allied with them. Others, however, found that they had become accustomed to—even dependent upon—the White House Office that had evolved during the previous decade and bitterly criticized Carter's decision to scale it back. The Carter campaign organization and Democratic party officials were incensed that Carter had created a purely clerical White House Personnel Office, bereft of meaningful influence over appointment choices and incapable of meeting their needs. "One party person, [PPO head] King recalled, came to the White House after the inauguration looking for a job. In spite of King's repeated assertions that there was nothing he could do, the Democratic hopeful sat in the anteroom for three days. On the third day, having watched personnel office traffic and operations, the aspirant came to King and said, 'You know, you weren't kidding about not being able to help me. But it's not supposed to work that way after you've won.' "[87] Veterans of Carter's own campaign organization, his Peanut Brigade, were likewise dissatisfied, complaining that Carter's embrace of decentralization had shunted them off to departments, where their campaign work on Carter's behalf "was a kiss of death."[88]

Members of Congress were displeased with the sharply scaled back role that the Carter White House had adopted in handling appointments. The departments, now solely in control of appointments, showed little consideration for their recommendations and denied them courtesies they had traditionally been accorded. Tip O'Neill, for example, was infuriated to discover — in the newspapers — that Elliot Richardson, a potential rival of his son for the governorship of Massachusetts, had been chosen to be ambassador at large and the president's representative to the Law of the Sea Conference.[89] Dan Rostenkowski, Chair of the House Ways and Means Committee, was angered to learn that Chris Cohen, an independent alderman and foe of the Daley machine, had been appointed to head HEW's Midwest regional office in Chicago, rather than the candidate that he (and the Cook County Democratic organization) had backed.[90] As one appointment aide acknowledged: "From the very beginning, Congress was very mad at us, and part of the reason was appointments."[91] Carter PPO head Arnie Miller described Carter's predicament well:

The president is much more personally identified in the political community with the business of governing — or at least the White House staff is, especially in appointments. Partly this is due to changes in nominations: you used to have the national committee, but now the president picks up support by building his own organization. Also, expectations have developed that you can't shake. John Macy told me to get out of handling things like regional directors — things that were of no business to the White House in the past. But you can't do this.[92]

Worse still, a purely clerical White House appointments staff failed, in the end, to meet the expectations of the Washington press corps and the mass public outside Washington. Sharply criticized by leaders inside Washington and beset by contending voices within his own administration, Jimmy Carter found his ability to control and lead his administration, and the wider government, called into question. Carter could not ignore the weight of public expectations — that the president will be the "master of his own house" — regardless of his personal inclinations. Speaking at a conference of White House Personnel heads, Arnie Miller observed:

Carter thought that he could return to that earlier decentralized approach, but he failed to understand how interwoven the fabric of the presidency is. You pull a little string here and everything unravels. He tried to decentralize personnel. He tried to cut back on the size of the Presidential Personnel Office staff. He bumbled it. Midway through his presidency he realized that he had given away the store. The expectations are still there on a President. The demands are so concentrated now on the president. Television has done a lot of that.[93]

Bill Walker, head of Ford's PPO, concurred: "It takes a tremendous management effort for the president, for the administration, to present a coherent voice on any topic." "So in order to countervail all that out there," Miller added, "you've got to build your own in the White House."[94]

Thus, slowly and grudgingly, Jimmy Carter did "build his own in the White House" during the final two years of his presidency, abandoning his commitment to "cabinet government." In April 1978 Tim Kraft was designated assistant to the president for Political Affairs and Personnel, and four months later Kraft turned to Arnie Miller, a veteran Democratic operative, to take charge of rebuilding the Carter personnel staff. Called into the White House at midstream, Miller was uncertain how to proceed and reached out to trusted sources for advice — including John Macy, Lyndon Johnson's chief appointments aide. When Miller queried John Macy about how to organize a White House appointments staff, Macy urged him to emulate his own practices: create a small staff of a dozen aides or so and stay away from all but the most senior policymaking positions. "You can't decentralize it now," Miller argued, spurning Macy's advice. Instead — in a supremely ironic move — Miller sought out the advice and assistance of veterans of the *Nixon* personnel office. Recalled Miller: "We tried to model, frankly, your system, Fred [Malek]. The first thing I did was hire one of the people who worked for you as my deputy, Harley Frankel, who worked for you at HEW. I brought him in immediately as the number two guy and then tried to develop a system in the midstream of the Carter administration."[95]

In three years the Carter administration had come full circle: from reviling the Nixon White House to emulating its structure and routines. To be sure, the Carter appointments staff was smaller than Nixon's (about two-thirds its size), and less powerful as well. But, it was dramatically different from the staff two years earlier: it was larger, more specialized, more powerful, and much nearer the path of the office's long-term, institutionally driven evolution. The experience of Jimmy Carter — like that of Richard Nixon — offers strong support for the central claim of rational choice accounts: "For the most part, politicization and centralization have grown not because of who presidents are or what they stand for, but because of the nature of our institutions and the role and location of presidents within them. The basic causes are systemic."[96]

THE CLINTON WHITE HOUSE: CARTER REDUX?

After Carter's debacle in the White House, it would be twelve years before another Democrat, Bill Clinton, returned to the presidency. Not surprisingly, Clinton and his senior aides viewed Carter's experiment with a vastly reduced White House (and Personnel Office) as a failure, not something to be emulated. Said a senior Clinton aide, "We didn't feel that Carter's experience with cabinet government worked well. That [decentralization] is totally different from the way we wanted to do it. We wanted this president to have the benefit of having *his* people in place to push *his* program and *his* plans."[97] Observed another:

> People make policy, and unless you look for the people who have policy visions that track with the president, you are not going to have policies emerging from the departments that track with the president. There are enormous centrifugal forces out there. There are powerful, important constituencies out there at work in the departments, and the minute a cabinet secretary takes office, they are tugged this way and that. If you don't have your people in the departments, there will be no balance [between the centrifugal forces and the president's aims].[98]

To this end, Clinton's aides constructed a personnel staff that resembled Ronald Reagan's in its size, procedures, and influence. Transition personnel chief Richard Riley met with the secretaries-designate prior to the announcement of their selection and told them, "This is the process. The rules are . . . you may submit names [of potential appointees]. But it is the *president's* decision on these presidential appointments. We had a previous president [Carter] who said 'I'm going to pick my cabinet and they're going to pick their people.' That is *totally* different from the way we're going to do it."[99] As the *New York Times* trumpeted, "Clinton Taking Big Role in Picking in Cabinet Aides."[100] Clinton's control over the staffing of his administration, it was planned, would extend downward through all presidential policymaking posts — deputy secretaries, assistant secretaries, and even top-level noncareer Senior Executive Service (SES) jobs. Thus, the Clinton personnel organization created "agency teams": groups of six to eight aides (roughly eighty-five in all), each of which was responsible for preparing job descriptions and assembling slates of six to seven candidates for each post to present to the incoming secretaries-designate.[101]

As it had hoped to do, Clinton's staff left a large mark on the staffing of departments and agencies during the transition and opening days of the administration. Asked whether half of all presidential appointees were drawn from lists prepared by Clinton's personnel aides, a senior PPO staffer exclaimed, "I'd say *at least* that. *Absolutely.* It was never lower than 60 percent, and in some departments, like independent agencies, it was about 100 percent. When we picked the head of the Peace Corps we said, 'You're making the selection for deputy from one of two people.' We've maintained a great deal of control."[102] Another aide, a veteran of an "agency team," recalled:

> When she [the cabinet secretary] first came in with our lists—we hadn't met her face to face yet—she said, "These lists are horrible." She blasted the search manager I was working with. She came back later and we made peace. In the end about two of the 17 PAS positions in her department didn't come from our lists. Now, as to how these results were produced: by the time the lists got to her, it didn't look like a Reagan or Bush list with a lot of unacceptable candidates. She had less grounds to fight.[103]

During the late spring and summer of 1993, however, the Clinton Personnel Office went through a wrenching "downsizing" that sharply circumscribed its role. During the 1992 presidential campaign candidate Bill Clinton, much like Jimmy Carter a dozen years earlier, pledged to reduce the size of the Executive Office of the President and White House Office by 25 percent by fiscal year 1994. Thus, as 1993 progressed—and the number of vacant posts slowly diminished—the Presidential Personnel staff was slashed from 105 (in March 1993) to 55 (in late August 1993).[104] With the new fiscal year looming, Clinton's PPO aides privately warned, "We're losing control. It's not like a car driving off a cliff, but we can see it happening already. [As we get smaller] we lose the ability to set direction; we become hostage to what the agencies want to do."[105] Bolstered by comparisons with the larger Reagan and Bush Personnel Offices, Clinton's personnel aides pleaded with Chief of Staff McClarty to halt the cuts, but to no avail. By October 1 (the start of 1994 fiscal year) the staff had been reduced to thirty-five—and by late November 1993 Clinton's PPO staff had been pared back to twenty-five aides, smaller than any since Carter's PPO of 1978-1979.[106]

Greatly diminished in size, the Clinton PPO was sharply circumscribed in its capacity to exercise influence over the staffing of the government as well. Where responsibility for the thirteen cabinet departments and agencies had once been divided among seven "associate directors" (and their five deputies), only two PPO staffers remained. Observed one veteran of the Clinton PPO:

> We did go down to GS-15 jobs, if they were program directors. Now, we can't. And with PAS jobs, we're going to ask "is this a technical job"? To the extent they are technical, we will defer to the agency. We also ask, do we have an interest in this job? Do we have any alternative candidates? Does the campaign have a candidate for this job? If so, then

we engage. If not, if the White House says no, then we go back and look at a few performance measures, a few parameters. How are we doing on diversity at this agency? It's all we can do. It is what we can realistically do, rather than a content based model.[107]

So frustrated were PPO aides that they complained to nominees — and they, in turn, to news reporters, "that its [the PPO's] own understaffing is causing delays."[108] More important, though, were the criticisms of the PPO that were sounded outside the White House Office.

By the waning days of 1993 the Clinton Personnel Office became a regular target of press criticism, much of it centering on the limited size and capabilities of the staff. Describing the selection of a new PPO head, Al Kamen of the *Washington Post* wrote acidly:

> The Clinton administration yesterday named Atlanta Bank executive Veronica Biggins . . . to take over the much-maligned White House personnel operation. Her first task will be to find candidates to fill the 105 senior-most jobs that are still wide open. Even before that, she may want to go around to the agencies, which have been in a chronic high-pitched whine over the tortoise-like pace of the personnel shop, and make nice to them. Another matter still in flux is the vetting operation, which is down to two lawyers. The sometimes months-long background checks have caused considerable, often needless, anguish for job-seekers, at least to hear them talk about it.[109]

The *Post* was by no means alone. The *New York Times*[110] and the *National Journal*[111] raised similar questions about the wisdom of White House staff cutbacks; so too did pundits and scholars.[112]

In short, by 1994 Bill Clinton was bumping up against the "lower bounds" of the modern White House Office, much as Jimmy Carter had a dozen years earlier; the costs of staffing reductions were becoming palpable and painful, particularly to Clinton's PPO staffers. As one of Clinton's PPO aides wryly observed, "You could theoretically have a PPO with only one aide. It all depends on what outcomes you're trying to produce. Political leadership? Policy leadership? [Smiling]. Now, *those* are interesting outcomes that are difficult to achieve with 23 people in the PPO."[113]

Will Clinton or his successors be able to sustain a Presidential Personnel Office so sharply limited in its capabilities while protecting the president's political stakes and policy leadership in the executive branch? The experience of the past twenty-five years and the logic of rational choice institutionalism suggest not. Presidents may disregard the institutional constraints within which they work, but only at their peril.

6

The Fruits of Their Labors:
The Consequences of Aggrandizement

What are the consequences of a large and specialized White House Personnel Office? Has the pursuit of centralization in an expanded Personnel Office given presidents what they want—a team of appointees that is responsive to their leadership? Or, has the aggrandizement of the Presidential Personnel Office been feckless, yielding only a bloated staff?

The emergence of a specialized staff to make political appointments has significantly centralized appointments, permitting recent presidents to exercise more influence over a larger number of appointment decisions than their predecessors. Nonetheless, presidents (and their aides) cannot control all of the choices all of the time; they still face constraints, both internal and external, that make control costly. Seen in this light, an expanded staff may allow presidents to structure and monitor the choices that they allow other politicians to make for them—and, sometimes, to dispense with the assistance of other politicians altogether. But all presidents must rely, to some degree, on the political intelligence and candidates that other politicians can provide. What happens when they do?

All politicians, including the president, establish what they commonly refer to as their "network": a set of people to whom they are linked by trust, reciprocal obligation, or belief. When faced with the task of assembling an administration, presidents draw upon their own networks for both people and political intelligence. Different politicians assemble very different political networks. Some politicians have very broad and deep networks to draw on, such as John F. Kennedy.[1] Others, like Jimmy Carter, find that their network is neither extensive enough nor specialized enough to reach far into departments and agencies, or even to assist them in peopling a handful of positions in a department.[2] But all presidents must rely to some degree on the political intelligence and candidates that other politicians can provide, be they members of Congress, campaign contributors, or leaders of interest groups.

Will dependence upon others yield an administration that is unresponsive to presidential leadership? Perhaps not. A "government of strangers"[3] is not necessarily a government of adversaries. Even if a president must rely heavily upon others to staff his administration, he will not necessarily find himself atop an executive branch whose members are reluctant to follow his lead. Contracting out to other politicians may yield a highly responsive administration, or a fractious set of executives who are reluctant to defer to presidential leadership.

When the president's party embraces a heterogeneous set of politicians and clientele groups, contracting out will yield a highly fractious and unresponsive administration—as Jimmy Carter discovered. Midway through his administration Jimmy Carter and his aides concluded that they had permitted others to "staff the government with McGovern people, Kennedy people— people with no loyalty to him and, more important, with different views of government." They then tried to recentralize control over staffing decisions in the White House Office. But, there was nothing Carter could do to alter the fact that the Democratic party consisted of "people with no feeling of loyalty towards him and . . . [with] different views of government."[4]

Conversely, when the president's party consists of a highly homogeneous set of officeholders, activists, and clientele—as the Republican party did in the 1980s,[5] the opposite results. Ronald Reagan's widely heralded success in eliciting responsiveness from the men and women who served him, I suggest, stemmed from his unprecedented control over who served in his administration and from his ability to draw upon a Republican party that was remarkably unified on major questions of domestic policy. In sum, responsiveness emerges from the confluence of two conditions: centralized control over staffing, and access to fairly homogenous networks of politicians and clientele.

I test the account against the experience of the Nixon and Reagan administrations; in particular, I assess the responsiveness of political appointees at the Department of Health, Education,and Welfare (HEW) to their leadership.[6] I have chosen to examine the Nixon and Reagan administrations because both built a large and powerful appointments staff, and both attempted to harness political appointments as an instrument of presidential leadership: if the president's staff does make a difference, then these administrations should clearly reveal its effects. I have chosen to examine HEW/HHS because it offers a "critical test" of presidential leadership: if control and responsiveness can be sustained in a setting that is this inhospitable to conservative Republican presidents, then it should be able to thrive throughout the executive branch. Though HEW/HHS offers a critical test, it is certainly not an unrealistic test. A liberal Democratic president faces similar problems in obtaining responsiveness from military and intelligence bureaucracies.[7]

Richard Nixon began his presidency with a staff of modest size and limited capabilities, relatively little control over appointments to HEW, and a fairly meager and heterogenous political network. Therefore, I expect to find that HEW was weakly responsive to Nixon's political leadership in 1969–1970. Because Nixon was able to "pull together the pieces" of responsiveness during his tenure at the White House, that is, able to assemble a serviceable political network and an influential staff, I expect that HEW became significantly more responsive to his leadership in 1972 and 1973 than it had been at the outset of his administration. Ronald Reagan, by way of contrast, began his presidency with an immense and powerful appointments staff and a remarkably homogenous political network. Hence, I anticipate that Ronald Reagan's HHS was highly responsive to his leadership throughout his tenure.

RICHARD NIXON AND HEW

When John Kennedy was faced with the task of assembling an administration, he lamented "People, people, people. I don't know any people. I only know voters. How am I going to fill these 1200 jobs?"[8] For no politician, however, was this observation more apposite than for Richard Nixon. He arrived at the presidency with a considerably narrower and shallower political network than either John Kennedy or Ronald Reagan. The paucity of political followers was not so much a product of his personal qualities, but rather his ascent to the White House. The meagerness of Nixon's own political network, combined with the heterogeneity of the Republican party in 1968, was instrumental in producing an administration that was unresponsive to his leadership.

Nixon's path to the presidency was an unusual one. By 1968 it had been eight years since Richard Nixon had last held office. Nixon lacked the traditional political base of a gubernatorial or senatorial post and therefore had neither the opportunity nor incentive to assemble a retinue of loyal followers that he could tap in staffing his administration. In contrast to Ronald Reagan, Nixon was a party politician, not the leader of a political movement. Indeed, on the eve of his presidential bid Nixon was "as close to being a stateless person politically as there has ever been in this country." Some described him as a "politically displaced person."[9]

In 1968 presidential candidates did not need to assemble their own national political organization to win their party's nomination or the general election. When Nixon chose to "return from exile" and seek the presidency again, he assembled a relatively narrow and shallow network of political supporters. His immediate political retinue consisted of one or two dozen Nixon loyalists and a handful of associates from the Eisenhower years (such as Burns, Stans) and the 1960 campaign (Flanigan).[10] Beyond this, however, Nixon relied heavily upon other politicians—governors, congressmen, and (particularly in the South) party officials—to deliver convention delegates and to lend him their political organizations for the autumn contest.[11]

Richard Nixon's pursuit of his party's nomination and a general election victory did little to extend the breadth or depth of his personal network. Upon his entry into the White House Nixon was endowed with neither John Kennedy's "band of brothers" nor Ronald Reagan's layers of personal and ideological followers.[12] In seeking nomination and election Nixon assiduously sought—and won—the support of Congressional candidates, governors, and party officials. However, these were not men and women bound to Richard Nixon by personal or ideological fealty. As Nixon would soon learn, they were independent politicians with their own ambitions, agendas, and networks to nurture. As a result of the limited network upon which he could draw, Nixon found it necessary to rely upon these politicians to staff his administration—to "contract out" to them, as he had in the election. As Evans and Novak observed:

> On the day the president took up transition residence at the Pierre Hotel, he could count on fewer close associates to help him run the government than any recent predecessor. The handful of trusted lieutenants and advisors would, of course, take up key positions in the White House and the administration. But almost to a man they were sadly unprepared in the ways of Washington, government, public affairs, and politics. To supplement them, Nixon would have to call on outsiders that would make his, at the beginning, an administration of strangers.[13]

Strangers are not necessarily adversaries. Even if presidents must rely heavily upon other politicians to staff their administrations, they will not necessarily find themselves atop an administration whose members are reluctant to follow their lead. If there are relatively small policy or ideological differences between the president and the other politicians in his party, relying upon them will yield an administration that is reasonably consistent with the president's own policy inclinations and responsive to his leadership.

By any measure, the Republican party at the outset of the Nixon administration was considerably less homogeneous—and less conservative—than it became in the late 1970s and early 1980s.[14] Consider the politicians who have the greatest hand in shaping the president's administration: members of the Congressional party. If we use conservative coalition support scores to measure the ideology of the party's members, and the standard deviation of these scores to measure the heterogeneity of the party, we can see that the Republican party was significantly more heterogeneous in the late 1960s and early 1970s than it would become in the ensuing decade. As late as 1973, the Senate Republicans had a mean Conservative Coalition score of 72.26, with a standard deviation of 27.14. By 1982, the mean Conservative Coalition score had risen to 80.4, while the standard deviation, the heterogeneity of the Senate party, declined sharply to 19.89.

Hence, Richard Nixon was confronted with a difficult problem in November 1968. Without a sizeable network of his own, he found himself forced to rely upon a heterogenous set of Republican politicians to staff his administration. The strategic choice that he made in the first two years of the administration — decentralization — would make the worst of a difficult situation. Decentralization meant that staffing decisions were not in the hands of the president or his aides, but rather other politicians. Given Nixon's meager political network and the diversity of the Republican party in 1969, these "other politicians" were often unsympathetic to his policy agenda, or unconcerned with his political fortunes. This was particularly true at the Department of Health, Education, and Welfare, as I show below.

"With Friends Like These . . .": Staffing HEW

Nixon's Secretary of Health, Education, and Welfare (HEW), Robert Finch, was a close political ally who had served as Vice-President Nixon's chief of staff and the director of Nixon's gubernatorial campaign in 1962. By the mid-1960s, Finch had established himself as a moderately liberal and ambitious politician. In California politics he aligned himself with the progressive wing of the Republican party, and his successful campaign for lieutenant governor in 1966 — in which he received even more votes than Ronald Reagan — was seen to be a harbinger of a promising political career. Though Finch declined Nixon's offer of the vice-presidential nomination in 1968, he eagerly accepted Nixon's offer of the HEW secretaryship, anticipating that HEW would be "where the action was."[15] Finch was right — though not in ways that he could anticipate.

Delegated responsibility for staffing his department during the transition, Finch was free to fill the senior political posts as he saw fit — subject to a rarely used (and therefore toothless) ex post veto by the president for candidates who were politically unacceptable. In practice, since Finch was free to proceed as he wished in staffing his department, he turned to men whom he trusted, and whose political beliefs he shared: not the president's staff, but his *own* political network.

Upon arriving in Washington, Finch summoned two trusted and long-standing political allies from California, Lewis Butler and John Veneman, and he assigned them the responsibility for staffing his department.[16] Both were acquainted with Richard Nixon, and Veneman had even played a significant role in the 1968 election, directing Nixon's California campaign on behalf of Finch, the nominal Nixon head in California. However, neither Butler nor Veneman was cut from the same cloth as Richard Nixon. Butler was a liberal Republican who had been a law partner with Congressman Pete McCloskey, and he had worked closely with Sargent Shriver at the Peace Corps. Veneman, who had served as Finch's campaign director in 1966, was a liberal Republican state legislator in California. As the Committee chairman with jurisdiction over health insurance, he was a veteran of many political battles with Governor Ronald Reagan.[17]

In staffing HEW during the transition, Butler and Veneman made no use of Flanigan's staff at the Pierre, and they made no attempt to reach out to the constellation of politicians who were "Nixon men" (part of his political network) and knowledgeable on questions of social policy.[18] Instead, they put together a department by reaching out to Republican politicians who were familiar and politically congenial to them and by tapping HEW's professional communities for advice and candidates. They assembled a set of presidential appointees that was largely Republican, but decidedly liberal. Those who came to the department from political careers — men such as (assistant secretary for administration) James Farmer, the former head of the Congress of Racial Equality (CORE) and unsuccessful Republican/Liberal party candidate from New York — displayed no inclination to depart from the Democratic policy agenda of the Kennedy and Johnson administrations. Creed Black, assistant secretary for legislation, was similarly inclined.[19] The professionals that Butler and Veneman chose for leadership positions in the department were drawn from among the more liberal elements in their communities. James Allen, assistant secretary for education was "politically liberal nonpartisan" and an exponent of busing who had served New York's Governor Nelson Rockefeller. John Knowles, Finch's personal choice for assistant secretary for health, was sympathetic to the creation of a national insurance plan — and anathema to the American Medical Association.[20] Finch's presidential appointees, in turn, brought equally liberal Republicans — or Democrats — to the layer of positions below them — deputy assistant secretaries and bureau chiefs holding "schedule C" appointments, such as Leon Panetta (director of the Office of Civil Rights) and Tom Joe (chief welfare aide). Finally, in deference to Congressional committees and professional groups that had close working relationships with the traditionally autonomous line bureaus within HEW,[21] Finch permitted many Democratic program executives to remain in their posts, such as Bob Ball (commissioner of the Social Security Administration)[22] and Mary Switzer (administrator of the Social and Rehabilitation Service).[23]

Once the administration began, Finch and Veneman — like their counterparts in other departments — remained reluctant to rely upon Nixon's White

House staff for personnel advice.[24] Seen from the perspective of Finch and his immediate circle, the White House personnel operation was not a useful resource to which they could turn in staffing their departments, but rather a "group of advance men" who were simple, narrow Republican partisans concerned only with rewarding the faithful. The concerns of the Flemming staff were unpleasant "constraints" that were grudgingly met – and skirted if necessary.[25]

To be sure, Nixon's staff did become engaged in struggles with Finch over appointments to HEW, but only in response to "fire alarms" from aggrieved Republican politicians and constituencies – when "a red flag went up," as one aide commented. When the American Medical Association found that its slate of candidates for the Assistant Secretary of Health had been ignored – and that a politically unacceptable candidate had been nominated by Finch – they quickly rounded up their supporters on Capitol Hill, such as Senator Everett Dirksen.[26] Flemming and his aides, eager to assuage congressional anger, quickly joined the fray.[27] Republicans on Capitol Hill voiced displeasure that Bob Ball, a Democratic holdover and brilliant architect of the Social Security system remained as the head of Social Security Administration; again, Flemming did battle with Finch.[28] Seen from the narrowly political vantage point of Flemming and Flanigan, the HEW staff that John Veneman assembled was troubling *not* because it threatened to lead HEW policy in directions that were antithetical to Nixon. Rather, Finch's appointees were a problem because they threatened to sour Nixon's relationship with important Republican politicians (Ronald Reagan, for example) or constituencies (the AMA).[29]

In the end, Nixon's appointments staff played only a minor role in determining who held senior policymaking posts at HEW. Only two of the twelve presidential appointments at HEW (17 percent) were importantly influenced by the president's staff – a proportion that was dwarfed by Reagan's staff of 1980–1981 and, as expected, virtually identical to the Eisenhower and Truman staffs.[30] Of the dozen senior political executives at HEW, only two had unmistakable links to Richard Nixon, and both were political backers who were rewarded for their political service to the president: Patricia Hitt, chair of Women for Nixon in the 1968 campaign and Nixon supporter since 1946; and Robert Mardian, a senior political adviser to Barry Goldwater in 1964 and western political director for Nixon in 1968.[31] Neither gave Richard Nixon much of a foothold at HEW: both were novices on questions of social policy. Mardian was closely tied to a number of White House aides, including Flemming, who used him as a "back door into the department." However, Mardian had few allies and many foes within the department and, dispirited, he moved to the White House in 1970.[32] The bulk of the department's senior political appointees were unacquainted with Nixon or estranged from him on matters of policy (as were appointees in other social service agencies)[33] – which provided fertile soil for unresponsiveness at HEW.

"Marching to a Different Drummer": Unresponsiveness at HEW

What did Richard Nixon want from "his team" at HEW? Nixon's own ideas about domestic policy were moderately conservative and never coherently and systematically expressed. His policy agenda for HEW was modest: he clearly wanted a Nixon HEW to break with Great Society policies aimed at the mobilization of the poor, to pursue policies that relied upon transfer payments for services to individuals, to substitute block grants for categorical grants-in-aide, and to slow the rising public expectations and expenditures of the 1960s. Throughout his first term Nixon's basic need "was to keep the home front tranquil while large foreign policy strategies evolved." Hence, Nixon was willing to "give a great deal of ground on the domestic [policy] side," so long as his HEW appointees did nothing to erode his political base.[34] In sum, Nixon offered a great deal of political guidance but relatively little policy guidance. And, as we will see, HEW appointees often failed to respond to either of these concerns.

As 1969 got under way, the president's staff quickly discovered the fruits of permitting HEW to be staffed by politicians who shared few of the president's views and were unconcerned with Nixon's political fortunes. Seen from the perspective of the White House, the political leadership of Nixon's HEW was "not marching to the president's drumbeat" and "not with the team": it was unresponsive to the president's policy aims and inattentive to his political concerns.[35]

Leading appointees responsible for mental health policy[36] publicly opposed key initiatives of the Nixon administration, such as the decentralization of program authority,[37] and surreptitiously lobbied for restoration of program cuts on Capitol Hill.[38] Leading health policy staffers protested the president's funding levels for their programs.[39] Those who controlled welfare policymaking were equally likely to "march to their own drummer." As Derthick notes, "The change in party control of the executive branch [after the 1968 election] brought no change in attitude towards social services within HEW. If anything, the change in leadership [and organization] that occurred in 1969–70 encouraged expansion."[40] Most important to the president and his staff, though, was HEW's role in civil rights enforcement. No domestic political issue loomed as large as school desegregation for Richard Nixon.[41] Nixon had relied heavily upon southern support to win his party's nomination and the presidency in 1968, and he believed that support among southern congressmen was crucial to the adoption of his legislative program and his reelection prospects. Southern political leaders were keenly aware of Nixon's past commitments, and clearly expected that Nixon would honor his tacit commitment to ease the "dislocations of desegregation."[42] Moreover, Nixon was hopeful that he could woo ethnic Democrats in the 1972 election by visibly opposing "forced busing," providing his appointees did not "blur his message."[43]

Hence, Nixon was intensely concerned that those responsible for civil rights enforcement at HEW do only what the federal courts required of them and nothing more—and that they do this with assiduous attention to the political repercussions of their actions.[44]

Unfortunately for Nixon, HEW's Office of Civil Rights, which shared responsibility with the Justice Department for school desegregation, was headed by Leon Panetta. Panetta, a liberal Californian, was staunchly committed to the vigorous use of the office's enforcement powers: the cut-off of funds to public institutions that violated constitutional standards of desegregation articulated by the Supreme Court. As 1969 unfolded, Panetta publicly chafed at the willingness of the Nixon White House to condone further delays in complying with court directives and prodded Finch to proceed with funding cutoffs to noncomplying southern schools. Nixon, in turn, was obsessed with the political damage inflicted by Panetta and supervised him so closely that "he knew of Panetta's travel plans before Panetta's wife did."[45] After several meetings directing Panetta to pay greater heed to the political problems of the president—and less attention to the instructions of federal courts—Nixon's senior aides adopted a policy directing the Justice Department to take the lead in enforcing school desegregation, rather than HEW. By early 1970 Nixon was unconvinced that Panetta was any more attuned to his political predicament. Rather, Nixon remained "very unhappy with some decisions that were being made, particularly at HEW on civil rights. He felt that Secretary Finch had been captured by his bureaucracy and that the civil rights lawyers were leading him around by the nose. Didn't they understand that he was the President and that he was going to have to run for reelection? The policies in this government had to be his; they could not be Finch's."[46] Hence, Nixon moved to "make the policies his." In February of 1970, Panetta, "the symbol of all that was wrong at HEW" was fired, and the White House staff (under the direction of Leonard Garment) assumed control over desegregation policymaking.[47]

HEW remained a cauldron of political problems for the White House. In the spring of 1970 the *New York Times* regularly trumpeted HEW–White House conflicts with stories such as "The Revolt of the Civil Servants" and "Health Part of HEW in Serious Trouble," and HEW employees publicly protested the president's Vietnam War policies and his civil rights policies. In June 1970 Nixon introduced much broader shake-ups at HEW. On June 5, 1970, Secretary Finch was "promoted" to the White House to serve as Counsellor to the President. At the direction of the White House, he supervised the ousting of a host of liberal appointees who had openly disagreed with the White House, including Commissioner of Education James Allen; Director of the National Institute of Mental Health, Stanley Yolles; the head of the Health Services and Mental Health Administration, Stephen English; and others.[48]

Although these moves were dramatic, they were only a palliative. Not all politically sensitive decisions within HEW's jurisdiction could be taken over by the president's White House staff as school desegregation had been; the list of sensitive problems was simply too long.[49] More importantly, the White House still had no reliable means to ensure that its concerns were foremost in the restaffing of HEW, as Elliot Richardson's tenure at HEW revealed.

In June 1970 Elliot Richardson took over HEW from Finch. Richardson was not only a veteran of Eisenhower's HEW, but had also been responsible for social welfare policy during his tenure as lieutenant governor of Massachusetts. Richardson restaffed HEW by relying upon his own well-developed political network, rather than turning to Flemming's staff for guidance or candidates.[50] For Richardson, like his cabinet counterparts, candidates from Flemming's "talent bank" were "a last resort — at best."[51] A top HEW official recalls: "I don't recall anybody that we appointed to a significant job who originated with the White House staff. I think the woman we put in charge of consumer affairs [Virginia Knauer] was a White House name."[52] Moreover, Richardson was quick to protect program executives that White House staffers were eager to dismiss for disloyalty to the administration, such as Robert Ball and Bertram Brown, director of the NIMH.[53] In the eyes of White House staffers, Richardson assembled "a little cadre of Elliot Richardson's friends; liberals from the Eastern establishment" who "did not have the interests of the man who had been elected president in mind."[54] Flemming's staff tried to "sit" on the HEW candidates it viewed with disfavor — such as Sid Marland, assistant secretary for education — but it lacked the stature to win these battles.[55]

As Nixon had hoped, Richardson did manage to "put out fires" at HEW in the coming months. Richardson and Stanley Pottinger, the new head of the Office of Civil Rights, proved to be more solicitous of the president's political concerns about school desegregation than their predecessors.[56] Moreover, HEW appointees were less likely to "go public" with criticism of the president and his policies than they had been during Finch's tenure.[57] As the *New York Times* pronounced, "Richardson, after Year on Job, Hailed for Ending Chaos at HEW." "In his first year as boss of Washington's most unwieldy bureaucracy, the moderate Republican from Massachusetts has defused an area of government that Mr. Finch once described as 'a political minefield,' one that was exploding daily and causing considerable embarrassment to the administration."[58] Nonetheless, working relations between the White House and HEW remained strained.

The White House staff remained deeply skeptical about the loyalties of HEW appointees. In part, their mistrust was a product of active resistance to the president's initiatives among HEW executives (and, occasionally, Richardson himself).[59] Bertram Brown, director of the National Institutes of Mental Health, publicly contradicted the president's position concerning the legalization of marijuana and orchestrated congressional and professional group opposition to the president's fiscal year 1972 proposal to terminate federal funds for an HEW grant financing psychiatric residency programs. Both incidents were instantly reported to the White House staff — the former by press reports, and the latter by OMB's HEW watchdog, Richard Nathan — and confirmed the worst fears of Nixon aides.[60]

Suspicion among White House staffers was bred not only by the active opposition of HEW appointees, but also — as they saw it — by a more subtle form of unresponsiveness: persistent attempts by HEW executives to redirect the president's initiatives in a liberal direction, as typified by HEW leadership on the paramount item in Nixon's legislative agenda, the Family Assistance Plan (FAP). As Richard Nathan notes:

> Nixon believed his family assistance plan was a balanced plan that involved both more generous benefits to some recipients and a strong work requirement for all able-bodied adults on welfare. Liberal Republicans in HEW tended to emphasize the first part and forget the second part of this equation. Richardson worked closely with this liberal group. The reaction in the White House can be described as extreme irritation — irritation that Nixon's welfare reform plan was getting away from him. When the FAP finally died . . . one of the reasons for its demise was this conflict between the White House and HEW officials over its nature and purposes.[61]

When Harry Flemming's staff compiled a government-wide list of appointees slated for dismissal in the summer of 1970, it was Richardson's HEW that topped the list. After investing "over 1,000 man hours and conducting 278 interviews with White House staff, Congressional personnel, and . . . agency personnel" Flemming's staff identified eighty-one political appointees they judged to be "out of step" with the administration — and twenty-three of the eighty-one (28 percent) were from HEW![62] More importantly, Nixon himself remained dissatisfied with HEW, as late as 1972 imploring Haldeman to "clean the whole damn place out."[63]

Turning the Screws: The Nixon White House and HEW, 1972–1973

The moves toward centralization that Nixon and his senior aides began in 1970 were redoubled after the 1972 presidential election, yielding a White House Personnel Office of unprecedented size and prerogatives. What were the fruits of Richard Nixon's assiduous pursuit of centralization? As Nixon's second term got under way, a new and substantially different team of appointees was assembled at HEW, reflecting the shifting political circumstances that Nixon faced. In November of 1972 Nixon's overwhelming victory over

McGovern indicated to him that he need no longer court the favor of blacks, Northeastern Republicans, or other constituencies that nudged his domestic policies to the center (or left). Instead, the future lay with the "New Majority" —a majority that was right of center.[64] Moreover, by late 1972 direct United States participation in the war in Southeast Asia was clearly ending.[65] These developments enabled Nixon to depart from his policy of the first administration: giving ground on questions of domestic policy in order to buy maneuvering room on foreign policy. Hence, the second term would feature a still newer Nixon, supplying more consistently conservative leadership to social service agencies—including HEW—than he had during his first term.[66]

Reflecting this change, Elliot Richardson, who was seen by White House aides as "too soft" on social issues and too attentive to career bureaucrats, was moved out of HEW (to the Defense Department).[67] Richardson's departure was accompanied by a wholesale shift in the political leadership of HEW. Those who were part of Richardson's own retinue left with him. As Richard Nixon had hoped, his victory permitted him to oust a host of senior program executives (such as Social Security Commissioner Bob Ball) with remarkably few adverse political repercussions.

Richardson was replaced with Caspar Weinberger, former director of the Office of Management and Budget and a longtime political ally of Governor Ronald Reagan—a man who earned the sobriquet "Cap the Knife" while Reagan's budget director. As one HEW holdover recalled, "We got Weinberger. Why? They [in the White House] were unhappy about [rising] expenditures. He was put there to control expenditures, not for any particular policy reason. Also, we were blithering liberals, and Cap Weinberger would not listen to us [as Richardson had done]."[68] Not surprisingly, Weinberger's HEW was populated by OMB alumni and veterans of Reagan's gubernatorial administration. As Derthick noted, "Like their predecessors in 1969, many of the new Nixon appointees in HEW came from the West Coast. It was still a California crowd, but a very different crowd. The men of 1973 were the fiscal controllers who had fought the liberalization of California welfare programs and administered governor Ronald Reagan's cutbacks in welfare after 1970."[69] Nixon and his senior aides believed Weinberger to be a champion of welfare state retrenchment, and they assumed that he would recruit officials who shared these convictions.[70] Even so, there would be no repetition of the permissiveness of 1969 in staffing HEW—even Weinberger would not have a free hand. As one senior personnel staffer recalled, the White House was firmly in control of staffing decisions:

In 1970–71 we got some of it [control over appointments] back. But we got almost the whole thing back in 1972. I remember having violent arguments with Weinberger over who he and Carlucci were going to appoint at HEW. I would say to Haldeman "Cap says he wants these guys.

They're not with us, they're not on the team, we can't have them." And Haldeman said, "Fine. Right on." Dang it, I had control. I had absolute political control over who those fellows would be.[71]

Did Nixon get the responsiveness he sought from HEW (and the remainder of the government)? News reports from the first year of Nixon's second term suggest that HEW was far more quiescent than it had been in 1969, and its executives were willing to accept directions set by the White House without public opposition.[72] One cannot say whether Nixon's appointees would have been more responsive in a positive sense — willing to take heat on behalf of the president. Certainly the social spending reductions Richard Nixon had in mind for fiscal year 1974 would have called for this.[73] However, the mettle of HEW appointees was never tested: as Watergate engulfed the administration, Nixon retreated from battles over HEW's programs to conserve his political capital for the most important battle: his political survival. There was no White House leadership for HEW appointees to follow.

REAGANISM COMES TO HHS

Like Richard Nixon, Ronald Reagan chose a seasoned Republican politician to head his Department of Health and Human Services (HHS): Richard Schweiker.[74] Like Finch, Schweiker had his own notions about his department's policies and his own political network upon which he wanted to draw. "Schweiker had spent 20 years on the Hill and he had spent 10 years in the Health Committee of the Senate Appropriations Committee. He was ranking Republican on the Health Subcommittee on the Labor and Human Resources Committee. So he had a number of contacts and a lot of policy experience . . . and his own list of folks as well."[75] As always, others championed their own candidates for the senior political posts at HHS — including Republican congressmen and trade and professional associations linked to the Republican party. Some of these groups, such as antiabortion groups, concentrated their energies on a single post; others — such as the AMA — went so far as to present a slate of candidates, one for each position in the department. However, the department that emerged from the claims of Republican politicians and clientele in 1981 was far different from that assembled a dozen years earlier: it was more Republican, more conservative, and more responsive to the policy agenda and political needs of its president, Ronald Reagan. Why was there such a difference between the two departments? The answer comes in two pieces: the centralization of political appointments, and the large and highly homogeneous political network of Ronald Reagan.

Centralization

In contrast to Robert Finch, Richard Schweiker found that his search for HHS subordinates was organized and manned by Reagan's transition aides and guided by Ronald Reagan's policy concerns and political needs. Well before Schweiker had been chosen to head HHS, a transition appointment staff for HHS had been selected, and it quickly set to work laying out job descriptions, interviewing prospective candidates, and assembling a slate of candidates into a "black book" for the secretary-designate.

The staff had been given two instructions: "reach beyond the in-box" and "make certain that all candidates met Ed Meese's five standards of fitness for service in the Reagan administration."[76] Like Pen James, transition staffers who tried to recall the five criteria found that they could bring only one to mind: ideological fidelity to the principles of Ronald Reagan. "We [associate directors] were all there in a big room on M Street [the transition headquarters]. I remember getting a white note card with some basic principles. There were five points to keep in mind. I don't even remember what they were—there was something about people having to fit the Reagan philosophy."[77]

The Reagan aides who were charged with overseeing the staffing of the department did not simply yield to the candidates proposed to them by Republicans on Capitol Hill, professional groups, or the incoming Secretary. Rather, they could—and did— draw on the president's political network in locating potential appointees and gathering political intelligence about candidates proposed by other Republican politicians. This network was an amalgam of health and welfare staffers from the Reagan gubernatorial administration, people from a nationally based conservative social policy network, and Republican veterans of the Weinberger HEW. Those who worked on the Reagan transition staff stood at the confluence of these three streams and drew upon each to recruit and evaluate candidates for HHS positions. Not surprisingly, the candidates they championed—John Svahn, Dorcas Hardy, David Swoap, and others—had circulated though each of these streams: John Svahn (Social Security commissioner), for example, had served in HEW under Weinberger, in Reagan's gubernatorial administration, and was a figure of some reputation in conservative social policy circles.

Although the Republican politicians and clientele groups advanced candidates who were largely attuned to Ronald Reagan's political needs and policy agenda, Reagan aides were not willing to leave other Republican politicians to their own devices. Rather, the transition staff conducted lengthy interviews, winnowing out those candidates whose political and ideological credentials were not in order: job candidates who had not worked in a Reagan campaign, congressional aides who had served as staffers to relatively liberal Republicans (such as Senator Danforth), and specialists whose views on policy were ideologically unacceptable — whether the candidates were proposed by clientele and professional groups, or Republican politicians.[78]

When informed of his selection, Schweiker was told, like other cabinet secretaries, that "the White House is going to control the appointment process; all of them are going to be controlled right here by Pen James."[79] December 12, the day after he was named, he was presented with a slate of candidates for his department's senior posts that had been scrutinized by James's associate directors, James himself, and Reagan's Kitchen Cabinet.[80] And, in the remaining weeks of the transition, he would work closely with Reagan's transition personnel aides, who generated names, conducted interviews, and checked on the political credentials of candidates before referring them to Schweiker for his consideration. In short, Schweiker was not left to his own devices; instead, his choices were thoroughly structured by Reagan's staff. Schweiker, in turn, proved to be remarkably willing to accept presidential leadership and work with a degree of central control that his predecessors might have found intolerable. A transition staffer remarked: "I think there was always one thing that Schweiker always understood, no matter what his private thoughts may have been: that he was the president's appointee, and that he and his appointees would have to be compatible with and supportive of the goals of the president."[81] An aide close to Schweiker seconded this view: "There was no question that these [PAS] appointments belonged to the president. We had no problem with that. We wanted people who the president and his immediate staff would feel comfortable with. . . . There was a desire on our part to staff up with people who were loyal to what the president wanted."[82]

Homogeneity

Why was Schweiker so willing to defer to presidential leadership in assembling his department? Establishing fairly centralized control for the purpose of assembling a uniformly conservative, loyal, and presidentially oriented HHS was a great deal easier in 1980 than it had been in 1968, because the intellectual and political progeny of Republican progressivism had disappeared in the intervening years. As Miller and Jennings show, the mobilization of the New Right, the demobilization of moderately liberal Republicans, and the conversion of other Republicans to a more conservative brand of Republicanism meant that an unusually homogeneous (and conservative) set of party activists were in command of the Republican party in the 1980s.[83] Much the same holds true for the Republican party's officeholders as well: between the early 1970s and early 1980s a series of elections moved the party well to the right and sharply diminished the heterogeneity of the Republican party.[84]

No more stunning example of the transformation of the Republican party exists than Schweiker himself. In the early to mid-1970s Schweiker was a liberal Pennsylvania senator with especially close ties to organized labor and who earned high marks from the Americans for Democratic Action (ADA): in 1970 his ADA score was 75, and in 1976 it was 84. However, like Paul on the road to Damascus, Schweiker on the road to Kansas City (the site of the Republican party's national convention in 1976) underwent a profound conversion. In a desperate and unsuccessful move to shake loose a few Ford delegates among moderate eastern delegations, John Sears instructed Ronald Reagan to pledge the vice-presidential nomination to Richard Schweiker in advance of the convention's presidential ballot. Schweiker accepted Reagan's offer, pronouncing himself a conservative. Upon his return to the Senate, Schweiker was a new politician, one whose voting record received a paltry ADA rating of 17 in 1980. Schweiker's would-be candidacy also enlarged his ties to the New Right and Reagan's entourage. By 1980 Reagan's social policy entourage and Schweiker's congressional policy team overlapped a good bit, and staff from each camp circulated freely between them. David Winston, who headed up the staffing efforts on behalf of the Reagan administration at HHS, nicely exemplified this pattern: he had served as Governor Reagan's assistant secretary of health in California, and came to Washington, D.C., in 1977 as the senior health policy aide to Senator Schweiker. After drafting the chapter on HHS for the Heritage Foundation's *Mandate for Leadership*, he was summoned by Reagan's personnel office to develop HHS policy and personnel planning for the Reagan transition. As one longtime Schweiker aide observed, "We sort of had our guy there, and Ronald Reagan sort of had his guy there—all rolled into one."[85]

The repercussions of this convergence were twofold. First, homogeneity mitigated conflict between the White House and the department and lowered the costs of centralization. Second, homogeneity permitted the president's staff to cede control over some posts without doing damage to the president's agenda. For example, the Reagan staff wanted *all* presidential appointees at HHS to be philosophically compatible with Reagan and to bring Reagan campaign credentials to their job—even appointees who held specialized and traditionally "nonpolitical" posts, such as the director of the Cancer Institute. However, for highly specialized posts—such as director of the National Institute of Health—the Reagan team had to rely more heavily upon Schweiker, professional groups linked to HHS, or other Republican politicians to staff the department.[86] Nonetheless, even when the Reagan staff had to depend upon the political networks of other Republican politicians— either Schweiker himself or his former colleagues on Capitol Hill—the candidates they championed were attuned to the policy agenda of the Reagan White House.

In the end, though, the president's political and policy concerns had come to figure more prominently in the filling of many more HHS positions than they did a decade earlier. Of those who received presidential appointments at HHS during the first two years of Reagan's presidency, all were screened for evidence of their "commitment to the Reagan agenda," and roughly half were first proposed by the Reagan staff to Schweiker.[87] Even the second layer of political appointees, departmental political appointees (SES and schedule C), did not escape the attention of the White House staff.[88] Drawing upon the practice of the post-1970 Nixon White House—and the Civil Service Reform Act of 1977—the Reagan staff turned to the Office of Personnel Management (OPM) as its strong arm: the OPM refused to authorize departmental posts unless the department's candidate had first received a clearance from the Presidential Personnel Office.[89] A senior member of the OPM staff recalled: "The agency would not send paperwork up [to OPM] until they had cleared the candidate with the White House. . . . I controlled the position, and the White House controlled the person. I wouldn't give them a position until I knew who was going in it, and they had been approved by the White House. That was the backstop."[90]

In spite of the increasing homogeneity of the Republican party and the willingness of senior HHS staff to accede to the president's prerogatives, the relationship between the HHS and the PPO was not free from conflict. As Reagan's first term progressed the attention of the PPO staff shifted away from PAS slots, which had largely been filled, and towards lower-level political appointments. Health and Human Services, like other departments, increasingly chafed at the PPO's claims on "its" departmental appointments. An aide close to Secretary Schweiker complained: "In the early days, at the PAS level, with Winston and Bailey, I thought that worked very well. . . . As PPO got staffed up more and more, and really ran out of things to do, they became more and more intrusive into the process [of departmental appointments], to the point of saying, 'Even if you want to promote someone who is a schedule C, or transfer them to another post, you have to clear it with us.' It got absurd."[91] Nonetheless, the president's staff had achieved much of what it had set out to achieve: the senior political ranks at Ronald Reagan's HHS were bereft of inappropriate types—civil servants, liberal Republicans, and Democrats.[92] And, more important, the political leadership of HHS steered the department in the directions charted by Ronald Reagan.

Responsiveness at HHS, 1981–1983

As one might expect, political executives in the Department of Health and Human Services were far more willing to look to the Reagan White House for guidance on questions of politics and policy than they had been during the opening years of Nixon's presidency. Many of Nixon's own executives in HEW rebelled against policy changes proposed by the White House; Reagan's team of executives at HHS, in the judgment of Washington insiders, was willing to "surrender control over policy to OMB and White House officials" without a fight,[93] to quietly acquiesce to the retrenchment of its programs,[94] and to "take the [political] heat" for White House political failures, such as a quickly aborted package of 1981 social security cutbacks.[95]

More important, Reagan's HHS team did more than sit still for White House initiatives: many HHS appointees waged their own campaigns to reshape ongoing programs to be consonant with the "Reagan agenda." Dorcas Hardy, a veteran of Reagan's gubernatorial administration and head of the Office of Human Development Services (1981–1986), proposed massive cuts in her programs as a means of "building self-sufficiency of clientele" and a "conservative opportunity society."[96] Hardy routinely and eagerly sought cuts in her programs five to ten times larger than those adopted by Congress, though with little success.[97] Although she was sharply criticized by careerists, research groups, and advocacy groups, Hardy used what authority she had over programs to steer research funds towards supporters of the administration and away from those critical of its policies, such as the Child Welfare League.[98] Jack Svahn, Reagan's first Commissioner of Social Security, was another Californian who showed equal zeal in trimming the welfare state. Like Hardy, Svahn championed rather ambitious reductions in his programs, which typically met with congressional opposition. Svahn, too, pushed for stringency in his programs (for example, the Social Security Disability Insurance Program), often in the face of fierce criticism from program advocates.[99] By the end of 1982 Richard Schweiker, weary of being squeezed from above by the Office of Management and Budget and from below by "Reaganauts" in his department, chose to resign, and in early 1983 Margaret Heckler (R-Mass.) was chosen to head the Department of Health and Human Services.

Stalemate at HHS, 1983–1985

As Chief of Staff James Baker saw it, the selection of Margaret Heckler to head the Department of Health and Human Services presented the White House with an opportunity to kill two birds with one stone: finding a plum for a House member defeated in the 1982 mid-term election and mitigating the widely heralded "gender gap" by appointing a Republican woman to a highly visible post in the Reagan administration. However, while in the House of Representatives Margaret Heckler had neither proven herself to be a capable administrator nor a reliable ally of the administration: in 1981 and 1982 she had supported the president less frequently than any other Republican in the House, and her voting record led the *National Journal* to classify her as one of only three liberal Republicans in the U.S. House of Representatives.[100] In short, Heckler had much in common with Robert Finch. Would Ronald Reagan soon find himself saddled with a Robert Finch of his own and an HHS that was "marching to its own drummer"? Familiar with the tenure of both Finch and Joseph Califano, Reagan's aides took a page from Richard Nixon's postelection strategy of 1972: Heckler would be the Secretary of HHS, but her undersecretary would be devoted 'Reaganaut' John Svahn, and Svahn would control policy and staffing. David Stockman, meanwhile, would select Heckler's assistant secretary for management and budget and control budgetary decisions.[101]

These arrangements soon collapsed in a miasma of mistrust. In the months after her appointment, Heckler resisted White House attempts to dictate policy and personnel choices and complained that Svahn was trying to run the department. Summoned to the White House in April 1983 for a meeting with Svahn, John Herrington, and Cabinet Secretary Craig Fuller, Herrington reminded Heckler, "You're supposed to be the fucking figurehead" and demanded that she acquiesce to White House leadership.[102] Despite such bullying, little changed in the coming months. Heckler refused to approve the candidates sent her by the White House, fearing that they would have stronger ties to the White House than she.[103] And, in spite of Heckler's attempts to generate support for her candidates on Capitol Hill, the White House personnel staff refused to approve them for department posts, claiming that they were far too liberal and insufficiently competent.[104] Svahn eventually departed HHS in frustration, and the White House appointments staff let Heckler select her own undersecretary—the only Heckler candidate for a presidential appointment to which the staff acceded during her two and one-half year tenure as Secretary.

Hence, from mid-1983 through 1985, virtually all senior leadership posts at HHS remained vacant or were filled by subordinates who served in an acting capacity.[105] By the spring of 1984 the vacant leadership ranks of HHS became a target of criticism among Congressional Democrats[106] and a joking matter among trade associations and professional groups that dealt with HHS: "How is HHS like a thespian society? Because everyone there is in an acting capacity."[107] Occasionally, even acting heads were absent, and HHS officials were forced to improvise their own leadership arrangements. As one deputy assistant secretary recalled, "We had what we jokingly called a 'provisional revolutionary committee': there wasn't even anybody in an acting capacity for a few months [in the assistant secretary post], so we had a committee [of deputy assistant secretaries] running the office."[108]

The Reagan White House staff was largely unable to compel acceptance of its candidates. However, in contrast to the Nixon White House staff of 1969–1970, the Reagan White House (and OMB) were consistently able to veto any personnel and policy choices they judged to be inconsistent with the president's priorities. As one senior White House staffer boasted: "I didn't give a shit about that woman. We had the policy taken care of. I mean, she was just an embarrassment, that's all. There was nothing going on over there that was sneaking through. Between the Domestic Council and OIRA [OMB's

Office of Information and Regulatory Affairs] and the [OMB] budget analysts
. . . we managed to take care of everything except for the woman herself."[109]

Though the department was responsive in a minimal, negative sense—it
made no policy commitments that the president's staff opposed—there were
opportunity costs to this stalemate. As one assistant secretary lamented: "After
Heckler took over, the conservative political appointees who cared about policy
were still there. But there was a real vacuum in leadership in the secretary's
office. Ronald Reagan was still there, nothing had changed about that. You
were looking for opportunities to carry that [your philosophy] out, but you
were getting no assignments. There was never any indication of where to go or
what we were to do in terms of policy."[110] In the absence of positive political
leadership, HHS drifted along "doing some things that were consensual and
routine activities" and eschewing "bold new ideas."[111] Heckler's stalemate with
the White House persisted from the summer of 1983 until the autumn of 1985,
when the presidential election was safely over and Heckler could be "promoted"
to the post of Ambassador to Ireland and replaced by Otis Bowen.

Ebbing Centralization and Its Consequences, 1985–1988

Sustaining systematic influence over the staffing of an administration is a
precarious business for the White House Personnel Office. It faces constant
challenges to its prerogatives from inside the White House, from rivals in
the executive branch, and from others in the Washington community. And,
as Ronald Reagan's second term began, the appointments staff's hold over
the selection of departmental executives was gradually eroding.[112] By June
of 1985, seasoned Washington journalists noticed the ebbing influence of
Reagan's personnel staff, announcing that the "White House Personnel Office
Struggles with More Vacancies, Less Influence,"[113] while staff members themselves acknowledged the same.[114] With control from the center ebbing and an
entirely new slate of appointees to bring on board at HHS, would the Reagan
administration finally find itself saddled with a team of HHS appointees who
succumbed to the importunings of HHS clientele and civil servants?

Without question, during Otis Bowen's tenure as Secretary of Health and
Human Services the political leadership of the department was significantly
less pugnacious in attacking the welfare state than it had been during the
opening years of the administration. Moreover, for the first time in Reagan's
presidency, HHS sponsored a program that promised to significantly expand
the welfare state: the Catastrophic Insurance Coverage Act. This proposal
evoked sharp criticism from the right wing of the Republican party. As the
Heritage Foundation's *Mandate for Leadership III* complained:

> The most serious policy error of the Reagan administration may be its
> support for an expansion of Medicare to provide catastrophic acute care

protection for the elderly. Reagan was persuaded by Administration officials and Republican lawmakers to endorse an expansion of Medicare
and hence of the federal government. It was a serious blunder . . .
[which] resulted in the biggest expansion of Medicare since it was created
in 1965 . . . [and] gave unexpected momentum to lawmakers who seek
to create a federally funded national health system in the America.[115]

These developments led some on the Republican right to complain that HHS
had reverted to its old ways: it had become a home to liberals and inhospitable
to Reagan loyalists and Reagan's ideas. As one Heritage Foundation official
complained in 1988, "Heckler was actually better than Bowen. He is not doing
anything that is consistent with the philosophies of Ronald Reagan or the directives coming out of different points in the White House. He has done nothing to
reduce the largest department imaginable—the one with the third-largest budget
in the world."[116] Did HHS actually stray from "the philosophies of Ronald
Reagan" as a result of a breakdown in the ability of Reagan's White House staff
to sustain its control over the staffing of the department? Probably not.

When Otis Bowen, a physician and former governor of Indiana, became
Secretary of Health and Human Services in November 1985, he was faced
with rebuilding the political leadership of his department, much as Richard
Schweiker had been at the start of the Reagan administration: thirty-eight
of the forty senior appointive posts at HHS were either vacant or filled by
people in an acting capacity.[117] The White House appointments staff, much
as it had in 1981, quickly furnished Bowen with a briefing book containing
a slate of candidates it had accumulated during its long stalemate with
Heckler. However, the Personnel Office was to play a somewhat smaller role
in assembling the political leadership of HHS in 1985 than it had four years
earlier. Unlike Schweiker in 1981, Bowen relied upon a personal staff of
trusted Hoosiers to help him staff his department, rather than a team chosen
by the White House.[118] More importantly, the White House Personnel Office was smaller, less expert, less highly regarded than it had been four years
earlier. Moreover, unlike 1981, the Personnel Office was only weakly supported by the president's chief of staff, Donald Regan: Robert Tuttle had
been stripped of the rank (assistant to the president) and West Wing Office
that his first term predecessors possessed, and Regan had pledged to some
cabinet members—among them Bowen—that they could enjoy a good bit
of latitude in staffing their departments.[119] In the end, approximately one-
third of the appointees to senior political posts originated in the White House,
a proportion that was quite large by historical standards but smaller than
that of the administration's first two years.

Even though the White House appointments staff exerted less control over
staffing decisions in 1985 than it had in 1981, the administration as a whole
remained uniformly Republican and overwhelmingly conservative. One survey

of political appointees midway through the second Reagan administration reveals that virtually every appointee (94 percent) was a Republican, and the overwhelming majority (75 percent) were right-of-center;[120] another survey, taken a year earlier, yielded virtually identical results.[121]

Moreover, the partisan and ideological composition of Reagan's HHS remained largely unchanged as well. Neither White House aides responsible for staffing HHS nor their counterparts in the department could identify any HHS appointees who were Democrats. A senior official at HHS responsible for staffing could only volunteer "someone that was an Independent came on board."[122] More importantly, neither could identify any HHS appointees who disagreed with the principal tenets of Reagan's conservatism.[123] If the political leader of Bowen's HHS had any disputes with the president or his program, they kept these objections to themselves, studiously avoiding open criticism of their president.[124] In fact, the bete noire of the Republican right, catastrophic insurance, was championed only by Bowen and his chief of staff. Reagan's men and women at HHS, as one might predict, strongly opposed it. Said one assistant secretary:

> I tried to talk Bowen out of it, but couldn't. I objected to it because it violated the goal of diminishing the role of the government and leaving more for private insurance. The premium thing just really ran the private insurance industry out of this, and turned it into a government insurance program. Here we have this expansion of a government program, which was in a lot of ways was the oddest thing to have happened in the Reagan years. There was strong opposition in Treasury, OMB, and here [but] when the Iran-Contra thing broke, the White House needed something to offer, so they reached down into the Domestic Policy Council and they pulled it up.[125]

In short, the administration's political appointees remained remarkably conservative and responsive to the concerns of their president. The raw material from which the Reagan administration was fashioned, Republican elites, was sufficiently homogeneous to permit a weakened White House grasp with little loss of responsiveness — even at a department long the bane of conservatives, the Department of Health and Human Services.

THE BEST LAID SCHEMES . . .

The best laid schemes o' mice an' men gang aft a-gley.
— Robert Burns

The experience of the Nixon and Reagan administrations demonstrates that political appointees are, under some circumstances, fairly reliable instruments of presidential leadership. Responsiveness can emerge even in the most challenging environments, such as a social service bureaucracy, when presidents are able to piece together a specialized staff that permits them extensive control over staff choices, and they can draw upon a fairly homogenous political network, either their own or that of other politicians.

However, the aggrandizement of the president's appointments staff has yielded far more than presidents had bargained for. A burgeoning appointments staff has given rise to a host of unintended consequences, many of which are every bit as important for the larger political system as the results that presidents had hoped to achieve. A balanced evaluation of centralization requires that we move beyond a presidential perspective and its preoccupation with control and responsiveness.

Burgeoning Demands and Expectations

First, the aggrandizement of the president's White House appointments staff has produced a tremendous surge in demands and expectations aimed at the White House. The White House appointments staff has absorbed the prerogatives and responsibilities of other politicians, particularly cabinet secretaries and national party officials. Other members of the Washington community — individual job-seekers, interest groups, congressmen, or campaign contributors — are well informed and rational, and they have adjusted their behavior accordingly: they press their claims directly on the White House staff, rather than (or, in addition to) their traditional points of access. When Dan Fenn met with scholars and civic leaders in 1962 to discuss (and promote) the Kennedy administration's moves to expand the president's appointments staff, one participant cautioned: "It seems to me that if we recommend [to the White House appointments staff] approaching the Chamber of Commerce and Rotary Clubs and business organizations and professional organizations all over the United States regarding available positions that they [the president's staff] would have to put another wing on the White House to handle all of the recommendations."[126] He was prescient: by the 1980s and 1990s, another wing — or at least a staff exponentially larger than the appointment staff of 1962 — would be necessary to meet the demands now channeled to the White House appointments staff. To those who headed the appointments staff in the Kennedy or Johnson presidencies, the burgeoning demands of the modern era are "horrifying."

> *[Dan Fenn]:* You know, the world was different for you [Reagan] people. When John [Macy] and I were doing this, nobody realized it was here, and that was good. I mean when you say 500 letters a month, that's horrifying.
> *[Pen James]:* I would get that [500 letters] in a day.
> *[Arnie Miller]:* I would get 100 [phone] calls a day.[127]

Though these demands may be "horrifying," they are not fleeting. Rather, they are grounded in two decades of experience. They will not go away, and they cannot be avoided. The president's appointment staffers may wistfully recall the quiet days of the Kennedy or Johnson administrations, but they cannot return to them, because other influential individuals and groups will not let them — or will make presidents pay a high price, as the Carter administration discovered. In short, the president's staff, like the president it serves, is no longer free to be "as small as it might like."

Intramural Conflict

A second unanticipated change wrought by the centralization of appointments in a White House staff is the intensification of conflict within the White House Office. Conflicts that were once played out outside of the White House — among departments, party officials, clientele groups, and congressmen — have increasingly been drawn inside the White House.

During the Truman, Eisenhower, and Kennedy presidencies, the party's national committee and congressmen typically found themselves enmeshed in disputes with departmental executives over the division of political spoils. The president's staff — lacking control over most posts — was either uninvolved in these disputes, or acted as a referee, mitigating and structuring conflicts. Within the White House, the president's appointments aides cut a small swath. The staff's responsibilities remained heavily clerical, and few other staffers cared about their actions. What working relations they had with other staffers were coordinated informally and marked by little conflict.

However, as the White House appointments staff tried to garner control over choices that once rested outside the White House, its relationships with others inside the White House were transformed. First, controlling choices necessitated drawing upon the competence of others in the White House and Executive Office, such as the president's National Security Council staff, the Domestic Policy staff, and even the OMB. Hence, relationships of informal coordination gave way, by the Nixon presidency, to an elaborate set of clearances with other specialized staff units. As the staff shifted from largely clerical responsibilities to substantial control over a large number of posts, other staffs inside the White House, each with its own axe to grind and its own constituencies to serve, took a far greater interest in its actions, hoping to use appointments choices to solve its own problems or pursue its own concerns.

The tensions that were just emerging during the Johnson presidency — between John Macy and the president's nascent Domestic Policy staff (Califano), Political Affairs staff (Marvin Watson), and Congressional Liaison Office (Mike Manatos) — blossomed into full-scale contentiousness during the Nixon and Reagan presidencies. The president's aides, we may presume, are no more disagreeable than they once were. Instead, conflicts that were played out between the party's National Committee, Senate aides, and departments in 1951 became, by 1981, conflicts among the presidential staffs that had absorbed many of their responsibilities: the Political Affairs Office, the Congressional Liaison staff, and the Presidential Personnel Office. Barring a much smaller, more modest White House Office, they will not go away.

The White House and Departments

Another pattern of conflict has intensified as the size and reach of the president's appointments staff has grown: conflict between the appointments staff and executive departments. During the Truman and Eisenhower presidencies, presidential appointments evoked precious little conflict between departments and the White House appointments staff: the White House simply acquiesced to department initiatives because its size and capabilities were too modest for it to challenge their choices.

As the size and responsibilities of the president's appointments staff have grown, it has become far more capable of vetoing departmental staffing decisions and forcing its candidates on departments. Hence, it is much more likely to find itself locked in heated struggles with departments — struggles that show up in the increasingly frequent and sour references to the staff in the memoirs of cabinet secretaries. Like other political conflicts, these conflicts are often resolved through reciprocity; what White House aides have dubbed "multiplayer deals" between the departments and the White House. Some measure of conflict and deadlock between the White House and departments is unavoidable. And, to the extent that this conflict pits the broad, national concerns represented by presidents (and their aides) against parochial and clientele-dominated concerns of departments, conflict and inaction are actually desirable.

However, recent experience suggests that too much conflict — and the wrong sorts of conflict — between the White House and departments have emerged. First, the stalemate between departments and the White House escalated sharply. At its worst — e.g., during Margaret Heckler's tenure at HHS — departments simply drifted, bereft of political leadership. Throughout the eight years of the Reagan administration, the presidentially appointed posts at HHS were, on average, unfilled for roughly two years, and when Otis Bowen took over the department from Margaret Heckler, fully thirty-eight of the forty senior posts were vacant (or filled by people in an acting capacity).[128]

In decades past, the conflicts that emerged between the White House staff and departments often centered on the reluctance of departments to service political obligations heaped upon them by appointments staff. Seen from the perspective of departmental appointees, the White House staff is often "political" in the narrow sense of the term. As I have shown, presidents' appointment staffs continue to advance the claims of electoral politics — albeit in the modern guise of candidate organizations. These conflicts between the White House and departments reflect an inescapable tension between elections and governance. However, in recent years — especially during the Nixon and Reagan presidencies — the president's appointments staff was sometimes "political" in the narrowest possible sense: aides used the staff as an avenue to pursue their personal aims, either pecuniary or ideological.

As the Presidential Personnel Office has grown in size and importance, it has became a more attractive place to work and a more difficult organization to monitor. Though the hours are long and the job can expose the staff to incessant importunings, the Personnel Office has acquired a reputation throughout the Washington community as a place to hunt for a choice job, where an ambitious person can "place six and grab one" — "you know, place six to twelve people so you've done your job for the president and then grab one for yourself."[129] Hence, many conflicts that have emerged between the White House and departments in recent years have pitted departments that sought to protect themselves from the personal ambitions of White House staffers — staffers who sought to place a cadre of like-minded acquaintances in departments to report on the loyalty of the president's senior appointees,[130] or staffers who sought to place people whose indebtedness they could exploit after leaving the White House appointments staff.[131]

To be certain, departments have not stood idly by in response to these pressures. Rather, they have learned how to insulate themselves from the claims of the president's staff: they cultivate allies on Capitol Hill to boost their own candidates or stymie those pushed by the White House staff, and they try to preempt the White House staff by "hitting the ground running." Frank Carlucci, a veteran of Nixon's ambitious attempts to gather control of staffing decisions, knew precisely what to expect at the outset of the Reagan administration. Hence, the advice he proffered to other cabinet secretaries was: "Spend most of your time at the outset focusing on the personnel system. Get your appointees in place, because the first clash you will have is with the White House personnel office. And if you don't get your people in place, you will end up being a one-armed paper hanger."[132] Departmental officials who are unable to avail themselves of these strategies have found yet another: they fill the secretary's office with a cadre of personal loyalists, and then isolate and disregard the "presidential agents" holding presidentially appointed posts, as Richard Schweiker did to ensure the loyalty of his top appointees.[133] However, the long-term flow of operating responsibilities into posts that are neither statutorily defined nor subject to confirmation has little to recommend it.

Can we do better than this? Is it possible to reform the way in which presidents go about selecting appointees and using their appointments staff, as some scholars have urged?

7

The Institutionalized Presidency: Theory and Practice

I conclude by addressing two questions: the first, theoretical, and the second, practical. What does the evolution of the Presidential Personnel Office between 1948 and 1994 tell us about our theories of the presidency's institutional development — and about the modern presidency more generally? And what does the evolution of the Personnel Office tell us about our prospects for improving presidential leadership of the bureaucracy, as scholars and reformers — such as the Volcker Commission — have urged?

PRESIDENCY THEORY

It is clear that the evolution of the White House Office is shaped by the propensities of the presidents who occupy it, and sometimes importantly so. Richard Nixon and Ronald Reagan significantly accelerated the aggrandizement of the Presidential Personnel Office, while Dwight Eisenhower retarded its development and Jimmy Carter reversed it (albeit briefly). Taken singly, as is often the case in presidency scholarship, these presidencies suggest that the White House Office is, in fact, the "shadow of the man." But, if one examines the evolution of the White House Office across the span of a few decades — or if one observes the repercussions of presidents' efforts to reshape the personnel staff in ways that violate the expectations and neglect the needs of others — what clearly emerges is the extent to which presidents, like other politicians, are creatures of the institutions they inhabit. In the long run, the Presidential Personnel Office, like the larger White House Office, is far more a product of the institutional system than the leaders who occupy it.

The aggrandizement of the Presidential Personnel Office was, as rational choice accounts argue, rooted in the atrophying of traditional constraints outside of the White House Office. As political parties lost control over

153

electoral politics and became less useful as political intermediaries between elections, their leverage ebbed sharply, and putting decisions into the hands of an expanded White House staff became significantly more attractive to presidents and their aides. By the mid to late 1960s, party leaders' access to appointment decisions had been withdrawn, and their ability to shape the president's appointments staff to suit their needs had essentially vanished.

However, one cannot fully account for the emergence of the modern Presidential Personnel Office simply by tracing the waning influence of political parties—as rational choice accounts have done. Throughout the decades during which presidents most aggressively sought to take control of appointment choices, the president's party was a relatively insignificant impediment to centralization: party leaders were enfeebled well *before* the most rapid growth of the Presidential Personnel Office got under way. It was not party officials with whom Kennedy, Johnson, or Nixon vied for control over appointment choices; rather, it was the leaders of executive departments and the policy networks allied with them who most powerfully constrained the size and influence of the White House appointments staff.

Department heads and policy network leaders had powerful incentives to curb the reach of a White House appointments staff. Seen from their vantage point, the president's staff was a disruptive influence, one that threatened to subordinate their professional or programmatic concerns to the president's "political" considerations, be they repaying campaign contributors and workers, promoting diversity, or enforcing personal loyalty. Well after party politicians had lost most of their hold over presidents, these members of the Washington community were endowed with formidable political resources, and it was they who made a strategy of centralization costly—too costly—for presidents and their aides to openly and aggressively pursue.

If one wishes to explain why centralization became increasingly attractive to presidents, one must show why presidents who have held office in the past quarter-century found the sanctions and rewards wielded by the leaders of departments and policy networks to be less constraining than their mid-century predecessors did. The increasing attractiveness of centralization to the presidents who followed Truman and Eisenhower was rooted in two very basic changes in the presidency's institutional setting: the vastly increased importance of television news, and the disintegration of "policy networks" in response to the multiplying of interest groups and the dispersion of authority within the U.S. Congress. Taken together, these changes swiftly increased the costs—and diminished the rewards—of permitting departments to operate as "semi-independent fiefdoms." Predictably, presidents responded by sharply accelerating the personnel staff's size and reach.

The evolution of the Presidential Personnel Office reveals one final limitation of existing rational choice accounts of the presidency's evolution: having fastened onto the attenuation of traditional constraints, these accounts have made little room for the emergence of new constraints in the presidency's institutional setting. Take, for example, the electoral environment of the presidency. The collapse of parties was accompanied by the rise of new electoral organizations, such as presidential campaign organizations. The White House staff remains intimately linked to the demands of electoral politics, albeit not through political parties. Still closely bound to electoral claimants, the Presidential Personnel Office that emerged in the 1970s, 1980s, and 1990s was far less an instrument of "policy control" than rational choice accounts would lead one to believe—and far more a "political organization," in the estimation of its leaders as well as its detractors.

In sum, the assumptions rooted in existing rational choice accounts mischaracterize the presidency's institutional setting in a few important ways and lead us to conclusions about the evolution of the White House Personnel Office that are wide of the mark. Nonetheless, rational choice accounts remain the most fruitful and promising way of theorizing about the presidency: what has been mischaracterized can be revised. Those who study the presidency would be wise to emulate scholars who study the U.S. Congress or political parties. Their theories have moved in the direction of increasingly sophisticated accounts of institutional settings and motivations[1]—while maintaining a level of abstraction that is all too rare in theories of the presidency.

Seen more broadly, this study complements and extends a body of scholarship that posits the emergence of a "plebiscitary" or "post-modern" presidency during the last quarter of the twentieth century. As a host of scholars have observed,[2] the disintegration of political parties and policy networks—in combination with the proliferation of new technologies of mass communication—has transformed the modern presidency. "Using mass communication technologies," Stephen Skowronek writes, "presidents now cultivate a direct political relationship with the public at large. The plebiscitary presidents routinely appeal over the heads of the elites of the Washington establishment, hoping to use their public standing to compel that establishment into following their lead."[3]

The changes the expositors of the plebiscitary presidency point to have had a greater effect, though, than they acknowledge. Consider, for example, the consequences of a vastly expanded flow of television news from Washington, D.C., into American homes. To be sure, television has permitted presidents to "go public" with increasing frequency—and it has *also* reshaped the institutional presidency. Bill Clinton's transition personnel organization dwarfed that of John Kennedy: his staff of thirty lawyers and researchers who vetted prospective Clinton appointees was the same size as John Kennedy's *entire* personnel transition staff. Why the efflorescence of presidential staff? A vastly more numerous and prominent Washington press corps is in large part responsible. As one Clinton aide observed:

> Let's face it, the way in which the media covers these things [presidential appointments] has changed dramatically. You've got CNN and all these new shows, and USA Today, and all this instantaneous news. And there is much more appetite for information, and there are more reporters and more digging. People who got famous [i.e. whose appointments became controversial and newsworthy] wouldn't have years ago, because there wasn't the availability in air time or newspaper space to write about it, and there weren't the reporters to cover it.[4]

Hoping to fend off critical media coverage of their nominees — and eager to ensure that their administration "speaks in one voice" — presidents have responded to the vastly increased importance of the news media by expanding their personnel staffs. Simply stated, the displacement of a presidential politics rooted in parties and policy networks and the emergence of a media-centered presidential politics has fueled not only plebiscitary leadership, but the aggrandizement of White House Office as well: the strategy of "going central" is the progeny of the same forces that have fueled "going public."

PRESIDENTIAL PRACTICE

Alarmed by the proliferation of political appointees and the increasingly assiduous efforts of presidents to centralize control over appointments, scholars and reformers have called for far-reaching reforms in the way presidents exercise leadership through political appointments. The National Commission on Public Service, popularly known as the "Volcker Commission," urged presidents to reduce the number of appointive posts, to halt their efforts at centralizing control over departmental appointments, and to handle presidential appointments with a greater regard to "neutral competence" by establishing "explicit criteria for the qualifications of people nominated to each position" and by emphasizing "managerial experience and substantive expertise" in defining these criteria."[5]

During the 1980s the National Academy of Public Administration, too, sounded warnings about the evolving system of political appointments, sponsoring conferences and studies and issuing its own recommendations in its *Leadership in Jeopardy: The Fraying of the Presidential Appointment System.* Drawing upon the National Academy's findings, Hugh Heclo proposes that presidents repair the "in-and-outer" system of administrative leadership by assuming responsibility for the system — and vesting their new responsibility in a "much-enhanced" Presidential Personnel Office. The new Personnel Office, the "Office of Executive Appointments, would be the only executive branch center for overseeing the operation of the political appointments system, as a system and through the president accountable to Congress."[6] Headed by "a senior presidential appointee subject to Senate confirmation," the Office would

> clear . . . the statutory creation or renewal of all positions filled by presidential appointment; offer advice to department heads on the appropriate scope of all nonpresidential appointments, reporting to both houses of Congress on the qualifications of all persons occupying such positions; maintain for disclosure to . . . Congress the full record of endorsements and recommendations made by people or groups pertaining to executive political appointments . . . ; [and] periodically evaluate the performances of presidentially appointed executives on a confidential basis.[7]

And, more recently, a trio of distinguished public administration scholars, John DiIulio, Gerald Garvey, and Donald Kettl, has urged — yet again — that by "reducing the number of mid-level political appointees" we can improve the quality of federal governance.[8]

What can we say about these and similar proposals in light of the study's findings? When viewed from the perspective of presidents, the centralization of appointment decisions in an expanded White House staff has been rewarding, yielding increased control and responsiveness. However, if we examine the *full* set of consequences that centralization has produced — especially the way in which it has permitted relatively narrow sorts of political concerns to crowd out the programmatic perspectives of departments and their allies, it appears to be an equivocal, even harmful development for the capabilities of the administrative establishment. But, because the public does not hold presidents accountable for disrupting the continuity and integrity of the administrative establishment, presidents simply have no incentive to worry about its health — or that of the "political executive system" taken as a whole. It is very unlikely that presidents will choose to embrace the role that Heclo has carved out for them.

Even if presidents were willing to accept responsibility for the "in and outer system," would we really want them to have this responsibility? The Presidential Personnel Office is the focus of fierce political pressures, and its leaders have found it difficult to uphold considerations of expertise and programmatic integrity in the face of importunings from the president's political supporters and demands for presidential fealty. If, in fact, the PPO is "a political organization" whose members "must have worked for the president's election," as one head of the PPO remarked, do we want it to be center of responsibility for the political appointment system? Probably not.

Finally, not only are presidents unlikely to superintend the political appointment system — or to do so in a way that reformers find appropriate — but they may also be more "politicizing" than the Volcker Commission has requested. The central claim of the rational choice approach — that politicization and centralization have grown "because of the nature of our institutions and the role and location of presidents within them"[9] — is, I have argued, well supported. Since presidents are institutionally induced to centralize, it does no more good to enjoin them to stop centralizing than it does to implore members of Congress not to seek spending projects for their constituency. And, as the experience of Jimmy Carter shows, it does little good to elect presidents who are not personally disposed to pursue centralization. In the end, the only thing that *will* work is to change the institutions that presidents inhabit in such a way that further centralization is no longer attractive. However, it is possible to conclude with a glimmer of hope for reformers: the organizational costs of centralization have become increasingly burdensome to presidents and have slowed the growth of the Presidential Personnel Office (and even halted it during the past decade). The Presidential Personnel Office and, more generally, the White House Office have settled into a period of stability. The White House Office has adapted to the disintegration of policy networks and the sharply increased significance of the electronic media, and the rewards of further aggrandizement are offset by its costs — until another round of changes in the presidency's institutional setting is initiated.

Appendix: Data and Methods

GATHERING OF DATA

There are no consistent and reliable White House Office records on the size of the PPO staff. Therefore, the data on staff size are drawn from personal interviews with PPO aides and cross-checked against contemporaneous accounts of the staff that appear in the press or White House files. The data include both professional staff and support staff within the PPO. PPO veterans report that since 1970 about one-fourth of the PPO's aides have been support staffers and the remainder have had some hand in its substantive business.

Because the PPO must cope with an enormous number of vacant posts and deluge of job-seekers, its staff is unusually large during the opening year of a presidency. Hence, in Figure A.1, I report the size of the PPO for the opening month of each even-numbered year.

The data in Table A.1 are taken from *Policy and Supporting Positions*, prepared quadrennially by the House or Senate Post Office and Civil Service Committee, a publication popularly known as "the plum book." The data in column one, "Total PAS," are all full-time presidentially appointed and Senate-confirmed posts in federal departments and agencies (these data exclude judicial posts, posts in the EOP, and part-time posts). The data in column two, PAS policy-determining, are full-time PAS posts in the executive branch, excluding U.S. attorneys and marshals, ambassadors, representatives to international organizations, and customs officers. The data in column three are "schedule C" positions: "confidential or policy-determining" positions outside of the civil service at grade GS-15 or below. By law, these posts are filled by appointment by department and agency heads. Noncareer Executive Assignment (NEA) posts (1968–1976) and Senior Executive Service (SES, noncareer) posts are filled, likewise, by appointment of department and agency heads.

159

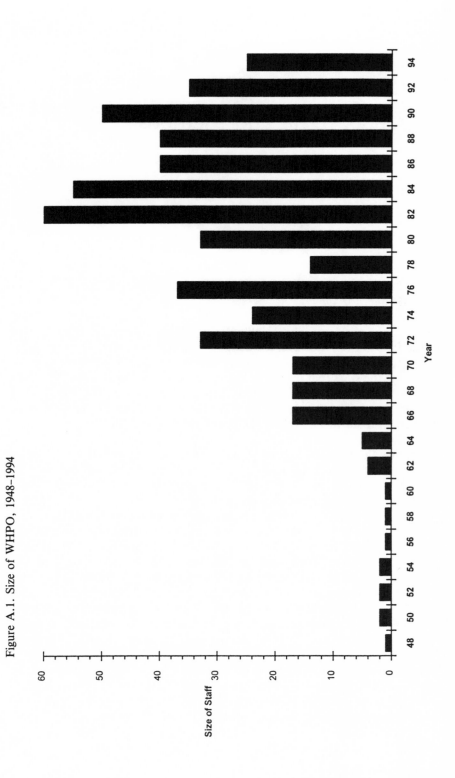

Figure A.1. Size of WHPO, 1948–1994

Table A.1. Full-Time Appointments in the Executive Branch, 1952–1992

Date	Total PAS	PAS[a]	Schedule C	SES/NEA	Total Non-Pres.	All Full-Time Appointments
1952			871		871	
1956			1,212		1,212	
1960		395	1,349		1,349	
1964	560	420	1,590		1,590	2,150
1968	578	441	1,105	504	1,609	2,101
1972	902	464	1,292	564	1,856	2,758
1976	823	477	1,138	533	1,671	2,494
1980	1,054	536	1,518	824	2,342	3,396
1984	857	527	1,682	693	2,375	3,232
1988	873	529	1,655	760	2,415	3,288
1992	921	581	2,034	732	2,766	3,687

[a]Excludes ambassadors, U.S. attorneys and marshals, international organizations, and customs.

A NOTE ON METHOD

Between November 1987 and May 1994 I conducted 115 interviews with 105 respondents (10 respondents were interviewed two times); all but 15 of the interviews were conducted in person. The interviews were semistructured and ranged from twenty minutes to two hours; on average they lasted about forty-five minutes. Each respondent was told that the interview was not for attribution, and the interviews were taped and transcribed.

The respondents were drawn from nine administrations: Truman (2), Eisenhower (9), Kennedy/Johnson (17), Nixon (18), Ford (1), Carter (9), Reagan (37), Bush (3), and Clinton (9). Of the 105 respondents, 65 were White House aides (57 from the PPO and 8 from other staffs); 22 were party, campaign, or transition staffers; and another 18 were cabinet secretaries or subcabinet officials.

Personal interviews were supplemented by materials drawn from archives, special collections, and oral histories, including: presidential libraries (Truman, Eisenhower, Kennedy, Johnson), the National Archives, the Nixon Collection of the National Archives, the archives of the Brookings Institution, the National Academy of Public Administration's Presidential Appointee Project, and the Columbia University Oral History Collection (a detailed description of the materials drawn from these collections is contained in the section "Sources Consulted").

As a rule, the more recent the administration, the more heavily one must rely upon personal interviews. Modern White House files are voluminous, and they are accessioned slowly: one decade after the end of Carter's presidency less than one-fourth of the 27 million pages of Carter White House files were available for research. Moreover, personnel files are among the most heavily restricted and slowly opened White House files. Thus, for example, evidence about the Reagan White House Personnel Office is drawn largely from personal interviews, which is why I interviewed an especially large and diverse set of respondents—37 in all—in order to ensure reliability.

Because the veterans of earlier presidencies disperse and die, relatively few respondents from mid-century presidencies were available. In such cases, however, personal interviews could be supplemented by a rich body of oral histories (housed in the Eisenhower Library and the Columbia University Oral History Collection), by White House and departmental files housed at the Eisenhower Library, and by memoirs and unpublished diaries of the administration's members.

Notes

CHAPTER 1. A HISTORY OF AGGRANDIZEMENT

1. For a discussion of the intellectual and political milieu within which the White House Office was conceived, see Louis Brownlow, *A Passion for Anonymity* (Chicago: University of Chicago Press, 1958), and *The President Needs Help*, ed. Frederick C. Mosher (Lanham, Md.: University Press of America, 1988).

2. Theodore J. Lowi, *The Personal President* (Ithaca: Cornell University Press, 1985), 5.

3. Arthur W. Macmahon and John D. Millet, *Federal Administrators* (New York: Columbia University Press, 1939), 302.

4. Stephen Hess, *Organizing the Presidency*, 2d ed. (Washington D.C.: Brookings Institution, 1988), 98–99.

5. Richard Nixon "trusted few people, and this distrust brought about a predominance of activity in the White House, with extraordinary power vested in his assistant for national security affairs" (Cecil V. Crabb and Kevin V. Mulcahy, *American National Security: A Presidential Perspective* [Pacific Grove, Calif.: Brooks/Cole, 1991], 143).

6. Colin Campbell, *Managing the Presidency: Carter, Reagan, and the Search for Executive Harmony* (Pittsburgh: University of Pittsburgh Press, 1986).

7. Terry Moe, "The Politicized Presidency," in John E. Chubb and Paul E. Peterson, eds., *The New Direction in American Politics* (Washington, D.C.: Brookings Institution, 1985).

8. Thomas Cronin, "The Swelling of the Presidency: Can Anyone Reverse the Tide?" in Peter Woll, ed., *Debating American Government*, 2d ed. (Chicago: Scott, Foresman, 1988), 221.

9. Hugh Heclo, "The Changing Presidential Office," in James P. Pfiffner, ed., *The Managerial Presidency* (Pacific Grove, Calif.: Brooks/Cole, 1991). Heclo observes: "The office of the president has become so complex, so propelled by its own internal bureaucratic dynamics, that it now presents every new president with a major problem of internal management" (p. 33).

10. "Presidential staffs tend to bring into the presidency conflicts and controversies raging among departments, congressional committees, and interest groups." (Heclo, "Changing Presidential Office," 40). See also Hess, *Organizing the Presidency*, 171–173.

11. Ben W. Heineman, Jr., and Curtis A. Hessler, *Memorandum for the President: A Strategic Approach to Domestic Affairs in the 1980's* (New York: Random House, 1980), 189.

12. The average tenure of political appointees is reported in Hugh Heclo, *A Government of Strangers: Executive Politics in Washington* (Washington, D.C.: Brookings Institution, 1977); G. Calvin Mackenzie, ed., *The In-and-Outers: Presidential Appointees and Transient Government in Washington* (Baltimore, Md.: Johns Hopkins, 1987).

13. See, however, Francis E. Rourke's "Executive Responsiveness to Presidential Policies: The Reagan Presidency" (Paper Presented to the 1989 meeting of the American Political Science Association, Atlanta, Georgia).

14. See, for example, Bernard Rosen, "Effective Continuity of U.S. Government in Jeopardy," *Public Administration Review* (September/October 1983): 383-391; Volcker Commission, *Leadership for America: Rebuilding the Public Service*, Report of the National Commission on the Public Service (Washington, D.C., 1989).

15. *Leadership for America*, 18. Because appointive posts are numerous and the tenure of appointees is brief, large numbers of posts are vacant. For a description of the disabling effects of turnover in political leadership, see Martha Derthick's *Agency under Stress: The Social Security Administration in American Government* (Washington, D.C.: Brookings Institution, 1990), 122-126.

16. *Leadership for America*, 18. On the damage done by the neglect of career perspectives at the State Department, see Anthony Lake, *Somoza Falling* (Boston: Houghton Mifflin, 1989).

17. See, for example, Morris P. Fiorina, *Congress, Keystone of the Washington Establishment*, 2d ed. (New Haven, Conn.: Yale University Press, 1989).

18. Jeremy Rabkin, *Judicial Compulsions: How Public Law Distorts Public Policy* (New York: Basic Books, 1991).

19. Richard Nathan, *The Administrative Presidency* (New York: John Wiley and Sons, 1983), 93.

20. For a careful and critical evaluation of this claim, see Joel D. Aberbach and Bert A. Rockman, "Mandates or Mandarins? Control and Discretion in the Modern Administrative State," *Public Administration Review* (March/April 1988).

21. Edward J. Lynch, "No, We Don't Have Too Many Political Appointees," *The Bureaucrat* (April 1991): 55. See also Terry Eastland, *Energy in the Executive* (New York: Free Press, 1992), ch. 9, "Picking the Instruments of Execution."

22. Bradley H. Patterson, Jr., *Ring of Power: The White House Staff and Its Expanding Role in Government* (New York: Basic Books, 1988), 343.

23. Ibid., 342-343.

24. For a discussion of these topics, see Lowi, *The Personal President*, 134-137; Terry M. Moe, "Presidents, Institutions, and Theory," in George C. Edwards III, John H. Kessel, and Bert A. Rockman, eds. (Pittsburgh, Pa.: University of Pittsburgh Press, 1993); Betty Glad, "The Idiosyncratic Presidency," *Presidency Research* (Winter 1990-1991): 6-20.

25. Louis J. Cordia, "The People Factor: Managing Presidential Personnel," in Charles Heatherly and Burton Pines, eds., *Mandate for Leadership III* (Washington, D.C.: Heritage Foundation, 1989), 116-117.

26. *Leadership for America*, 17. Counting political appointees is fraught with difficulties: the number and complexity of appointive posts is extraordinary, and reasonable scholars employ different rules in counting appointees. The Volcker Commission derived its figures for the 1933-1965 increase from Stanley et al., *Men Who Govern* (see *Leadership*, p. 170 n. 11). Stanley et al. apply a restrictive definition of

PAS. As a result, the Commission's 1985 numbers, which are based upon a more liberal way of classifying appointees (see Patricia W. Ingraham, "Building Bridges or Burning Them?" *Public Administration Review* 47 [September/October 1987]: 427), overstate the rate of growth in political appointees between 1965 and 1985. Applying the Stanley counting rules in 1985 yields 290 PAS appointees, rather than 527 (see Mackenzie, ed., *The In-and-Outers*, xiv, 2). The basic claim of the Volcker Commission argument is nonetheless sound: the number of political appointees roughly doubled in the thirty years separating the New Deal and Great Society (1933 and 1965) and roughly doubled again in the following twenty years (1965–1985), a still shorter interval. My own data on the number of political appointees between 1952 and 1992 are presented in Table A.1.

27. Samuel Kernell and Samuel L. Popkin, *Chief of Staff: Twenty-Five Years of Managing the Presidency* (Berkeley: University of California Press, 1986), xiii.

28. Ronald Brownstein, "White House Personnel Office Struggles with More Vacancies, Less Influence," *National Journal*, June 15, 1985, 1410.

29. Personal interview, Reagan PPO aide.

30. Moe, "The Politicized Presidency," 254.

31. Personal interview, Reagan White House aide.

32. Interview with Graham Claytor, National Academy of Public Administration Presidential Appointee Project, 1985.

33. *Leadership for America*, 18.

34. Joseph Pika, "Moving beyond the White House: Problems in Studying the Presidency," *Congress and the Presidency* 9:1 (Winter 1981–1982): 22.

35. See, for example, Bert Rockman's essay "The Style and Organization of the Reagan Presidency," in Charles O. Jones, ed., *The Reagan Legacy* (New York: Chatham House, 1987). Rockman argues that the president's operating style ("detachment") and agenda (conservative activism) guided the "structures, systems, and strategies of the Reagan administration" (p. 8). Other examples include Richard Johnson, "Presidential Style," in Aaron Wildavsky, ed., *Perspectives on the Presidency* (Boston: Little, Brown, 1975); Hess, 1990; and Richard Neustadt, *Presidential Power: The Politics of Leadership from FDR to Carter* (New York: John Wiley and Sons, 1980).

36. Richard Fenno, "Observation, Context, and Sequence in the Study of Politics," *American Political Science Review* (March 1986): 14.

37. W. Lance Bennett observes that the foremost characteristic of the mass media is its tendency to "personalize" the news. "Personalized news," he writes, "can be defined as the journalistic bias that gives preference to the individual actors and human-interest angles in events while downplaying institutional and political considerations that establish the social contexts for those events" (*News: The Politics of Illusion*, 2d ed. [New York: Longman, 1988], 26). Gaye Tuchman, *Making News: A Study in the Construction of Reality* (New York: Free Press, 1978), and Stephen Hess, *The Washington Reporters* (Washington, D.C.: Brookings Institution, 1981).

38. Johnson, in Wildavsky, ed., *Perspectives on the Presidency*, 1975, 262.

39. "The Washington focus tends to be short-term and immediate: What is happening today? Who is doing what to whom? Who is adept? Who is inept? Who is in? Who is out? In many ways, Washington is as much a town made for gossip as is Hollywood" (Bert Rockman, *The Leadership Question: The Presidency and the American System* [New York: Praeger, 1984], 178–179).

40. Henry Kissinger, *The White House Years* (Boston: Little, Brown, 1979), 47.

41. Tower Commission, *The Tower Commission Report: The Full Text of the President's Special Review Board* (New York: Bantam and Times Books, 1987), 13.

42. Pika, "Moving beyond the White House," 18.

43. Philip G. Henderson, *Managing the Presidency: The Eisenhower Legacy—From Kennedy to Reagan* (Boulder, Colo.: Westview Press, 1988), 180.

44. Hugh Heclo and Lester Salamon, eds., *The Illusion of Presidential Government* (Boulder, Colo.: Westview), 1981, 317.

45. Hess, *Organizing the Presidency,* 154.

46. See, for example, Jeffrey Hart, *The Presidential Branch* (New York: Pergamon Press, 1987), and Cronin, "The Swelling of the Presidency."

47. Cronin, "The Swelling of the Presidency," 225.

48. Hess, *Organizing the Presidency,* 225.

49. The data are presented in Table A.1.

50. Lyndon Johnson's domestic program was as large and complex as that of any of his successors (Mark Peterson, *Legislating Together* [Cambridge, Mass.: Harvard University Press, 1988]). However, his White House domestic policy staff was far smaller than that of his successors. Johnson's domestic policy aide, Joseph Califano, began with one aide in 1965, but had a staff of four aides by the end of the Johnson administration. Emmette S. Redford and Richard T. McCulley, *White House Operations: The Johnson Years* (Austin: University of Texas Press, 1986), 82–83. By the early to mid-1970s the staff had blossomed to a small bureaucracy of forty to eighty, and by 1985, two decades after its inception, the domestic policy staff consisted of roughly fifty aides (Hart, *Presidential Branch*, 44).

51. One might argue that appointment politics is more labor-intensive than it once was, either because appointive posts are more complex than they were twenty-five years ago, or because there is more scrutiny of candidates due to conflict-of-interest legislation. Except for 1993, the White House Counsel's Office, not the PPO, has been responsible for conflict-of-interest investigations. The technical complexity of positions subject to appointment may be marginally greater, but the president's appointment staff made no more extensive efforts to master the technical demands of appointive posts in 1981 than it did in 1965.

52. David Mayhew, *Congress: The Electoral Connection* (New Haven, Conn.: Yale University Press, 1974), esp. 81–105.

53. See Gary Jacobson, *The Politics of Congressional Elections*, 3d. ed. (New York: Harper Collins, 1992).

54. Moe, "The Politicized Presidency." Moe elaborates upon this framework in "Presidents, Institutions, and Theory," in George Edwards, John H. Kessel, and Bert A. Rockman, eds., *Researching the Presidency: Vital Questions, New Approaches* (Pittsburgh, Pa.: University of Pittsburgh Press, 1993). See also Samuel Kernell's essay, "The Evolution of the White House Office," in *Can the Government Govern?*, ed. John E. Chubb and Paul E. Peterson (Washington, D.C.: Brookings Institution, 1988), 54.

55. Moe, "The Politicized Presidency," 238.

56. Ibid., 240.

57. Ibid., 243.

58. Ibid., 246.

59. As Moe acknowledges, "The Politicized Presidency" is "not thoroughly documented" or tested. Rather, the essay "illustrates certain portions of the argument, outlining some of the patterns, events, and personalities involved in the historical emergence of centralization and politicization" (ibid., 246).

60. A few studies have aimed at examining the entire White House Office, including Hess, *Organizing the Presidency;* Hart, *The Presidential Branch;* and Patterson, *Ring of Power.* These studies encompass the entire White House Office at a price. They

have little to say about individual staff units within the White House and still less to say about the political environment that has shaped the evolution of the White House. Instead, they typically focus on the managerial arrangements that presidents impose on the White House Office (e.g. Hess) or the aggregate size of the White House Office (Hart).

61. Heclo, *A Government of Strangers*, 88.

62. See, for example, Francis Rourke's essay, "Presidentializing the Bureaucracy: From Kennedy to Reagan," in Pfiffner, ed., *The Managerial Presidency*. Rourke suggests that "the presidentialization of the bureaucracy through the president's power of appointment has today come to represent the chief means by which the White House bends the executive branch to its will" (124).

63. This book does not offer a comprehensive description of "the politics of the appointment process." I do not examine appointments outside of the executive branch, the Senate confirmation of presidential appointees, and a host of other topics that would fall within the purview of such a project; this is a task that has been capably handled by others. See G. Calvin Mackenzie, *The Politics of Presidential Appointments* (New York: Free Press, 1981), and Mackenzie, ed., *The In-and-Outers*. Rather, my aim is to bring to light those aspects of political appointments that tell us why the modern White House Office has grown, and to explore the repercussions of its growth.

CHAPTER 2. LOOSENING THE TIES THAT BIND

1. In this chapter I am concerned with those who spoke on behalf of political party organizations. Hence, I focus chiefly the national committees of the Democratic and Republican parties and, to a lesser degree, state and local party figures (e.g., state chairs) and state and local officeholders to the extent that they act as agents of the organizations that they control—either by law or in practice.

2. Francis J. Sorauf and Paul Allen Beck, *Party Politics in America*, 6th ed. (Glenview, Ill.: Scott, Foresman, 1988), 152–153.

3. See, for example, Ann Devroy, "Envoys without Experience; Bush Favors GOP Donors as Ambassadors," *Washington Post*, July 18, 1989, A1; Helen Dewar, "Envoy-Designate on Hold; 'There Is No There, There,' Senator Says of Credentials," *Washington Post*, November 10, 1989, A25.

4. At the urging of the Nixon administration, Congressman George Bush sought—unsuccessfully—the Senate seat from Texas. Bush's career, however, was safe: he was rewarded by the Nixon White House with an appointment as U.S. representative to the United Nations.

5. V. O. Key, *Politics, Parties, and Pressure Groups*, 5th ed. (New York: Cromwell, 1964), 384.

6. Nixon succeeded: 42 percent of these votes he received in 1972 were cast by Independent and Democratic voters. Martin P. Wattenberg, *The Decline of American Political Parties, 1952–1992* (Cambridge, Mass.: Harvard University Press, 1994), 141.

7. In addition, presidents may be faced with a Congress controlled by the opposition party. The need to obtain votes from Democrats has sometimes compelled Republican presidents to award political appointments to Democrats or Independents—and put them at odds with fellow partisans. The evidence of this is clearest for Eisenhower and Ford. On the case of Eisenhower, see Roger Olien's *From Token to Triumph: Texas Republicans since 1920* (Dallas: Southern Methodist University Press, 1982).

8. Interview, Republican National Committee staffer.

9. In 1933, for example, of the 14,509 presidentially appointed posts located outside of Washington, D.C., 14,112 were postmasters, and the remainder were concentrated in the Justice Department (184) and the Treasury Department (134). Harold W. Metz, "Presidential Appointments, 1913–1953." (Unpublished paper, Republican National Committee Files, National Archives, n.d.)

10. Interview, Eisenhower White House aide.

11. For a discussion of appointments to field posts, see Dorothy Fowler, "Congressional Dictation of Local Appointments," *Journal of Politics* 7 (1945): 25–57, and Joseph Harris, *The Advice and Consent of the Senate: A Study of the Confirmation of Appointments by the U.S. Senate* (Berkeley: University of California Press, 1953).

12. See John Corson's unpublished study, "Staffing the Executive Branch at the Policymaking Level," in Charles F. Willis, Jr., Files, Eisenhower Library.

13. For an extended discussion of this point, see Chapter 4.

14. For new agency or a particularly important post, the president might play a larger role, as FDR did in the staffing of some New Deal agencies, such as the Social Security Board. See Paul Van Riper, *History of the United States Civil Service* (Evanston, Ill.: Row, Peterson, 1958), 324–328.

15. Dean E. Mann with Jameson W. Doig, *The Assistant Secretaries: Problems and Processes of Appointment* (Washington, D.C.: Brookings Institution, 1965), 269.

16. Dawson held the title of administrative assistant to the president, and served from 1947 though the end of the administration in January 1953. He was assisted by Martin L. Friedman from 1950 to 1953. Dawson's other responsibilities on the Truman White House staff are described by Richard Neustadt in "The White House Staff," in Frances Heller, ed., *The Truman White House* (Lawrence: University Press of Kansas, 1980), 114.

17. Key, *Politics, Parties, and Pressure Groups*, 384. For example, after the 1948 campaign Dawson handled the sensitive job of deciding which Democratic politicians merited consideration and which should be denied the privilege of submitting candidates for appointment — such as the Southern Democrats who had deserted Truman to support Thurmond's Dixiecrat candidacy.

18. Interview, Truman White House aide.

19. Heclo, *A Government of Strangers*, 93.

20. Dawson "did not get into those appointments except to OK the appointments recommended by Vince Burke [Deputy Postmaster General] or the deputy Attorney General." He "insisted that they be cleared politically with the people in the field," but he "didn't go much further than that" (Interview, Truman White House aide).

21. Interview, Truman White House aide.

22. Interview, Truman White House aide. Dawson's relationship with the DNC is described in Harold F. Bass, Jr., "Presidential Responsibility for National Party Organization, 1945–1974" (Ph. D. dissertation, Vanderbilt University, 1976), 109–110.

23. Interview, Truman White House aide.

24. India Edwards Oral History, Truman Library, 66–67.

25. Gary King and Lynn Ragsdale, *The Elusive Executive* (Washington, D.C.: Congressional Quarterly Press, 1988), 295.

26. Interview, Truman White House aide.

27. Interview, Truman White House aide, Martin Friedman Oral History, Truman Library. Good-government groups also believed the situation to be deplorable. The Carnegie Corporation, for example, commissioned a study by John J. Corson, *Executives for the Federal Service; A Program of Action in a Time of Crisis* (New York: Columbia University Press, 1952).

28. Friedman Oral History, 17-18. The members of the committee were: John E. Peurifoy, deputy undersecretary of state; H. Graham Morison, assistant attorney general; Philip M. Kaiser, assistant secretary of labor; Eugene M. Zuckert, assistant secretary of the air force; Archibald Alexander, assistant secretary of the army.

29. Diary of meetings, Martin Friedman Files, Truman Library.

30. The committee was assisted by a full-time staff member, John Mee, chair of Indiana University's management department, and commissioned a research project by John Fly, professor of political science at Princeton University. The committee also sought — unsuccessfully — to enlist the assistance of the Ford Foundation's staff director.

31. Philip Kaiser's proposal was drafted May 17, 1950, approximately two weeks after Morison presented his proposal to the committee (H. Graham Morison, "Personnel Needs for Federal Appointments in the Executive Branch" [H. Graham Morison Papers, Truman Library, n.d.]).

32. Friedman Oral History, 17.

33. Untitled memo, May 1950, Philip M. Kaiser Papers, Truman Library.

34. Memorandum for the file, Paul T. David, June 3, 1957, box 7, President's General Files, Brookings Archives.

35. Talking points, "Presentation to the Cabinet" (Friedman Papers, Truman Library, n.d.).

36. Interview, Truman White House aide. See also Memorandum for the file, Paul T. David (Friedman interview, June 3, 1957), Brookings Archives: "The Democratic National Committee did not like the place assigned to it on a proposed organization chart in the report."

37. Ibid.

38. Interview, Truman White House aide. Dawson explained the demise of Operation Best Brains this way: "We wanted to reduce the whole political appointment thing to more of a science, to get the best brains. I had to conclude that it couldn't work because of the political facts that you have to deal with. Appointing this guy will displease Senator X or we need to do something else for Mr. Y in the House" (quoted in Heclo, *A Government of Strangers*, 89).

39. Interview with Donald Dawson, conducted by Samuel Kernell, Washington, D.C., June 1988.

40. Memorandum for files (Friedman interview, July 3, 1957), Brookings Archives.

41. Interview, White House aide.

42. Memorandum for files (Friedman interview), Brookings Archives.

43. For a description of nomination politics at mid century, see Paul T. David, Ralph M. Goldman, and Richard C. Bain, *The Politics of National Party Conventions* (Washington, D.C.: Brookings Institution, 1960).

44. Larry M. Bartels, *Presidential Primaries and the Dynamics of Public Choice* (Princeton, N.J.: Princeton University Press, 1988), 15.

45. See, for example, John H. Aldrich, "Presidential Campaigns in Party and Candidate-Centered Eras," in Mathew D. McCubbins, ed., *Under the Watchful Eye: Managing Campaigns in the Television Era* (Washington, D.C.: Congressional Quarterly Press, 1992). Aldrich writes (p. 76): "It was not until the 1960s . . . that [new campaign] technology [and other changes] made it possible for a presidential candidate . . . to build an effective personal campaign organization."

46. Sorauf and Beck, *Party Politics in America*, 354.

47. As late as the 1950s, "the parties, especially the Republican party, still functioned as major financial intermediaries. Candidates and their volunteer committees raised a good deal of money directly, but the parties controlled the major share of

it" (Francis J. Sorauf, *Money in American Politics* [Glenview, Ill.: Scott, Foresman, 1988], 22–23).

48. Memo, Clark Clifford to John Kennedy, November 9, 1960, Transition Files, Kennedy Library.

49. Fundraising for Truman's campaign is described in George Thayer, *Who Shakes the Money Tree?* (New York: Simon and Schuster, 1973), 74–76.

50. On the role of the DNC during the 1948 campaign and the Truman presidency, see Matthew Connelly Oral History, Truman Library; Ken Hechler, *Working with Truman: A Personal Memoir of the White House Years* (New York: Putnam, 1982); Lester Seligman, "The Presidential Office and the President as Party Leader (with a Postcript on the Nixon-Kennedy Era)," in Jeff Fishel, ed., *Parties and Elections in an Antiparty Age* (Bloomington: Indiana University Press, 1978) 295–302; Harold Gosnell, *Truman's Crises: A Political Biography of Harry S. Truman* (Westport, Conn.: Greenwood Press, 1980).

51. When Biffle returned from his trip "he reported to Truman that from his soundings he thought he could win, and Truman was much impressed by his advice" (Jules Abels, *Out of the Jaws of Victory* [New York: Henry Holt, 1959], 163).

52. Jim Farley claimed that state and local Democratic organizations could mobilize roughly 140,000 workers around the nation during the mid-1930s (Charles Michelson, *The Ghost Talks* [New York: G.P. Putnam's Sons, 1944], 133–134). Most accounts of local party organization suggest that Truman could count on Democratic organizations to mobilize roughly the same number of workers. On state and local party organizations in the postwar years, see David Mayhew, *Placing Parties in American Politics* (Princeton, N.J.: Princeton University Press, 1986).

53. Jack Redding, a longtime DNC official, offers a vivid account of "group liaison" on behalf of President Harry Truman in his memoir, *Inside the Democractic Party* (Indianapolis, Ind.: Bobbs-Merrill, 1958).

54. However, White House aides were far from satisfied with the support that the Democratic National Committee provided the president on Capitol Hill. See, for example, Hechler's memoir, *Working with Truman*, esp. 154, 162.

55. Harold Stanley, Dean Mann, and Jameson Doig, *Men Who Govern* (Washington, D.C.: Brookings Institution, 1967), 31–33 and Table E-1, 132.

56. Laurin Henry, "The Presidency, Executive Staffing, and the Federal Bureaucracy," in Aaron Wildavsky, ed., *The Presidency* (Boston: Little, Brown, 1969), 529.

57. Nelson Polsby, *The Consequences of Party Reform* (New York: Oxford University Press, 1983), 64.

58. James W. Davis, *Presidential Primaries: Road to the White House* (New York: Crowell, 1967), 2.

59. "The organizations were Business and Professional Men and Women for Kennedy-Johnson, and Citizens for Kennedy-Johnson" ("Financing the 1960 Election," in Herbert Alexander, ed., *Studies in Money in Politics*, 3 vols. [Princeton, N.J.: Citizen's Research Foundation, 1965–1974], 32). Spending for Nixon's 1960 bid was roughly evenly divided between party and candidate as well (p. 33).

60. On the role of labor in electoral politics, see David J. Sousa, *Union Politics in an Era of Decline* (Ph.D. Dissertation, University of Minnesota, 1991).

61. See James Q. Wilson, *The Amateur Democrat* (Chicago: University of Chicago Press, 1960), and Sorauf and Beck, *Party Politics in America*, 102–121.

62. Lawrence R. Jacobs, "The Recoil Effect: Public Opinion and Policymaking in U.S. and Britain," *Comparative Politics* 24:2 (January 1992), 209.

63. Lowi, *The Personal President*, 75–76.

64. Paul S. Herrnson, "Political Parties, Campaign Finance Reform, and Presidential Elections" (Paper presented to the annual meeting of the American Political Science Association, 1990), 4. See also Theodore White, *The Making of the President, 1960* (New York: Atheneum, 1961), for a description of the senior coterie of Kennedy advisers.

65. Cornelius P. Cotter and Bernard Hennessy, *Politics without Power: The National Party Committees* (New York: Atherton, 1964), 125.

66. For descriptions of the National Committee's capabilities, see Cotter and Hennessy, *Politics without Power*, and Hugh Bone, *Party Committees and National Politics* (Seattle: University of Washington Press, 1958).

67. John Anthony Maltese reaches this conclusion in *Spin Control: The White House Office of Communications and the Management of Presidential News* (Chapel Hill: University of North Carolina Press, 1992).

68. Jacobs, "Recoil Effect," 209.

69. Lawrence Jacobs and Robert Shapiro, "Leadership and Responsiveness: Some New Evidence on the Johnson Presidency" (Paper presented to the Annual Meeting of the American Political Science Association, 1992, Chicago), 4.

70. O'Brien's staff is discussed in Stephen J. Wayne, *The Legislative Presidency* (New York: Harper and Row, 1978).

71. Memo, Henry Hall Wilson to D. M. Wilson, deputy director, Voice of America, July 2, 1962 (Kennedy Library, GEN PE2).

72. Larry O'Brien Oral History, Tape 2, 27–46, John F. Kennedy Library.

73. OCR Files are replete with examples of petty patronage secured for state and local politicians. Dorothy Davies of the O'Brien staff proudly notified Ken O'Donnell that she had "placed a son of a friend of Governor DiSalle [D-Ohio] in a summer job, a GS-3 at the Immigration and Naturalization Service — as we did last year." Memo, Dorothy Davies to Ken O'Donnell, Kennedy Library, PE2, April 11, 1962.

74. Interview, Kennedy White House aide.

75. Ibid.

76. Thomas P. Murphy, Donald E. Neuchterlein, and Ronald Stupak, *Inside the Bureaucracy: The View from the Assistant Secretary's Desk* (Boulder, Colo.: Westview, 1978), 4–6. For a comprehensive discussion of "political layering," see Heclo, *Government of Strangers*, ch. 2.

77. Nearly all of the presidential appointments — 14,509 out of 14,723 (98.5 percent) — were to federal field positions, such as postmasters, U.S. attorneys, and customs collectors (Metz, "Presidential Appointments, 1913–1953").

78. Quoted in Mann, *The Assistant Secretaries*, 80.

79. Transition Files, Richard Neustadt, Kennedy Library.

80. Transition Files, Clark Clifford, Kennedy Library.

81. Interview, Kennedy White House aide.

82. Shriver's staff consisted of Adam Yarmolinsky (a foundation consultant), Harris Wofford (civil rights lawyer and Kennedy liaison to civil rights community), Louis Martin (black publisher and aide to Adlai Stevenson), and a host of informal "volunteers," including Paul Warnke (then of Covington and Burling) and Eugene Rostow.

83. Harris Wofford Oral History, 87, Kennedy Library.

84. Ibid, 93.

85. Mann, *The Assistant Secretaries,* 74–75.

86. Wofford Oral History, 97.

87. Sam C. Brightman Oral History, 5, Kennedy Library.

88. Interview, Kennedy White House aide.

89. Adam Yarmolinsky to Larry O'Brien, February 6, 1961, "Continuing the Talent Hunt," Ralph Dungan Files, Kennedy Library.

90. Joseph Califano to Adam Yarmolinsky, July 7, 1961, Dungan Files, Kennedy Library.

91. Group Oral History, Kennedy Library. Fenn was a member of Harvard's Class of 1944 and the editor of the Harvard *Crimson*. After graduating from Harvard, Fenn was appointed to the faculty of the Harvard Business School where he helped edit the *Harvard Business Review* and dabbled in Massachusetts Democratic politics, working with O'Brien and O'Donnell on the 1954 gubernatorial campaign. Equally important, Fenn's family had ties to the Kennedy clan, and Fenn was a longstanding friend of Ken O'Donnell.

92. Memo, Dan Fenn to Ralph Dungan, August 17, 1961. Ralph Dungan Files, Kennedy Library.

93. Ibid., 4–5.

94. The phrase is from a Brookings scholar, Laurin Henry (see Henry, "The Presidency, Executive Staffing, and the Federal Bureaucracy," 527).

95. National Academy of Public Administration, *Recruiting Presidential Appointees: A Conference of Former Presidential Personnel Assistants* (Washington, D.C., 1984), 3.

96. Macy "offered to provide me [Fenn] with full-time help, and he sent me a list of 3 or 4 people [from the Civil Service Commission staff] that I could choose from" (Group Oral History, Kennedy Library, 2).

97. Fenn also had two to three clerical assistants during this time. Transcript of Brookings Institution Los Angeles Conference (1962), 19.

98. "35–40 posts" (Brookings Los Angeles Conference [1962], 33); "One-third of vacancies" (Interview, Kennedy White House aide).

99. Fenn observed, "It is more 'What jobs are of particular importance to the President or the administration at any time?'" (Brookings Los Angeles Conference [1962], 21).

100. Interview, Kennedy White House aide.

101. Of those in the contact network, 15 to 20 percent were party figures. The contact network was developed by beginning with the president's White House staff (Dutton, Dungan, etc.) and respected figures within the administration (such as David Bell) and working outwards. Interview, Kennedy White House aide.

102. "Kennedy did not rely upon Bailey for appointment advice" (Cotter and Hennessy, *Politics without Power*, 141).

103. Group Oral History with Dan Fenn, Dave Jelinek, Dick Barrett, John Clinton, Ed Sherman, and Terry Scanlon, 72, Kennedy Library. See also GOH 8–9: "It is a truism that the people who came through Dorothy Davies and . . . from the [National] Committee just didn't measure up. I think that is a general statement that we will hold up, don't you agree?" (Fenn): "Yes. The chances that you are going to turn up people out of the campaign . . . the National Committee or on the Hill . . . to be Assistant Secretary of the Air Force for Financial Management or Deputy Director of the Arms Control Agency . . . are slim."

104. Interview, Kennedy White House aide. Many party figures, particularly the DNC Chair, John Bailey, also found themselves unable to veto pending appointments. "They were not in a position to say no," Larry O'Brien recalled (O'Brien Oral History II, Kennedy Library, 30).

105. Interview, Kennedy White House aide.

106. Group Oral History, Kennedy Library, 70. DNC staffers, too, acknowledged the Committee's ebbing fortunes. Said one: "Tom [Brislin, chief patronage aide at

the DNC] is in charge of petty patronage — the kind the White House can't be bothered with" (Cotter and Hennessy, *Politics without Power*, 142).

107. On the allocation of Justice Department job patronage, see Anthony Dolan Oral History, Kennedy Library. On Post Office job patronage during the Kennedy administration, see J. Edward Day, *My Appointed Round: 929 Days as Postmaster General* (New York: Holt, Rinehart, Winston, 1965), 8-14. Fenn also skirted the roughly fourteen hundred "schedule C" jobs that were keenly sought after as the currency of congressional and (less often) local patronage, leaving these to the patronage staff housed within the Office of Congressional Relations (Group Oral History, Kennedy Library).

108. "Actually, the people on the political side weren't all that interested in the jobs that we were dealing with, positions like an assistant secretary at Interior or HEW. These jobs don't matter a damn to a county chairman in Keokuk; county chairmen want postmasters and other local jobs" (interview, Kennedy White House aide).

109. "Bailey . . . worked much more closely with Dorothy Davies" (interview, Kennedy White House aide). See also Group Oral History, 8: "The people that came through Dorothy Davies and behind her from the Committee just didn't measure up." The Davies staff was the same size as Fenn's, and its focus was low-level federal field posts and schedule C jobs.

110. Interview, Johnson White House aide.

111. Johnson and Macy became acquainted in 1951 when Macy was senior aide to Frank Pace, Secretary of the Army. Throughout Johnson's service as vice-president, Macy and Johnson worked closely on a number of projects, such as the Equal Employment Opportunity Commission (Macy Oral History, Johnson Library, Tape 3, 6-7).

112. Interview, Johnson White House aide.

113. Interview with John Macy, conducted by Richard L. Schott, Austin, Texas, December 14, 1976 (Macy interview 2).

114. Ibid., 22.

115. Ibid.

116. Interview with John Macy, conducted by Richard L. Schott, Washington, D.C., November 9, 1976.

117. Macy Oral History, Johnson Library, Tape 3, 24.

118. Bradley Patterson interview with Matthew Coffey, September 19, 1986, Washington, D.C. (Macy Oral History, 3, 8-10).

119. Macy interview, 2.

120. Macy Oral History, Tape 3, 8.

121. James Farley Oral History, Johnson Library, 39-40.

122. India Edwards Oral History, Johnson Library, 5-39.

123. Joseph I. Lieberman, *The Power Broker* (Boston: Houghton Mifflin, 1966), 313-326.

124. Katie Louchheim Oral History, Johnson Library, Tape 2, 32 (see also Tape 3, 14-46).

125. Meeting notes, Johnson Daily Diary, Johnson Library.

126. Memo, Edward Sherman to John Macy, Personal Papers of Edward L. Sherman.

127. Interview, Johnson White House aide.

128. Ibid.

129. Memo, Jim Rowe to President Lyndon Johnson, April 28, 1965 (John Macy Files, Johnson Library).

130. James Rowe Oral History, Johnson Library, Tape 2, 46.

131. Memo, Jim Rowe to John Macy, June 10, 1965 (Macy files, Johnson Library).

132. Interview, Johnson White House aide.

133. Macy interview 2, 24–25.

134. Interview, Johnson White House aide.

135. Ibid.

136. Ibid.

137. Macy, for example, viewed the patronage that he handled as virtually worthless for the purpose of building political support (Macy interview 2).

138. For a discussion of the link between the two positions, see ch. 4, "Presidential Party Management," in Bass, "Presidential Responsibility for Party Organization."

139. See Jane Dick, Volunteers and the Making of Politics (New York: Dodd, Mead, 1980), 73–137.

140. Charles Willis, Columbia University Oral History Collection, 24.

141. Paul Van Riper, *History of the United States Civil Service* (Evanston, Ill.: Row, Peterson, 1958), 481.

142. Notes on June 26, 1953, cabinet meeting, Arthur Minnich Series, Office of Staff Secretary, Eisenhower Library.

143. Laurin Henry, *Presidential Transitions* (Washington, D.C.: Brookings Institution, 1960), 653.

144. Hall offered these comments at a July 1953 cabinet meeting (cited in Carl Brauer, *Presidential Transitions: From Eisenhower through Reagan* [New York: Oxford University Press], 41).

145. One of Eisenhower's leading supporters in Ohio, for example, complained that only Taft backers were receiving federal appointments in Ohio (Willis Files, Eisenhower Library).

146. Van Riper, *History of the United States Civil Service*, 495–496.

147. Notes on Cabinet meeting December 4, 1953, Arthur Minnich Series (January 13, 1954), Eisenhower Library.

148. Jerry Klutz, "New U.S. Job Set-Up Planned," *Washington Post*, December 20, 1953, 1.

149. Interview, Eisenhower White House aide.

150. Memorandum to the President, from Henry Cabot Lodge, Jr., January 27, 1954, Willis Files, Eisenhower Library. Lodge reports to Eisenhower on his meeting with Secretary of Defense Wilson, at which he pushed Wilson to open "the whole field of employment in the Department of Defense *outside* of Washington" to "recommendations from political quarters" and to "designate individuals in the Departments of Army, Navy, and Air Force to work on this [patronage] problem." For the reflections of the army's patronage officer, see National Academy of Public Administration, confidential interview with Eisenhower DOD appointee, Washington, D.C., 1985.

151. Interview, Eisenhower White House aide. Memo from Charles Willis to Sherman Adams, "Meeting at the National Committee, July 22, 1953," OF 138-C-1, Eisenhower Library.

152. Ibid.

153. See, for example, Memo from Charles Willis to Sherman Adams, June 25, 1953, OF 138-B, Eisenhower Library. Willis describes his efforts — and Hall's assistance — in resolving a dispute over the division of federal appointments in Tennessee between Taft and Eisenhower groups.

154. In 1953 Len Hall had a staff of twenty-nine aides working on political appointments at the Republican National Committee — a staff that dwarfed Willis's at the White House Office (Memo, Willis to Adams, August 13, 1953, OF 138-B, Eisenhower Library).

155. In fact, the plan was devised by a Civil Service Commission staffer, William

Coulson, who was detailed to the White House and first proposed to Sherman Adams by Civil Service Commission Chair Philip Young! Adams approved the plan and assigned its implementation to Willis.

156. Charles Willis to Sherman Adams, May 6, 1955, Willis Files, Eisenhower Library.

157. Thomas J. Weko, 'A Good Man is Hard to Find': Presidents and Their Political Executives (Ph.D. dissertation, University of Minnesota, 1991), 93–95.

158. A. James Reichley, "The Rise of National Parties," in Chubb and Peterson, eds., The New Direction in American Politics, 181.

159. Herbert Alexander, Financing the 1968 Election (Lexington, Mass.: D.C. Heath, 1971).

160. Reichley, "The Rise of National Parties," 181.

161. Interview, Nixon White House aide.

162. Ibid.

163. Ibid.

164. Peter Flanigan continued to play a limited role in appointment staff work for the president, too: he supervised the selection of ambassadorial nominees and, to a lesser degree, regulatory appointments. Flanigan, who had helped finance Nixon's 1968 bid, helped ensure that the president's leading campaign donors and the Nixon's allies in the business community were given consideration as the posts were being awarded.

165. Interview, Nixon White House aide.

166. Ibid.

167. Memo, George Bell to H. R. Haldeman, September 16, 1970, Haldeman Files, Malek Name File, September 1970, Nixon Archives.

168. Malek Name File, March 1971, Haldeman Files, Nixon Archives.

169. Maltese, Spin Control.

170. In the estimation of Sorauf and Beck, "the Nixon administration carried the dominance of the presidential campaign [by the president's personal campaign organization] to new lengths in 1972" (Party Politics, 354).

171. Interview, Nixon White House aide.

172. Ibid.

173. Ibid.

174. Memo, Highby to Haldeman, February 7, 1973, "RNC" File, Nixon Archives.

175. Interview, Nixon White House aide.

176. Ibid.

CHAPTER 3. POLICY NETWORKS AND THE EVOLUTION
OF THE WHITE HOUSE PERSONNEL OFFICE

1. Memo, Highby to Haldeman, "The Second Administration, A Concept" (Haldeman Files, Nixon Collection, National Archives).

2. Following John Mark Hansen (1990) I have chosen "policy networks" to describe the close working relationship that links members of Congress, clientele groups, and their executive branch allies. Other scholars have adopted other appellations, including "iron-triangles" and "subgovernments."

3. Interview, Nixon HEW appointee.

4. Roland Evans and Robert Novak, Nixon in the White House: The Frustration of Power (New York: Random House, 1971), 68.

5. Nathan, *The Administrative Presidency*, 1983.

6. See, for example, Becky Norton Dunlop, "The Role of the White House Personnel Office," in Sanera and Rector, eds., *Steering the Elephant* (New York: Universe Books, 1987), 145–155.

7. Interview, Nixon White House aide.

8. So frequent were the importunings of Senator Hugh Scott (R-Pa.), the Senate minority leader, that the General Services Administration provided a long-distance telephone line, billed to the GSA, for the use of his office. The phone line was well used: between 1969 and 1972 Scott succeeded in placing thirty-four of the ninety-five deserving Pennsylvanians that his office had referred to the GSA (Joseph Gebhardt, William Dobrovir, and Thomas M. Devine, *Blueprint for Civil Service Reform* [Washington, D.C.: A Fund for Constitutional Government, 1976], 97).

9. "Securing a regulatory appointment expands the Congressman's zone of influence and extends his philosophy to agencies with which he is directly concerned" (U.S. Congress, *Study on Federal Regulation*, vol. 1 [Washington, D.C.: Government Printing Office, 1977], 381).

10. As Bryce Harlow warned Pen James, "Never, ever, appoint a Hill staffer to a regulatory post, because if you do, they are never the president's appointee, they are always the appointee of the senator or congressman who supported them" (Interview, Reagan White House aide).

11. Harvey C. Mansfield, "Political Parties, Patronage, and the Federal Government Service," in Wallace Sayre, ed., *The Federal Government Service: Its Character, Prestige, and Problems* (Englewood Cliffs, N.J.: Prentice Hall, 1954), 147.

12. "One thing is certain: over the years, the private sector has taken a more systematic interest in regulatory appointments than any other group — whether it be the public, the party, the agency, the Congress, or the White House. Their interest . . . is consistent and unceasing. *Broadcasting* magazine, for example, probably monitors the vacancies on the FCC with greater care than the White House" (*Study on Federal Regulation,* 378).

13. Ibid.

14. Henry, "The Presidency, Executive Staffing, and the Federal Bureaucracy," 534.

15. Joseph Califano, *Governing America: An Insider's Report from the Cabinet and White House* (New York: Simon and Schuster, 1981), 38.

16. As Terry Moe observes, presidents "do not want the kind of bureaucracy that the other players [members of Congress and clientele groups] are trying to create. . . . Presidents pursue interests that are often incompatible with, and indeed very threatening to, the interests of most of the other major players" ("Presidents, Institutions, and Theory," 363).

17. Interview, National Academy of Public Administration Presidential Appointee Project.

18. Interview, Bush White House aide.

19. Presidents and White House aides have permitted clientele groups and their congressional backers to play a leading role in the selection of candidates for posts outside of executive departments, such as regulatory commissioners, often soliciting candidates and recommendations from regulated interests. *Study on Federal Regulation.*

20. Mansfield, "Political Parties, Patronage, and the Federal Government Service," 147.

21. Interview, Nixon White House aide.

22. John Ehrlichman, *Witness to Power: The Nixon Years* (New York: Simon and Schuster, 1982), 94.

23. Mann, *The Assistant Secretaries*, 87–88.

24. *Study on Federal Regulation;* also, an interview with a Truman White House aide.

25. Talking points, "Presentation to the Cabinet" (n.d.), Friedman Papers, Truman Library.

26. Memorandum for the Files, Emil J. Sady and Paul T. David, Luncheon Conference with Martin Friedman and Dale E. Doty on Handling of Political Appointments During the Truman Administration, June 3, 1957, President's General Files, Robert D. Calkins, Brookings Institution Archives, 2.

27. Interview, Truman White House aide.

28. Samuel Kernell, *Going Public: New Strategies of Presidential Leadership*, 2d ed. (Washington, D.C.: Congressional Quarterly Press, 1993), 13.

29. Truman personal staff is described in Richard Neustadt's essay, "The White House Staff, The Later Period," in Heller, ed., *The Truman White House*, 93–117.

30. Wayne, *Legislative Presidency*.

31. Nelson Polsby, *The Consequences of Party Reform* (New York: Oxford University Press, 1983), 96.

32. R. Gordon Hoxie, ed., *The White House: Organization and Operations* (New York: Center for the Study of the Presidency, 1971).

33. Stephen S. Smith and Christopher Deering, *Committees in Congress*, 2d ed. (Washington, D.C.: Congressional Quarterly Press, 1990), 30.

34. Kernell, *Going Public*, 98–107.

35. Lowi, *The Personal President*.

36. Kernell, *Going Public*, ch. 4.

37. Neustadt, *Presidential Power*, 170–171.

38. Adam Yarmolinsky Oral History, Kennedy Library, 25.

39. Wofford Oral History, Kennedy Library, 93.

40. Interview, Kennedy White House aide. Wofford described their relationship with Ribicoff this way: "Ribicoff spent quite a few hours with us and seemed very anxious for suggestions and tapped us for a while thereafter" (Wofford Oral History, Kennedy Library, 94).

41. Udall, Carr, and Beaty Oral Histories, Kennedy Library. See also David T. Stanley's *Changing Administrations: The 1961 and 1964 Transitions in Six Departments* (Washington, D.C.: Brookings Institution, 1965), 60–63.

42. Interview, Kennedy White House aide.

43. Wofford Oral History, Kennedy Library, 115.

44. Mann, *The Assistant Secretaries*, 88.

45. Brookings Los Angeles Conference (1962), 65.

46. Fenn also had two to three clerical assistants during this time (ibid., 137).

47. Ibid., 33. The estimate that Kennedy personnel aides preferred candidates for one-third of vacancies comes from a personal interview with a Kennedy/Johnson White House personnel aide.

48. Brookings Los Angeles Conference, 16.

49. Ralph Dungan to Dean Rusk, October 17, 1961, Memo on Inspector General for AID, Dungan Files, Kennedy Library.

50. Regulatory Agency Panel Oral History, Kennedy Library, 145–147.

51. "When the cabinet secretary had no candidate of his own, he was stymied, or he was open to our suggestions" (Interview, Kennedy/Johnson White House aide).

52. Group Oral History, Kennedy Library, 10.

53. Ibid., 10. See also, p. 9: "Ralph Dungan was in on that because it was something that the President was intensely interested in."

54. Ibid., 10–11.

55. Ibid., 10.

56. Ibid., 12.

57. Ibid., 11.

58. Ibid., 14–15, 16–19.

59. Interview, Kennedy/Johnson White House aide.

60. Group Oral History, 26.

61. Ibid., 11.

62. "We didn't always know where the good [important] jobs were. We had a lot of trouble knowing what were the hot spots." Ibid., 45.

63. Interview, Kennedy White House aide.

64. Interview Kennedy/Johnson White House aide.

65. Macy had an agreement with Central Files (which got a copy of all written memos in the White House) — and with Johnson — that anything to do with appointments anywhere in the White House was routed through Macy's office (Interview, Johnson White House aide).

66. Memo, John Gardner to John Macy, September 21, 1965, Beechill Name File, Macy Files, LBJ Library.

67. Interview, Johnson White House Cabinet Secretary.

68. Ibid.

69. Ibid.

70. Ibid.

71. Interview, Johnson White House aide.

72. Ibid.

73. Ibid.

74. Macy Oral History, Johnson Library, Tape 3, 21–22.

75. *Study on Federal Regulation*, 122 n.7.

76. "John Macy was not involved (in other than a marginal way) in a single appointment to either the FCC or FTC during his tenure as Johnson's appointments chief" (ibid., 122).

77. Interview, Johnson White House aide.

78. Wilbur Cohen Oral History, Johnson Library, Tape 3, 9.

79. Macy Oral History, Johnson Library, Tape 3, 24.

80. Interview, Johnson White House cabinet secretary.

81. On "neutral competence" see Hugh Heclo, "OMB and the Presidency — The Problem of Neutral Competence," *Public Interest* (Winter 1975): 80–98.

82. Interview, Johnson White House aide.

83. Ibid.

84. Ibid.

85. Interview, HEW official, Johnson administration.

86. Ibid.

87. "The Loomis incident," Macy recalled, "reduced my effectiveness by at least 10%" (Schott interview 2, 60).

88. See Daniel Hallin, *The Uncensored War: The Media and Vietnam* (New York: Oxford University Press, 1986).

89. By May 1966 Johnson's approval had fallen below the 50 percent mark, and it very rarely reached this level again throughout his presidency (King and Ragsdale, *The Elusive Executive*, 298–300).

90. Michael B. Grossman and Martha Joynt Kumar, *Portraying the President* (Baltimore, Md.: Johns Hopkins University Press, 1981).

91. Interview, Johnson White House cabinet secretary. Watson's role is discussed

in Redford and McCulley, *White House Operations: The LBJ Years*; interview with Bill Moyer, conducted by Richard Schott. Officially the president's appointments secretary, Watson also managed the president's relationships with fellow Texans, campaign contributors, Democratic politicians around the country, and the DNC.

92. Macy interview 2, 59.

93. Ibid. "Some of those FBI reports were just ridiculous. We said, "Why in the hell are we dredging all this stuff up, about some meeting a person attended in 1927?" (Interview, Johnson White House aide).

94. Ibid.

95. Ibid.

96. Ibid. See, for example, "Memorandum for John Macy, State Department Honorary Appointments, August 3, 1965." He writes: "It is quite apparent now that Cieplinski at State has opened up a line of communication with Watson's office on the filling of honorary appointments." He continues: "We cannot be effective in this area unless there is one point of contact in the White House and one channel of communication to the Department. . . . In this manner we have been able to meet the really pressing requirements of Cliff Carter, O'Brien, Watson, and others. But the system is obviously breaking down as other channels between the White House and the Department come into being." At the Justice Department, Watson established a direct link to Johnson loyalist Harold "Barefoot" Sanders. By September 1967 Sanders proposed to cut Macy out of the channel, arguing that "the Macy role is unnecessary duplication, don't bother with Macy" — and Watson concurred (Edward Sherman, Personal Papers).

97. Interview, Johnson White House aide.

98. National Academy of Public Administration, Presidential Appointments Project Interviews, Sheldon Cohen (Commissioner IRS).

99. Interview, Johnson White House aide.

100. Ibid.

101. After John Gardner proposed that William Gorham be nominated assistant secretary of HEW for planning and evaluation, Macy and his staff examined Gorham's bona fides and "joined Gardner in recommending approval of this appointment." Watson met with Gorham (and another Gardner nominee, Robert G. Marston), after which he wrote Johnson: "I was much impressed with him [Gorham]. Both are much aware of your programs and ideas and are eager to serve" ("Gorham," Macy Name Files, Johnson Library).

102. Often, of course, the two would be combined. For example, after Ramsey Clark proposed that Ed Zimmerman be nominated to fill the post of assistant attorney general for antitrust, a Watson aide phoned longtime Johnson confidant Jake Jacobson to solicit his views of Zimmerman. After a personal meeting with Zimmerman and discussions with Harold "Barefoot" Sanders, a Johnson loyalist in the Justice Department, the aide placed his imprimatur on the candidate: "Barefoot and I are satisfied that . . . Zimmerman had been and would be loyal to the president and the policies of the administration" (Memo, Larry Temple to the President, April 27, 1968, White House Central Files, FG 135A, April 27, 1968).

103. "In the early period, before Marvin arrived, I can't recall a single instance of a question being raised about a schedule C" (Interview, Johnson White House aide).

104. Apparently little evidence was needed to establish the loyalty of most non-presidential appointees. Many supergrade recommendations from Macy to Johnson read like this: "Alan Boyd, Undersecretary of Commerce for Transportation, wants to appoint Albert S. Lang to be Deputy Undersecretary. . . . Alan Boyd personally attests that you can expect complete support and sympathy from Mr. Lang" (Memo

for Edward Sherman from Lou Schwartz, August 4, 1965, "Agency Requests for White House Clearance of Appointees to Supergrade Positions in the Excepted Schedule," Edward Sherman Personal Papers).

105. Interview, Johnson White House aide. See also Macy interview 2, 15: "In memoranda to the president, we always included aides' comments as part of the evaluation, since the president put a great deal of confidence in their judgement and as time went by it was more and more evident that the president was likely to give greater weight to the people that he knew."

106. Matt Coffey, Interview with Bradley Patterson.

107. On the reform of committees, see Smith and Deering, *Committees in Congress*. The authoritative treatment of floor activity is Steven Smith's *Call to Order: Floor Politics in the House and Senate* (Washington, D.C.: Brookings Institution, 1990).

108. Kernell, *Going Public*, 49.

109. Robert H. Salisbury, "The Paradox of Interest Groups in Washington—More Groups, Less Clout," in Anthony King, ed., *The New American Political System*, 2d version, (Washington, D.C.: American Enterprise Institute Press, 1990).

110. Ibid.

111. John Mark Hansen, *Gaining Access: Congress and the Farm Lobby, 1919–1981* (Chicago: University of Chicago Press, 1991).

112. Smith, *Call to Order*.

113. The number of articles about the White House rose markedly between 1953 and 1978 (Grossman and Kumar, *Portraying the President*, 256), and the trend continued through 1983 (Kernell, *Going Public*, 180–181).

114. For a discussion of efforts to center political communications in an expanded White House staff, see Maltese, *Spin Control*.

115. None of the aides who served in the Truman, Eisenhower, and Kennedy White House personnel office raised this concern; virtually every aide who worked in the Nixon, Carter, Reagan, and Bush White House did.

116. Interview, Nixon White House aide.

117. Interview, Reagan White House aide.

118. Quoted in David S. Broder, 'Canny Post-Campaign Predictions," *Washington Post*, April 6, 1994, A19. William Kristol, chief of staff to Dan Quayle, observed: "With the political challenges and the decline of parties, everything is so volatile [that] you need more control in the White House than perhaps you once did. The White House has to be on top of everything that gets into the evening news level of attention." George Stephanopolous added, "I agree that you do need control in the White House. There is no way around it. Right now we have 24-hour news cycles. . . . CNN assures that you are forced to react at any time." (*Campaign for President: The Managers Look at '92* [Hollis, N.H.: Hollis Publishing, 1994]).

119. Memo, Flanigan to Nixon, November, 1972, Haldeman Files, Nixon Archives.

120. Ibid.

121. See, for example: Hess, *Organizing the Presidency*; George Reedy, *The Twilight of the Presidency* (New York: American Library, 1970).

122. Califano, *Governing America*, 26.

123. Bruce Adams and Kathyrn Kavanagh-Baran, Volcker Commission, *Promise and Performance: Carter Builds a New Administration* (Lexington, Mass.: D.C. Heath, 1979), 187.

124. Joel Haveman, "The TIP Talent Hunt—Carter's Original Amateur Hour?" *National Journal*, February 19, 1977, 269.

125. Adams and Kavanagh-Baran, *Promise and Performance*, 22.

126. Califano, *Governing America*, 16.

127. Interview, Carter White House aide.

128. Haveman, "The TIP Talent Hunt," 270.

129. Califano, *Governing America*, 27–41.

130. Ibid., 33.

131. Ibid., 129–130.

132. Adams and Kavanagh-Baran, *Promise and Performance*, 64–65.

133. Haveman, "The TIP Talent Hunt," 272.

134. The staff also had roughly ten clerical assistants, bringing its total size to approximately fourteen. Interview, Carter White House aide.

135. Interview, Carter White House aide.

136. King, who got his start in politics doing advance work for John F. Kennedy, was chief of staff to Sen. Edward Kennedy from 1967–1975 and trip director for Carter's campaign.

137. Interview, Carter White House aide.

138. Ibid.

139. Ibid. Posts that fell outside the purview of departments, such as regulatory posts, were filled with little assistance from the president's appointments staff. Instead, Hamilton Jordan took responsibility for the posts, summoning other members of the president's staff—especially Domestic Policy Office aides and political advisers—to lend him assistance on an ad hoc basis.

140. Adams and Kavanagh-Baran, *Promise and Performance*, 72–73.

141. Haveman, "The TIP Talent Hunt," 273.

142. Califano, *Governing America*, 32.

143. Ibid., 41.

144. Griffin Bell, *Taking Care of the Law* (New York: Free Press, 1988), 22. Survey data bear out Bell's suspicions. Few members of the administration had strong personal ties to Carter, and many held political views that had little in common with Carter's. See Susan Carrol and Barbara Geiger-Parker, *Women Appointed to the Carter Administration: A Comparison with Men* (New Brunswick, N.J.: Rutgers University, Eagleton Institute, 1983).

145. Dom Bonafede, "Carter Sounds Retreat from Cabinet Government" *National Journal*, November 18, 1978, 1852.

146. Ibid., 1853.

147. Kernell and Popkin, *Chiefs of Staff*, 167.

148. Interview, Carter White House aide.

149. Bonafede, "Carter Sounds Retreat from Cabinet Government," 1852.

150. Interview, Carter White House aide.

151. Califano, *Governing America*, 23, 450–452.

152. Dunlop's aborted nomination is discussed in Polsby, *Consequences of Party Reform*, 134–135, and Adams and Kavanagh-Baran, *Promise and Performance*, 38–39.

153. Haynes Johnson, *In the Absence of Power* (New York: Viking Press, 1980), 229–230; Bonafede, "Carter Sounds Retreat from Cabinet Government," 1852; John P. Burke, *The Institutional Presidency* (Baltimore, Md.: Johns Hopkins University Press, 1992), 135–136.

154. Johnson, *In the Absence of Power*, 246. Bonafede, "Carter's Recent Staff Shakeup May Be More of a Shakedown," *National Journal*, June 17, 1978, 952.

155. Bonafede, "Carter Sounds Retreat from Cabinet Government," 1852; Johnson, *In the Absence of Power*, 245–248.

156. Johnson, *In the Absence of Power*, 247.

157. *New York Times*, November 6, 1978, cited in Bonafede, "Carter Sounds Retreat from Cabinet Government," 1852.

158. Bonafede, "Carter Sounds Retreat from Cabinet Government," 1852–1857.

159. Bonafede, "Carter's Recent Staff Shakeup May Be More of a Shakedown," 952–957.

160. Bonafede, "Carter Sounds Retreat from Cabinet Government," 1853–1854.

161. Dom Bonafede, "Signs of a Personnel Purge," *National Journal*, March 10, 1979, 391.

162. Ibid.

163. "Kraft and other political types, like Caddell, were making some adolescent efforts to purge the government that didn't go anywhere" (National Academy of Public Administration, *Recruiting Presidential Appointees*, 30) and interview, Carter White House aide.

164. The appointments staff had thirty-three members, of whom roughly two-thirds could be described as "professionals." Of the professional staffers, roughly eighteen to twenty conducted searches, interviewed job candidates, and worked at placing political referrals. Another three to four were responsible for supervising and coordinating their efforts (National Academy of Public Administration, *Recruiting Presidential Appointees*, 18, and interview, Carter White House aide).

165. Interview, Carter White House aide.

166. Ibid.

167. Ibid.

168. Ibid.

169. Ibid.

170. Ibid.

171. Ibid.

172. Ibid.

173. National Academy of Public Administration, *Recruiting Presidential Appointees*, 13.

174. Interview, Carter White House aide.

175. For a discussion of this episode, see Polsby, *Consequences of Party Reform*, 115–128, and sources cited therein. Arnie Miller observed of the July cabinet shakeout: "The fiasco in . . . 1979 was again without the personnel shop. This was done by people who had dabbled for a while, then pulled back, then all of a sudden decided to get back in, and saw what they had created and got away. But it was a disgrace, that whole process. I think Hamilton Jordan called me once during that whole process and asked me about one person. . . . That was apart from us" (National Academy of Public Administration, *Recruiting Presidential Appointees*, 30–31).

176. Interview, Carter White House aide.

177. Ibid.

178. National Academy of Public Administration, *Recruiting Presidential Appointees,* 35.

179. Ibid., 39.

CHAPTER 4. PLUS ÇA CHANGE?

1. Mayhew, *Placing Parties in American Politics*, 331. See also Thomas Byrne Edsall, *The New Politics of Inequality* (New York: W.W. Norton, 1984), ch. 2.

2. For a detailed discussion of these reforms and their effects, see Polsby, *The*

Consequences of Party Reform; Byron Shafer, *Bifurcated Politics: Evolution and Reform in the National Party Convention* (Cambridge, Mass.: Harvard University Press, 1988).

3. In 1968, 45 percent of all Republican National Convention delegates were chosen in primaries; by 1980, the proportion had soared to 75 percent (Polsby, *The Consequences of Party Reform*, 64).

4. Herbert Alexander, *Financing the 1976 Election* (Lexington, Mass.: D.C. Heath, 1983). The legislation (and its effects) are discussed in Polsby, *Consequences of Party Reform*, and Sorauf, *Money in American Politics.*

5. Alexander, *Financing the 1968 Election*, ch. 5.

6. Ibid.

7. Herbert Asher, *Presidential Elections and American Politics*, 4th ed. (Chicago: Dorsey Press, 1988), 214.

8. See, for example, David Menefee-Libey, *The Politics of Party Organization* (Ph.D.dissertation, University of Chicago, 1989).

9. John H. Aldrich, "Presidential Campaigns in Party and Candidate-Centered Eras," in Mathew McCubbins, ed., *Under the Watchful Eye* (Washington, D.C.: Congressional Quarterly Press, 1992), 76.

10. David Mayhew writes: "Local party organizations have declined decisively since the 1960s in the ability to influence nomination processes for local, state, or national offices. . . . The 1950's and 1960's were a golden age of sorts for American local organization. Traditional patronage organizations hung on quite successfully . . . and amateur organizations thrived. All of these forms of structure fared very badly in the 1970's, largely losing out to candidate organizations and capital-intensive campaigns" (Mayhew, *Placing Parties in American Politics*, 329–330; see also 321, 325).

11. Interview, Kennedy White House aide.

12. Mayhew, *Placing Parties in American Politics*, 330.

13. "Transcript of Press Conference," *Congressional Quarterly Weekly Report*, December 18, 1976, 3342.

14. Terence Smith, "It's Carter Folk vs. Regular Democrats," *New York Times*, December 11, 1977.

15. Mark Siegal, in Jonathan Moore and Janet Fraser, eds., *Campaign for President: The Managers Look at 1976* (Cambridge, Mass.: Ballinger, 1977), 115.

16. Interview, Carter White House aide.

17. Elizabeth Drew, *American Journal* (New York: Random House, 1977), 507–511; interview, Carter White House appointments aide.

18. Carter's relationship to the Democratic party is discussed in Drew, *American Journal*; Moore and Fraser, *Campaign for President*; and Robert Shogan's *Promises to Keep* (New York: Thomas Y. Crowell, 1977). Shogan writes: "Having waged and won a battle for the nomination, Carter's team of Georgians was reluctant to grant influence or access to outsiders. . . . For the most part Carter relied on the same advisors [in the general election] who had guided him to the nomination" (52–53).

19. "500 paid," interview, Carter White House aide. Elizabeth Drew estimates that the Carter organization relied upon roughly six hundred volunteers in its Atlanta headquarters and eight hundred in the field (Drew, *American Journal*, 475).

20. According to Mark Siegal, Carter's liaison to the Democratic National Committee, the DNC's contribution to Carter's campaign consisted of "one major task": voter registration. The Committee also served as "a complaint bureau for all our state chairmen, national committee members, and our county chairmen" (Moore and Fraser, eds., *Campaign for President*, 148–149).

21. For descriptions of the 1980 contest, see Jack Germond and Jules Witcover,

Blue Smoke and Mirrors: How Ronald Reagan Won and Jimmy Carter Lost the Election of 1980 (New York: Viking Press, 1981), and Jonathan Moore, ed., *The Campaign for President: 1980 in Retrospect* (Cambridge, Mass.: Ballinger, 1981).

22. Interview, Reagan White House aide.

23. Ibid.

24. Ibid.

25. James Ceasar, "Political Parties: Declining, Stabilizing, or Resurging?" in Anthony King, ed., *The New American Political System*, rev. ed. (Washington, D.C.: American Enterprise Institute Press, 1990), 110.

26. Clark Clifford to John F. Kennedy, Transition Files, Kennedy Library.

27. Unable to participate, Macy recommended a Civil Service Commission staffer who had served him in the Johnson White House Office, Matthew Coffey. Aided by four staffers, Coffey directed the "Talent Inventory Program," Carter's answer to the Kennedy Talent Hunt.

28. Interview, Carter White House aide.

29. Ibid.

30. Adams and Kavanagh-Baran, *Promise and Performance*, 183.

31. Interview, Carter White House aide.

32. Ibid.

33. James L. Sundquist, "Jimmy Carter as Public Administrator: An Appraisal at Mid-term," *Public Administration Review* (January/February 1979): 6. See also Polsby, *Consequences of Party Reform*, 132–140.

34. Interview, Carter White House aide.

35. Carrol and Geiger-Parker, *Women Appointees in the Carter Administration*, vii.

36. Ibid.

37. Although Tobin and Werthheim worked out of the DNC, they were part of the Carter organization – and grudgingly accepted at the DNC.

38. See the oral histories of Katie Louchheim, India Edwards, and Margaret Price.

39. The same observation could be extended to other Democratic party constituencies, such as African-Americans. As late as the 1950s and early 1960s politically active African-Americans worked through the Democratic party and its National Committee. The president's White House aides relied heavily upon party notables – most prominently, Louis Martin, Jr., of the DNC – as their link to the African-American community (interview, Kennedy White House appointments aide). When Jimmy Carter wished to strengthen his ties to the African-American community in preparation for his 1980 presidential bid, he did not use his party as an intermediary. Instead, he brought Louis Martin into his White House Office, whereupon Martin dealt directly with African-American groups and journalists (interview, DNC official).

40. Adams and Kavanagh-Baran, *Promise and Performance*, 19–21.

41. Carrol and Geiger-Parker, *Women Appointed to the Carter Administration*, x.

42. Interview, Carter White House aide.

43. And in processing nomination paperwork – a purely ministerial responsibility.

44. Rhodes Cook, "Carter and the Democrats – Benign Neglect?" *Congressional Quarterly Weekly Report*, January 14, 1978, 59.

45. The resolution reads, in part, "the Democratic National Committee requests that the Carter administration and the staff of the National Committee act to ensure that the state parties participate fully and meaningfully in all party affairs. Involvement includes but is not limited to: One, the solicitation of recommendations from state parties for the making of appointments; Two, consultation before making appointments; Three, notification before announcement of appointments" (Files, Democratic National Committee, April 1, 1977, p. 8 [Courtesy of David Menefee-Libey]). Warren

Weaver, Jr., "National Committee Scolds Carter for Bypassing State Party Chiefs," *New York Times*, April 2, 1977.

46. Cook, "Carter and the Democrats," 57-63.

47. Terence Smith, "It's Carter Folks vs. Regular Democrats," *New York Times*, December 11, 1977, 3. See also Adams and Kavanagh-Baran, *Promise and Performance*, 65-67.

48. Interview, Carter White House aide.

49. Nancy Hicks, "Women's Groups Want More Women Named to High Positions," *New York Times*, February 8, 1977.

50. Robin G. Kaiser, *Washington Post*, "The 2,000 Carter Jobs: Who Got Them?" June 6, 1977, 6.

51. Ernest Ferguson, "Women, Blacks in Bottom Cabinet Drawer," *Los Angeles Times*, December 27, 1976. In Carter's first interview after his inauguration he defended his record on the appointment of women and blacks. *New York Times*, January 25, 1977.

52. Hicks, "Women's Groups Want More Women."

53. In the end, the solicitude of the administration did bear some fruit: while some feminists continued to criticize Carter, others reported that women "got a lot more attention from the departments than they've ever got before" and that "our lists [of prospective appointees] were being taken very seriously" (Mercer Cross, "Interest Group Doubts Rise on Top Jobs," *Congressional Quarterly Weekly Report*, April 30, 1977, 806).

54. Interview, Carter White House aide.

55. After approving the appointment of Ben Heineman as Assistant Secretary of Planning and Evaluation for HHS Carter did pen a note warning Califano "this is the last white male I will accept" (Califano, *Governing America*, 41).

56. Interview, Carter White House aide. Califano's description of the conflict appears in *Governing America*, 229-230.

57. Smith, "It's Carter Folk vs. Regular Democrats," 3.

58. Cook, "Carter and the Democrats," 58. See also Smith, "It's Carter Folk vs. Regular Democrats": "They [the Carter network] will campaign for Carter priority items such as his energy program and the Panama Canal Treaty."

59. The succor, however, came in many forms and from many quarters. In December 1977 "in an effort to sustain the ties that bind the Carter network, the first batch of a projected 150,000 White House Christmas cards was sent out to Carter supporters." Smith, "It's Carter Folk vs. Regular Democrats," 3.

60. Adams and Kavanagh-Baran, *Promise and Performance*, 68.

61. In January 1977 the Civil Service Commission authorized departments to increase the number of allotted schedule C positions by 25 percent for 90 and 120 days "in order to facilitate the orderly transition of duties as a consequence of a change in presidential administration," creating roughly four hundred temporary positions in all.

62. Austin Scott, "Jobs Found for Carter Supporters," *Washington Post*, February 13, 1977, 1.

63. Interviews, Carter White House aides. This shift is discussed in Chapter 3.

64. Interviews, Carter White House aides.

65. Interview, Carter White House aide. The staff was so weak when Miller took over that he chose to rely upon lawyers and accountants *in private practice* to come up with job candidates for newly-created Inspector General posts.

66. National Academy of Public Administration, *Recruiting Presidential Appointees*, 13.

67. Ibid.

68. Ibid., 38.

69. Miller himself was a "politico." He had worked on Democratic campaigns since 1968, including Carter's campaign of 1976, and he had "never spent a single day inside of the government" (interview, Carter White House aide).

70. Interview, Carter White House aide.

71. National Academy of Public Administration, *Recruiting Presidential Appointees*, 9–10.

72. Ibid.

73. Ibid., 38.

74. For a description of the Reagan transition, see Carl Brauer, *Presidential Transitions: Eisenhower through Reagan* (New York: Oxford University Press, 1986), or James P. Pfiffner, *The Strategic Presidency: Hitting the Ground Running* (Chicago: Dorsey Press, 1988).

75. "As far back as 1976, when Reagan made his first serious try for the presidency, I discussed this problem [of staffing the government] with Ed Meese and recounted to him what had happened to Nixon. Meese had already thought about planning and, after hearing about the Nixon transition fiasco, was even more convinced that it was foolhardy not to do some extensive prior work" (Martin Anderson, *Revolution* [New York: Harcourt, Brace, Jovanovich, 1988], 195).

76. Meese told James, "What we want you to do is to put together a plan so that should we win the election we will have something ready to go" (National Academy of Public Administration, *Recruiting Presidential Appointees*, 13).

77. The New Right network to which Anderson and Meese were linked shared their views. Ed Feulner of the Heritage Foundation had made the phrase "personnel is policy" (that is, political appointments should be used solely as an instrument to promote policy control over the executive branch) his mantra throughout the 1970s.

78. Anderson, *Revolution*, 199.

79. Interview, Reagan White House aide.

80. Ibid.

81. Lawrence Barrett, *Gambling with History* (Garden City, N.Y.: Doubleday, 1983), 65.

82. Interview, Reagan transition aide.

83. As Martin Anderson cautioned: "The Nixon administration never recovered from the personnel blunder. Once Nixon missed that initial opportunity to put his people in key positions it was too late. Nixon lost his opportunity to govern before he started" (Anderson, *Revolution*, 195).

84. Interview with Pen James, conducted by Bradley Patterson, New York City, June 23, 1987. See also National Academy of Public Administration, *Recruiting Presidential Appointees*, 11.

85. "Reagan wanted to control the appointments. He did not want a Joe Califano who went in there and hired all his people and said, 'screw what Carter wants, we're going to run our own show here'" (interview, Reagan transition aide).

86. Ibid.

87. Interview, Reagan White House aide.

88. Ibid.

89. The "issue clusters" and their associate directors were: economic affairs, Annelise Anderson; human services, James Cavanaugh; legal and administrative agencies, Tim McNamar; national security, Dudley Mecum; resources and development, Donald G. Ogilvie. A sketch of the transition organization can be found in Dick Kirschten,

"Wanted: 275 Reagan Team Players; Empire Builders Need Not Apply," *National Journal*, December 6, 1980, 2077-2079.

90. Interview, Reagan White House aide.

91. Interview, Reagan campaign aide.

92. Interview, Reagan White House aide.

93. Ibid.

94. Interview, RNC staffer.

95. Mayhew, *Placing Parties in American Politics*, 331. See also ch. 2, "The Republican Party," in Edsall, *New Politics of Inequality*.

96. Adam Clymer, "Staff Quietly Planning for a Reagan Presidency," *New York Times*, September 14, 1980, 1.

97. "Thousands Seek a Niche in Reagan Administration," *New York Times*, November 23, 1980, 33.

98. Interview, Reagan transition aide.

99. Interview, Reagan White House aide.

100. Ibid.

101. Patterson, *Ring of Power*, 243.

102. Interview, Reagan transition aide.

103. One staffer recalled an exhausting schedule that he and his colleagues kept: "We worked from 7 A.M. until 11 P.M. five days a week, on Saturday from 9 A.M. until 6 P.M., and on Sunday from 10 A.M. until 4 P.M. — for four months straight" (interview, Reagan transition aide).

104. Ibid.

105. One aide estimated that "from the political point of view, [schedule C] is where 95% of the pressure comes, because all of the campaign workers across the country and all of the party are trying to put their people in there" (ibid).

106. Interview, Reagan White House aide.

107. Ibid.

108. Ibid.

109. Ibid.

110. Ibid.

111. Ibid.

112. On Reagan's relationship with the Kitchen Cabinet during his prepresidential years, see Bill Boyarsky, *The Rise of Ronald Reagan* (New York: Random House, 1968). During the first two years of the Reagan presidency, the members of the Kitchen Cabinet remained major figures in Republican financial circles: three members of the Kitchen Cabinet — Coors, Salvatori, and Dart — contributed roughly $200,000 to the Republican party and New Right groups (Edsall, *The New Politics of Inequality*, 102).

113. See Helene Von Damm, *At Reagan's Side* (New York: Doubleday, 1989), and Lawrence Barrett, *Gambling With History* (Garden City, N.Y.: Doubleday, 1983), 65-71.

114. According the Henry Salvatori, "The three criteria we followed were: one, is he a Reagan man; two, a Republican; three, a conservative. The most crucial element is conservatism." Dom Bonafede, "Reagan and His Kitchen Cabinet Are Bound by Friendship and Ideology," *National Journal*, April 11, 1981, 606.

115. Interview, Reagan White House aide (Barrett, *Gambling with History*, 78-79).

116. Interview, Reagan transition aide.

117. Interview, Heritage Foundation aide.

118. Willa Johnson, director of the Heritage Talent Bank, sat in on the defense and state presentations.

119. Jim Cavanaugh, James's deputy, was a veteran of the Nixon and Ford White House staffs, and had taken on Howard Phillips over his handling of the OEO. Predictably, Cavanaugh was a favorite target of the New Right.

120. Interview, Heritage Foundation aide.

121. "Cleaning Out the Kitchen," Roland Evans and Robert Novak, *Washington Post*, March 20, 1981.

122. Barrett, *Gambling with History*, 61.

123. Howell Raines, "Conservatives Cite Gains in Top Posts," *New York Times*, March 8, 1981, 1.

124. Interview, Reagan White House aide.

125. Ibid.

126. Ibid.

127. Ibid.

128. Ibid.

129. Ibid.

130. Interview, HHS official.

131. Interview, HHS appointee.

132. Interview, assistant to the president for domestic policy, Reagan White House.

133. Interview, Associate Director, Reagan PPO.

134. Ronald Brownstein, "White House Personnel Office Struggles with More Vacancies, Less Influence," *National Journal*, June 15, 1985, 1410.

135. Interview, senior Clinton transition aide.

136. Interview, transition personnel staff. The 250–270 includes both paid and volunteer staffers.

137. Interview, Clinton transition aide.

138. Ibid.

139. Senior Clinton-Gore campaign professionals estimated the organization's payroll at about eight hundred.

140. Interview, Clinton transition aide.

141. Ibid.

142. Ibid.

143. Ibid.

144. Interview, Clinton White House aide.

145. See, for example, Paul M. Barrett, "Conservatives Tear a Page from Liberals' Book, 'Borking' Clinton's Nominees for Legal Positions," *Wall Street Journal*, November 29, 1993, A14.

146. Ann Devroy describes a staff of "105 people, plus volunteers" in "Late for Appointments: Presidential Hiring Process Slower Than Ever," *Washington Post*, March 2, 1993, 1. Summer 1993 numbers are based upon discussions with Clinton PPO aides.

147. The politics of diversity invariably leaves out some claimants. Groups ranging from military veterans to lesbians voiced displeasure with the lack of solicitude shown them. The displeasure of the lesbians was noted in Michael Kelly and Maureen Dowd, "The Company He Keeps," *New York Times*, January 17, 1993, 20; that of military veterans, CNN Nightly News, March 24, 1994.

148. Ruth Marcus, "Clinton Berates Critics in Women's Groups," *Washington Post*, December 22, 1992, 1; Catherine S. Manegold, "Clinton Ire on Appointments Startles Women," *New York Times*, December 23, 1992, 15.

149. CNN News, June 20, 1993, "Clinton Continues Popularity among Women's Groups," Transcript 425, Segment 1, Early Prime News. Al Kamen, "Personnel Trend Pleases Women's Groups," *Washington Post*, April 5, 1993, 19.

150. Martha Farnsworth Richie, "The Bean Count Is In! A Promise Fulfilled: Clinton's Appointees Really Are as Diverse as America," *Washington Post*, January 23, 1994, C2.

151. Donnie Radcliffe, "The Women's Hour: Clinton Appointees Revel in Their First Year in Power," *Washington Post*, February 9, 1994, 1.

152. Interview, Clinton White House aide.

153. These six policy areas into which Clinton's PPO staff were organized were: Transportation and Commerce, Social Services, Energy and Environment, Legal and Financial, National Security, and Boards and Commissions.

154. "Maria Haley, who is an associate director for economic affairs, has a special responsibility in addition for being a point of contact for the Asian-American community, and also for Arkansans, because she is an Arkansan. Alfred Ramirez, who is another associate director, has an additional responsibility for Hispanic tracking" (interview, Clinton White House aide).

155. For a lengthy profile of Hattoy, see Richard Berke, "Time Bomb in the White House," *New York Times*, June 6, 1993, 29.

156. The Clinton diversity standards were popularly known as the "EGG standards," for "ethnicity, gender, and geography." See, for example, Al Kamen, "Administration Still Walking on EGG Shells," *Washington Post*, April 19, 1993, 18.

157. Interview, Clinton White House aide.

158. Ibid.

159. Jon Healey, "As Administration Fills Its Slots, Congress Plays Waiting Game," *Congressional Quarterly Weekly Report*, May 1, 1993, 1059–1061.

160. Douglas Jehl, "High-Level Grumbling over Pace of Appointments," *New York Times*, February 25, 1993, A16. See also, The Talk at the Top," *Newsweek*, June 7, 1993, 4.

161. Michael K. Frisby, "While Some Clinton Changes Make Big Waves, Others Trickle Down to Lower Levels," *Wall Street Journal*, November 3, 1993, 24.

162. Consider the case of the feminist movement. In 1976 it first became a significant presence in presidential election politics and, through the efforts of the Coalition for Women's Appointments (CWA), in political appointments. By 1992, the efforts of feminists to shape presidential politics and political appointments were vastly better financed and more sophisticated than they had been in 1976—and more successful, as well. On the CWA's efforts see Manegold, "Clinton Ire on Appointments Startles Women," 15; on the representation of women in the Clinton administration, see Richie, "The Bean Count Is In," C2.

163. The success of demands made by feminists, African-Americans, and other "blocs and movements" for representation in appointive posts depend heavily upon the legitimacy bestowed upon their demands by news organizations. By the 1980s and 1990s news organizations assiduously sought out information about the composition of presidential appointments and regularly reported the results. In 1992–1993, for example, the Associated Press interviewed Clinton nominees and researched their biographies, then compiled this material into a computer database. So, too, did other news organizations—significantly strengthening the claims of "blocs and movements." Describing Bush's appointments, Ruth Shalit writes, "Bush's preemptive bean-counting was a purely defensive measure." Bush aide Ed Rogers acknowledged as much, saying, "We were responding to pressure from the press corps. Much of the goal [of diversity] was just to have our talking points in order, to deflect criticism when it came" ("The Unwhite House," *New Republic*, April 12, 1993, 13).

164. Ibid., 14.

165. This development is analyzed in Kernell and Popkin, *Chiefs of Staff.*

166. Interview, Bush White House aide.

167. Interview, Kennedy White House aide.

168. Interview with Mike Manatos, conducted by Richard L. Schott, Washington, D.C., June 19, 1978.

169. See Chapter 4.

170. Interview, Reagan White House aide.

171. Discussing the PPO staff, a member observed, "Most of these people were hired and Pen didn't even know who they were. Pen's deputies would bring them in and introduce them to him." Interview, Reagan PPO aide.

172. Interview, Reagan White House aide.

173. Ibid.

174. National Academy of Public Administration, *Recruiting Presidential Appointees*, 14.

175. Interview, Reagan White House aide.

176. Brownstein, "White House Personnel Office Struggles," 1408–1410.

CHAPTER 5. DO PRESIDENTS MAKE A DIFFERENCE?

1. Stanley Kelley, *Professional Public Relations and Political Power* (Baltimore, Md.: Johns Hopkins University Press, 1956).

2. See, for example: Mansfield, "Political Parties, Patronage, and the Federal Government Service," 84–112; "Politics without Patronage," *Time*, June 7, 1954, 23; Richard Neustadt, "On Patronage, Power, and Politics," *Public Administration Review* (Spring 1955): 108–114; James Watson, "Is Patronage Obsolete?" *Personnel Administration* (July 1955): 3–9; Francis J. Sorauf, "The Silent Revolution in Patronage," *Public Administration Review* 20:1 (Winter 1960): 28–34.

3. See, for example, Paul T. David and Ross Pollock, *Executive for Government Service: Central Issues of Federal Personnel Administration* (Washington, D.C.: Brookings Institution, 1957), and Herbert Kaufmann, "Emerging Conflicts in the Doctrines of Public Administration," *American Political Science Review* 50 (December 1956): 1057–1073. Throughout the late 1950s the Brookings Institution sponsored a Conference on Federal Personnel Management. This group included prominent academics (e.g., Rensis Likert, Wallace Sayre), civil service leaders (e.g., Arthur Flemming and John Macy), government insiders (e.g., Elmer Staats and Rufus Miles) and management consultants (McKinsey's John Corson). The group "deplored the haphazardly organized" arrangements for recruiting political executives and called for "a more orderly and considered system"—under the leadership of the president. Transcript of March 23, 1957, meeting, Conference on Federal Personnel Management, President's General Files (Robert Calkins), Brookings Archives.

4. Henry, "The Presidency, Executive Staffing, and the Federal Bureaucracy," 529.

5. "The Changing Presidential Office," in Arnold Meltsner, ed., *Politics and The Oval Office* (San Francisco: Institute for Contemporary Studies, 1981), 165.

6. Those aspects of the White House Office that impinge least on the demands and expectations of leaders outside of the White House—that is, how presidents choose to manage the White House Office—are most responsive to the proclivities of presidents. Those aspects of the White House Office that importantly impinge on the needs and expectations of leaders outside the White House—such as the press office or political appointments staff—are least susceptible to presidents' proclivities. Hence, presidents have a good bit of latitude in deciding how to manage the White House Office but little latitude in deciding what gets done there.

7. A second set of Nixon staffers, headquartered in Washington, D.C., was responsible for overseeing low-level presidential appointments and the 1,700 posts outside the civil service filled by department and agency heads, chiefly "schedule C" positions.

8. The Pierre staff, Martin Anderson recalled, "never learned how many jobs were available," nor did it try to "analyze the positions, identify candidates for those positions, [or] interview the candidates" (Anderson, *Revolution*, 194).

9. Interview, Nixon transition aide.

10. Ibid.

11. Flemming relied heavily on the advice of Robert Hampton, Eisenhower's appointments aide during the final years of his presidency (and subsequently as Civil Service commissioner). Said Flemming, "You make sense of this for me. I'm certainly not walking into this with any experience. I don't know what I'm doing. I need your help." Hampton's advice was to "decentralize responsibility for the staffing of departments" (interview, Nixon White House aide).

12. Evans and Novak, *Nixon in the White House: The Frustration of Power*, 66.

13. Staff size during opening weeks: John Pierson, "Nixon Talent Hunt Off to Good Finish," *Wall Street Journal*, May 9, 1969, 18. Staff size at the end of the administration's first year: Dom Bonafede, "Nixon's First Year Appointments Reveal the Pattern of His Administration," *National Journal*, January 24, 1970, 182–192; U.S. Congress, *Final Report on Violations and Abuses of Merit Principles in Federal Employment Together with Minority Views (Violations and Abuses)*, Subcommittee on Manpower and Civil Service of the Post Office and Civil Service Committee, Committee Print, 94–28, 94th Congress, 2d session, (Washington, D.C.: Government Printing Office, 1976), 141. HEW, by way of comparison, had a staff of eighteen in its "Office of Special Projects" to handle job patronage requests — and other patronage activities (*Violations and Abuses*, 171).

14. Ibid.

15. Interview, Nixon White House aide. The staff was a busy one: it received five hundred job requests per month from Capitol Hill, governors, mayors, Maurice Stans (Nixon's campaign finance chairman), and elsewhere. After evaluating each candidate and ranking them on a 1–4 scale of "political weight," three hundred of these requests each month were forwarded to departmental liaisons — of which only ten were "musts" (see *Violations and Abuses*, 145–146).

16. In point of fact, candidates were rarely rejected by Flemming's office. Only 4–5 percent of candidates submitted to the Personnel Office were rejected, typically because they had failed to pass FBI clearance or political clearances. Bonafede, "Nixon's First Year Appointments Reveal the Pattern of His Administration," 186. More often than not clearance simply permitted the PPO to ensure that important presidential allies were "stroked" by notifying them of impending nominations. "When you have decided who the man should be for Medicaid," Peter Flanigan instructed HEW's chief of staff, "call Mr. Henry Scut. Remember that Scut was *the* insurance man who came out for the president hard and early" (Memo, Peter Flanigan to L. Patrick Gray, October 24, 1969, FG 23-8-1 [Appointments, HEW], Nixon Collection, National Archives [NCNA]).

17. Interview, Nixon White House aide. During June 1969, departments solicited the assistance of Flemming's office in filling forty-eight posts. "In response," Flemming aide George Bell wrote, "we have reviewed 700 folders, forwarded copies of 152 resumes with supporting letters, which appear to be applicable to 26 of the jobs." None of the requests were for senior, presidentially appointed posts such as assistant secretaries. Instead, candidates were requested for career and noncareer jobs ranging from the GS-12 to GS-18 level — with the majority of requests for posts below

the GS-16 level — positions that were least likely to entail significant policy responsibilities (Memo, George Bell to Charles Colson, NCNA).

18. Memos, George Bell to Harry Flemming, June 26, 1969; February 16, 1970. Haldeman Files, Malek Name File, September 1970, NCNA.

19. Memo, Bell to Colson, NCNA.

20. Interview, Nixon White House aide.

21. The president "lacks control of the IRS," personnel chief Fred Malek complained, because IRS executives "feel that it is more important to be responsive to the Chairman of the House Ways and Means Committee than to the President." Memo, Malek to Haldeman, December 15, 1970, Malek Name File, Haldeman Files, NCNA.

22. One senior White House aide described Social Security Commissioner Bob Ball this way: "I think Bob Ball was clearly one of the leading experts in the country. He was very well respected on the Hill, and he had a definite point of view. Clearly, if you wanted to accomplish any changes in the law and regulations, it was important to have Bob Ball on board" (interview, Nixon White House aide).

23. Lewis Butler, HEW's Assistant Secretary for Planning and Evaluation, warned that Robert Ball's assistance was crucial to the implementation of Nixon's proposed Family Assistance Plan. Butler wrote: "Dick Nathan spent all day with Bob Ball last Friday. He is very concerned that Ball may resign. He would regard Ball's leaving as disastrous to the Family Assistance Plan and has told Ed Morgan [of the Domestic Council] this. We need to move very fast with a demonstration of support for Ball. Our reasons should be pure selfish interest. We need him to launch the FAP administration. We can't make it without him, and will have a hard enough time making it with him." Recognizing Ball's importance, Ehrlichman scrawled on a copy of the letter, "Turn Flemming off re: Ball" (prevent personnel aide Harry Flemming from firing Ball). Memo, Lewis Butler to Secretary, Undersecretary, April 20, 1970, Finch Name File, Ehrlichman Files, NCNA.

24. Theodore Marmor, "Entrepreneurship in Public Management: Wilbur Cohen and Robert Ball" ch. 8 in Jameson W. Doig and Erwin C. Hargrove, eds., *Leadership and Innovation* (Baltimore, Md.: Johns Hopkins, 1987), 264. Ed Morgan, deputy to John Ehrlichman, alleged that other executives at SSA were also engaged in undermining the president to protect "their program." Writing to John Ehrlichman he complained that "Robert Myers [chief actuary for the Social Security Administration] has close personal relationships with Ways and Means Committee members" and that he is "purposely sandbagging us by providing the Hill with erroneous information" about the cost of the Family Assistance Plan (Memo, Morgan to Ehrlichman, FG 23-8-1, NCNA).

25. Memo, Larry Highby to H. R. Haldeman, "The Second Administration: A Concept," Haldeman Files, NCNA.

26. Malek shared responsibility for political appointments with another HEW staffer, Alan May, when he joined HEW in the spring of 1969. Within a few months he took over May's responsibilities as head recruiter for Finch's HEW (see *Violations and Abuses*, 171–177).

27. Frederic V. Malek, "Mr. Businessman Goes to Washington," *Harvard Business Review* (September-October 1972): 68.

28. "Malek's forte at HEW had been the removal and Siberian placement of HEW officials felt to be a problem for the new administration, as well as the selection of management-oriented new appointees" (Nathan, *Administrative Presidency*, 39).

29. Malek also concluded that he could not rely upon partisan networks to discover or evaluate prospective appointees. Politicians, in his estimation — and Haldeman's —

were not discerning judges of administrative or technical competence. A colleague of Malek's recalls: "Malek thought that if you had political experience you had to be incompetent" (interview, Nixon White House aide).

30. Dom Bonafede, "Nixon Personnel Staff Works to Restructure Federal Policies," *National Journal*, November 12, 1971, 2440-2448.

31. Daniel Guttman and Barry Willner, *The Shadow Government* (New York: Pantheon Books, 1976), 46-47.

32. Many of the managers recruited by Malek were politically unsophisticated and far more familiar with techniques of analysis and management than the substance and politics of the programs they administered. Martha Derthick, *Uncontrollable Spending for Social Service Grants* (Washington, D.C.: Brookings Institution, 1975), 36-37.

33. Memo, Fred Malek to H. R. Haldeman, August 21, 1970, "Strengthening the President's Ability to Manage the Government," Malek Name File, Haldeman Files, NCNA.

34. Ibid. "Breaking the link" between political executives and their allies outside the executive branch was a chief aim of both the administration's February 1971 proposal to establish a "Federal Executive Service" and its reorganization plan of 1970. On the administration's "Federal Executive Service Plan," see *The Government's Managers*, Report of the Twentieth Century Fund Task Force on the Senior Executive Service (New York: Priority Press, 1987), 42-43.

35. The strike force proposed by Malek first went to work on the IRS. Confidential Memo, Malek to Haldeman, December 15, 1970; Haldeman Files, NCNA. Later, Malek performed a similar service for Nixon at the Bureau of Labor Statistics. David Johnston, "GOP Official Made a Census of Jews at Agency," *New York Times*, September 11, 1988, 31; Charles Colson Oral History, NCNA.

36. Malek consciously rejected reliance upon universities, think tanks, and nonprofits. Relying upon them suited Lyndon Johnson's (and John Macy's) needs, but not Richard Nixon's. Interview, Nixon White House aide.

37. "Power centers": Interview, Nixon White House aide. "Pool of people": Marmor, "Entrepreneurship in Public Management: Wilbur Cohen and Robert Ball," 274.

38. Malek's office also had a small "special projects" unit. This unit was charged with tackling "trouble spots" of unresponsiveness, such as the IRS.

39. Interviews, Nixon White House aides.

40. Ibid.

41. John Osborne, *The Second Year of the Nixon Watch* (Washington, D.C.: New Republic Books, 1971), 190-191; Robert Sherrill, "Hatchman and Hatchetmyth," *Washington Post*, February , 1972, 11.

42. Flemming's list of eighty-one appointees targeted for removal had twenty-three names from HEW — 28 percent of all appointees slated for removal.

43. Memo, Malek to Haldeman, December 1970, Malek Name File, Haldeman Files, NCNA.

44. Malek's proposal for a new personnel office was approved by Nixon in late November 1970 and announced to the cabinet on January 29, 1971.

45. For a contemporaneous description of Malek's staff, see Bonafede, "Nixon Personnel Staff Works to Restructure Federal Policies," 2441-2448.

46. Memo, Malek to Haldeman, October 14, 1970, "Progress Report," Malek Name File, Haldeman Files, NCNA.

47. Ibid.

48. Members of the cabinet who carried political responsibilities — such as Maurice Stans, the president's fundraiser — also relied upon the office to service their claimants.

49. Malek to Haldeman, March 8, 1971, "Progress Report on Upgrading Personnel," Malek Name File, March 1971, Haldeman Files, Nixon Archives. Haldeman directed Harry Flemming to prepare a purge list as early as August 1970. His list — longer still than Malek's — was discarded in favor of Malek's (Highby to Flemming, August 6, 1970, Flemming Name File, Haldeman Files, NCNA). See Evans and Novak, *Frustration of Power*, 352–364, for a contemporaneous assessment of these events.

50. *Violations and Abuses*, 168; Bonafede, "Nixon Personnel Staff Works to Restructure Federal Policies," 2441–2448.

51. On Nixon's continued dissatisfaction with the political responsiveness of departments and agencies, see H. R. Haldeman, *The Ends of Power* (New York: Times Books, 1978), 167–173.

52. Memo, Malek to Haldeman, December 1970, Haldeman Files, NCNA.

53. Interview, Nixon White House aide.

54. Ibid.

55. Interview, Civil Service Commission.

56. Haldeman, *The Ends of Power*, 171.

57. Interview, Nixon White House aide.

58. *Violations and Abuses*, 154. "After the election we evaluated every one of the 555 presidential appointees in the executive branch" (interview, Nixon White House aide).

59. Pen James to Fred Malek, no date, Malek Files, NCNA.

60. "The Second Term: A Concept," attributed to Highby (n.d.) [forwarded to Ehrlichman, October 19, 1972], Haldeman Files, NCNA.

61. Haldeman, *The Ends of Power*, 173.

62. According to White House records, Fred Malek was to deliver a two-hundred-person "talent bank" to Richard Nixon by October 1, 1972, to be used in restaffing the administration. The restaffing would be completed by January 12, 1973, just weeks after the election. Malek Name file, October 1972, Haldeman Files, NCNA.

63. "White House Personnel Office Mission, Programs, and Staffing," Jerry Jones to Bob Haldeman, March 7, 1973. Jones Name File, Haldeman Files, NCNA.

64. Interviews, Nixon White House aides.

65. Interview, RNC aide.

66. See Chapter 2.

67. Interview, Nixon White House aide.

68. Ibid.

69. Ibid.

70. Malek scrambled and hastily assembled lists of Italians, Hispanics, Irish Catholics (Malek Name File, Haldeman Files, Nixon Archives). The lists were brief and unreliable. Malek recruited Claude Brinegar to be Secretary of Transportation, thinking he was an Irish Catholic. Brinegar was actually a German Protestant, and when he was queried by Nixon about "the cardinals," Brinegar replied that he was a Steelers fan. "No, no, you know," Nixon said, "like Kroll and those cardinals." Brinegar replied "Well, I don't know any of those cardinals. I'm an Episcopalian" (John Ehrlichman, "The White House and Policymaking," in Kenneth W. Thompson, ed., *The Nixon Presidency: Twenty-Two Intimate Perspectives on Richard Nixon* [Lanham, Md.: University Press of America, 1987], 136).

71. "Integrity in Numbers," *Washington Post*, May 26, 1973, A18. Professional groups were eventually joined by Senate Democrats and editorial writers — such as those at the *Washington Post*.

72. *New York Times*, January 25, 1973, 39.

73. Ibid., 30.

74. Ibid.

75. Interview, Nixon White House aide.

76. Haig took over as Chief of Staff on May 4, 1973.

77. Harold Seidman, *Politics, Position, and Power: The Dynamics of Federal Organization* (New York: Oxford University Press, 1980), 120.

78. *Violations and Abuses*, 183.

79. Interview, Nixon White House aide.

80. *National Journal*, October 6, 1973, 1475. See also *New York Times*, July 9, 1973, 24. "Departments and agencies are putting through appointments once blocked because appointees didn't have the dedication to Nixon that was previously required."

81. Ibid.

82. Interview, Nixon White House aide.

83. Ibid.

84. Ibid.

85. National Academy of Public Administration, *Recruiting Presidential Appointees*, 49.

86. See Chapter 3. Whether Carter actually reduced the size of the larger White House Office is arguable (see Hart, *Presidential Branch*, 180–181).

87. Adams and Kavanagh-Baran, *Promise and Performance*, 66.

88. Robin G. Kaiser, "The 2,000 Carter Administration Jobs: Who Got Them?" *Washington Post*, June 6, 1977, 1.

89. Johnson, *In the Absence of Power*, 247.

90. Califano, *Governing America*, 148–149.

91. Interview, Carter White House aide.

92. Ibid. See also National Academy of Public Administration, *Recruiting Presidential Appointees*, 15–16. John Macy recalled, "In . . . my day we would send those to the department." Miller replied: "We did that on some stuff, but there was such heat. We'd get held up on legislation by a Member of Congress over regional directors or other such jobs."

93. National Academy of Public Administration, *Recruiting Presidential Appointees*, 39.

94. Ibid., 39.

95. Ibid., 10.

96. Moe, "The Politicized Presidency," 269.

97. Interview, Reagan White House aide.

98. Interview, Clinton White House aide.

99. Interview, Clinton transition aide.

100. Thomas Friedman, "Clinton Taking Big Role in Picking Cabinet Aides," *New York Times*, November 17, 1992, A18.

101. Interview, Clinton transition aide.

102. Interview, Clinton White House aide.

103. Ibid.

104. By its own estimates, the Clinton PPO had completed about two-thirds of the full-time presidential appointments by August 1993. Interview, Clinton White House aide. By the reckoning of the *Wall Street Journal*, "about 150 slots still lacked appointees" by the end of 1993 (*Wall Street Journal*, "Washington Wire," February 11, 1993, 1).

105. Interview, Clinton White House aide.

106. Ibid.

107. Ibid.

108. *Wall Street Journal*, "Washington Wire," February 11, 1994, 1.

109. Al Kamen, "Banker's Ours: Clinton Snares Atlanta Executive," *Washington Post*, January 12, 1994, 17.

110. Douglas Jehl, "Clinton Nominations Come Slowly and with Many Setbacks," *New York Times*, January 30, 1994, 20.

111. Burt Solomon, "Scrimping on White House Staff Could Damage Clinton's Fortunes," *National Journal*, August 14, 1993, 2046-2047.

112. See, for example, James P. Pfiffner's essay, "Cutting Staff No Easy Task for Clinton," *Maine Sunday Telegram*, December 12, 1993, 1C.

113. Interview, Clinton PPO aide.

CHAPTER 6. THE FRUITS OF THEIR LABORS

1. One staffer who served three Democratic presidents recalls that the Kennedys could "get on the phone and touch base with people all over the country. They had people everywhere that owed them something. You can't imagine the connections of these people" (interview, DNC aide).

2. Carter's administration was indeed a government of strangers: among a sample of men who served in the administration, nearly 80 percent of cabinet and subcabinet appointees had not met Carter prior to receiving their post (Carrol and Geiger-Parker, *Women Appointed to the Carter Administration*, 35).

3. Heclo, *A Government of Strangers*.

4. Bell, *Taking Care of the Law*, 22.

5. On the increasing polarization of group politics in the early years of the Reagan administration, see Mark Peterson and Jack Walker, "The Impact of the Reagan Administration upon the National Interest Group System" (Paper presented to the annual meeting of the American Political Science Association, New Orleans, 1985).

6. Political leadership in the bureaucracy consists of setting directions and mobilizing political resources for one's agency. Responsive appointees do these things on the president's behalf: they look to the president for guidance when setting directions, and they mobilize their political resources — their reputation, skills, and political ties — on behalf of their president. Moreover, they take on those who oppose the president's program, be they careerists, professional groups, or the press. Unresponsive appointees do the opposite. Hence, evidence of the responsiveness of appointees is based upon two measures: the frequency with which the president (or EOP and White House staff) is publicly criticized by HEW/HHS appointees (in either the *New York Times* or the *Washington Post*), and the willingness of the president's appointees to come into public conflict with congressional, clientele, or career opponents of the president's proposals (as reported in congressional committee hearings and news stories).

7. Defense and intelligence careerists, for example, are far more conservative than their counterparts in social agencies — and more conservative than any foreseeable Democratic presidents. On the views of careerists in defense agencies, see Robert Maranto, "Still Clashing after All These Years: The Political Geography of Conflict in the Reagan Executive Branch" (Unpublished paper, 1990). For a discussion of Bill Clinton's problems with the Department of Defense, see Lawrence J. Korb, "The President and the Military at Odds," *Brookings Review* (Summer 1993): 5.

8. Arthur M. Schlesinger Jr., *A Thousand Days: John F. Kennedy in the White House* (Boston, Mass.: Houghton, Mifflin, 1965), 127.

9. David Broder and Stephen Hess, *The Republican Establishment* (New York: Harper and Row, 1967). See also Stephen Ambrose, *Nixon: The Triumph of a Politician, 1962-1972* (New York: Simon and Schuster, 1990), 66, 102, 106.

10. Broder and Hess, *The Republican Establishment*, 185-189, and Stephen Hess, "Nixon in Exile," in Thompson, *The Nixon Presidency*.

11. Reichley, "The Rise of National Parties." As late as 1976 the leading text on party politics observed that presidential campaigns — Goldwater's excepted — "work pragmatically through the maze of state and local organizations, finding useful leaders and contacts as best they can" (Francis J. Sorauf, *Party Politics in America*, 4th ed., [Boston: Little, Brown, 1976], 307).

12. Interview, Nixon White House aide.

13. Evans and Novak, *Nixon in the White House*, 11.

14. For data on beliefs of convention delegates, see Warren E. Miller and M. Kent Jennings, *Parties in Transition: A Longitudinal Study of Party Elites and Supporters* (New York: Russell Sage Foundation, 1986), and John Kessel, *Presidential Campaign Politics* (Chicago: Dorsey Press, 1988), 115-119. On the increasing conservatism of Republican officeholders, see Nicol Rae, *The Decline and Fall of Liberal Republicans: From 1952 to the Present* (Oxford University Press, 1989), esp. 157-196.

15. Vincent J. Burke and Vee Burke, *Nixon's Good Deed: Welfare Reform* (New York: Columbia University Press, 1974), 43.

16. Leon E. Panetta and Peter Gall, *Bring Us Together: The Nixon Team and the Civil Rights Retreat* (Philadelphia: J. B. Lippincott, 1971), 62-66. As of September 30, 1968, there were 12 presidential appointments and 76 nonpresidential posts in HEW: 31 NEA, 42 schedule C, and 3 schedule A jobs (U.S. Congress, *Policy and Supporting Positions*, House Post Office and Civil Service Committee [Washington, D.C.: Government Printing Office, 1968]). HEW had a smaller ratio of political to career positions than virtually any agency in 1969, which led HEW's chief patronage officer to request that three hundred additional posts be taken out of the civil service (*Violations and Abuses*, 171-184, 573-728).

17. Burke and Burke, *Nixon's Good Deed*, 43.

18. Panetta and Gall, *Bring Us Together*, 62-66. Had they made use of Nixon's political network, they would have found that this "constellation" was thin: among those politicians who were tied to Nixon, only two were unmistakably expert on questions of social policy, Arthur Flemming and Elliot Richardson — and both were liberal Republicans.

19. Ibid.

20. On Finch's struggle over the Knowles appointment, see Evans and Novak, *The Frustration of Power*, 59-66.

21. On the autonomy of bureaus within HEW, see John Iglehart, "Diffuse Nature of HEW Mission Challenges Republicans' Management Goals," *National Journal*, August 5, 1970, 1905-1915.

22. Ball's career is described in Marmor, "Entrepreneurship in Public Management."

23. This pattern was repeated throughout the government. One sample of political appointees revealed that 13 percent of all presidentially appointed executives in 1970 were Democrats — and that 29 percent of departmental appointees (NEA and schedule C) appointees were Democrats (Joel D. Aberbach and Bert A. Rockman, "Clashing Beliefs in the Executive Branch: The Nixon Administration Bureaucracy," *American Political Science Review* 70 [June 1976]: 456-468).

24. For a description of staffing at HUD, see Richard W. Waterman, *Presidential Influence and the Administrative State* (Knoxville: University of Tennessee Press, 1990), 51-70.

25. Interview, Nixon White House aide.

26. Evans and Novak, *The Frustration of Power*, 61-64.

27. Ibid.

28. Ibid., 68.

29. Interview, Nixon White House aide.

30. As one should expect — given the emulation of the Eisenhower administration's arrangements for staffing the government — the influence of the Nixon and Eisenhower staffs over the selection of senior political appointees was nearly identical. The Eisenhower staff played a prominent role in only eleven out of forty-seven (22 percent) appointments (Mann, *Assistant Secretaries*, 87–88).

31. Panetta and Gall, *Bring Us Together*, 93–95.

32. Ibid.; interview, Nixon White House aide. L. Patrick Gray, Finch's chief of staff, was also a Nixon loyalist. However, he, too, stayed only briefly at HEW (Thompson, *Nixon Presidency*, 165).

33. Republicans in the executive branch were predominantly centrist (50 percent moderate, 35 percent right-of-center, 15 percent left-of-center). However, "Republicans in the social service agencies [HEW, HUD, and OEO] were more liberal than Republicans serving in other agencies" (44 percent were moderate, 22 percent right-of-center, and 33 percent left-of-center). See Aberbach and Rockman, "Clashing Beliefs in the Executive Branch," 461–463.

34. Thompson, *Nixon Presidency*, 104.

35. Interviews, Nixon White House aides.

36. Among those who opposed key Nixon initiatives in mental health were Joseph English, administrator of the Health Services and Mental Health Administration (HSMHA) and Stanley Yolles, director of the National Institute of Mental Health (NIMH).

37. On the conflict over decentralization, see *National Journal*, May 23, 1970, 1080; Iglehart, "Diffuse Nature of HEW Mission," 1914.

38. Yolles blasted the president for his "lack of commitment to supporting mental health services for children" and reprimanded the administration for "introducing partisan political considerations into the appointment of individuals to scientific positions in the government." For charges of partisan interference and lack of concern with mental health, see Richard Lyons, "U.S. Health Aide Is Out in Dispute," *New York Times*, June 3, 1970, 1. These criticisms reverberated in the White House, causing H. R. Haldeman's assistant, Egil Krogh, to complain to Finch: "As you have read in the papers, Yolles has been repeatedly undermining the administration's position" (on mental health bloc grants). Memo, Egil Krogh to Peter Flanigan, October 31, 1969, FG 23-8-1 (HEW, Appointments), NCNA.

39. Roger Egeberg, assistant secretary of health, demanded to meet Nixon and discuss funding levels (Memo, Chapin to Ehrlichman, December 12, 1969, FG 23-8-1, Nixon Archives).

40. Derthick, *Uncontrollable Spending for Social Service Grants*, 35.

41. Ehrlichman, in Thompson, ed., "The White House and Policymaking."

42. Panetta and Gall, *Bring Us Together*. Memos, Harry Dent to John Ehrlichman, in Panetta Name file, Ehrlichman Files, NCNA.

43. Ehrlichman, *Witness to Power: The Nixon Years*, 220–224, 234–235.

44. Ehrlichman recalls Nixon's position as: "We'll do what the law requires — and nothing more" (*Witness to Power*, 227–228).

45. Ibid., 225.

46. Ehrlichman, in Thompson, ed., "The White House and Policymaking," 130.

47. Patterson, *Ring of Power*, 39–43.

48. On James Allen's departure, see *National Journal*, June 13, 1970, 1238.

49. John Ehrlichman reports that Richard Nixon wanted to handle "sensitive problems" personally — including "abortion, race, aid to parochial schools, labor legislation,

drugs, crime, welfare, and taxes." All of the issues except labor legislation, taxes, and crime fall within the jurisdiction of HEW (Ehrlichman, *Witness to Power*, 207).

50. Interview, senior HEW official.

51. Memo, George Bell to Charles Colson, NCNA.

52. Interview, senior HEW official.

53. Ibid.

54. Interviews, Nixon White House aides. One high-ranking White House aide observed that "Elliot was perceived to be too soft on the welfare and education [desegregation] issues."

55. Interview, Nixon White House aide.

56. Ehrlichman, *Witness to Power*, 207-234; Gary Orfield, *Must We Bus?* (Washington, D.C.: Brookings Institution, 1978).

57. The number of news stories in which HEW officials spoke critically of the president, his staff, and his policies declined from seventeen in 1970 to two in 1971.

58. *New York Times*, June 9, 1971, 22.

59. On Richardson's disagreements with the president's advisers: "Richardson Says He'll Fight Cuts," *New York Times*, December 18, 1971, 22; "Richardson Threatens to Resign over Rejection of His Austin Texas Desegregation Plan," *New York Times*, August 10, 1971, 52.

60. Memo, Richard Nathan to Jonathan Moore (blind carbon copy to Cole and Malek), FG 23-8-1, NCNA.

61. Nathan, *Administrative Presidency*, 31-32.

62. Memo, Malek to Haldeman, March 8, 1971, "Progress Report on Upgrading Personnel," Haldeman Files, Malek Name file, March 1971, NCNA.

63. Haldeman, *The Ends of Power*, 171.

64. Charles Colson Oral History, NCNA.

65. In January 1973 the United States and North Vietnam signed the Paris Peace Accords after months of intensive diplomacy by Kissinger.

66. Nathan, *The Administrative Presidency*, 48-49.

67. Interview, Nixon White House aide.

68. Interview, HEW appointee.

69. Derthick, *Uncontrollable Spending for Social Service Grants*, 104.

70. Interview, Nixon White House aide.

71. Ibid.

72. In calendar year 1973, the *New York Times* carried only one story in which HEW officials spoke critically of the president or his policies.

73. The budget that Nixon presented in January 1973 was a more conservative document than any he had previously presented. For a discussion of Nixon's rightward shift in domestic policy after the election of 1972, see Ehrlichman, *Witness to Power*, 240-241.

74. On the selection of Schweiker to be Secretary of HHS, see Von Damm, *At Reagan's Side*.

75. Interview, HHS official.

76. Interview, Reagan transition aide.

77. Ibid.

78. Ibid.

79. Interview, Reagan White House aide, and National Academy of Public Administration, *Recruiting Presidential Appointees*, 11.

80. The transition staffers were Pam Bailey, Jim Cavanaugh, and David Winston. Bailey and Cavanaugh served on the Nixon Domestic Council as health policy staffers; Winston was a Reagan and Schweiker aide.

81. Interview, Reagan transition aide.
82. Interview, HHS official.
83. Miller and Jennings, *Parties in Transition.*
84. Edsall, *The New Politics of Inequality*, ch. 2, "The Republican Party."
85. Interview, Reagan HHS official.
86. White House staffers initially refused to accept Schweiker's candidate for the NIH, Dr. Wynngarden, "because he hadn't done anything for Reagan." However, Schweiker and his staff "just kept arguing. We said, 'Who do you have that is better?' " The PPO staff relented and accepted Schweiker's candidate because "they had a problem coming up with someone" (interviews, Reagan HHS officials).
87. Interviews, Reagan HHS officials. Seen from the perspective of HHS, "the White House was more active than either the Hill or trade associations" in proposing candidates to the department. By way of contrast, only two out of the dozen senior political appointees in Robert Finch's HEW originated with the Nixon staff.
88. In FY 1983 HHS had 155 departmental posts: 52 SES noncareer positions and 103 schedule C positions. Figures courtesy of Government Operations Committee, U.S. Senate.
89. Interview, OPM aide.
90. Ibid.
91. Interview, HHS official.
92. Ibid.
93. Linda Demkovich, "Team Player Schweiker May Be Paying a High Price for His Loyalty to Reagan," *National Journal*, May 15, 1982, 848. By most accounts, Schweiker and his personal aides quietly surrendered control over income maintenance policy to the "California crowd" (Anderson, Carlson, and others) in the Domestic Policy Office and even permitted departmental staff to be detailed to the White House to assist in policy development (interview, HHS official).
94. A Nexis search of *Washington Post* and *New York Times* articles for the years 1981–1983, Schweiker's tenure, turned up only three articles focusing on conflict between HHS appointees and the White House or OMB staffs. Each involved budget cuts in highly popular HHS programs (such as Head Start). Spencer Rich, "Elite Medical Corps Is Facing Budget Surgery by Stockman," *Washington Post*, April 17, 1981, A1, and "Phase-Out of Head Start Proposed by Stockman," December 12, 1981, A1; Eric Pianin, "Budget Gives City Sweetened Setback," *Washington Post*, February 8, 1982, A1.
95. Demkovich, "Team Player Schweiker May Be Paying a High Price for His Loyalty to Reagan," 848–853.
96. Robert Pear, "Nominee for Social Security Defends Decisions on Grants," *New York Times*, May 15, 1986, 18:3.
97. *Washington Post*, February 22, 1983, A13b.
98. Ibid.
99. On the social security disability insurance program, see Jerry Mashaw, "Disability Insurance in an Age of Retrenchment: The Politics of Implementing Rights," ch. 6 in Jerry L. Mashaw and Theodore R. Marmor, eds., *Social Security: Beyond the Rhetoric of Crisis* (Princeton, N.J.: Princeton University Press, 1988).
100. *National Journal*, May 7, 1983, 951.
101. Interview, HHS official.
102. Interview, Reagan White House aide.
103. Ibid.
104. Ibid.
105. Only two of the HHS's sixteen PAS positions were filled during Heckler's tenure.

106. Interview, Reagan White House aide.

107. Ibid.

108. Interview, HHS official.

109. Interview, Reagan White House aide.

110. Interview, HHS official.

111. Ibid.

112. Interviews, Reagan White House aides.

113. Ronald Browstein, *National Journal*, June 15, 1985, 1408–1410.

114. Interview, Reagan White House aide.

115. Ronald Docksai, "Health," in *Mandate for Leadership III* (Washington, D.C.: Heritage Foundation, 1989).

116. Interview, Heritage Foundation official.

117. Interview, HHS official.

118. Ibid.

119. On Tuttle's loss of status within the White House Office, see Brownstein, "White House Personnel Office," 1408–1410. Interview, Reagan White House aide.

120. Joel Aberbach and Bert Rockman, "The Federal Executive Reexamined" (Paper presented at Hofstra Conference on the Presidency of Richard Nixon, November 19–20, 1987).

121. McKenzie, *The In-and-Outers*, 13. See also Maranto, "Still Clashing after All These Years: A Political Geography of Ideological Conflict in the Reagan Executive Branch." Maranto, too, finds that Reagan's political appointees — in both domestic and defense agencies — were overwhelmingly conservative and Republican.

122. Interview, Reagan White House aide. The two or three candidates proposed by HHS who were Democrats were promptly shot down by the White House. Interview, HHS official.

123. Officials were asked whether appointees embraced the assumptions that less government is better than more government, that state or local is better than national, and that markets (or market-like arrangements) work better than governmentally provided services.

124. A Nexis search of *Washington Post* and *New York Times* articles turned up only one article focusing on conflict between HHS appointees and the White House or OMB staffs during Bowen's tenure: "Bowen Resists Cutbacks," *New York Times*, December 21, 1985, 1:1.

125. Interview, HHS official.

126. Transcript of Brookings Conference, Los Angeles, California, 1962, 184–185, Brookings Archives.

127. National Academy of Public Administration (NAPA).

128. Interview, senior HHS appointee.

129. NAPA interview, S. John Byington.

130. Interview, senior HHS official.

131. Interview, Reagan White House aide.

132. Interview with Frank Carlucci, conducted by National Academy of Public Administration for its Presidential Appointee Project, 1985.

133. Interview, senior HHS official.

CHAPTER 7. THE INSTITUTIONALIZED PRESIDENCY

1. Compare, for example, Douglas Arnold's *The Logic of Congressional Action* (New Haven, Conn.: Yale University Press, 1990) to David Mayhew's *The Electoral*

Connection (New Haven,Conn.: Yale University Press, 1974), or John Aldrich's "A Downsian Spatial Model with Party Activists," *American Political Science Review* 77:4, (1985): 974–990) to Anthony Downs's *An Economic Theory of Democracy* (New York: Harper and Row, 1957).

2. See, for example, Lowi, *The Personal President*; Samuel Kernell, *Going Public;* Richard Rose, *The Post-Modern President: George Bush Meets the World* (Chatham, N.J.: Chatham House, 1988); Jeffrey Tulis, *The Rhetorical Presidency* (Princeton, N.J.: Princeton University Press, 1987).

3. Stephen Skowronek, *The Politics Presidents Make* (Cambridge, Mass.: Harvard University Press, 1993), 55.

4. Interview, White House aide.

5. *Promise and Performance: Strengthening the Executive Leadership System*, Report of the Task Force on the Relations Between Political Appointees and Career Executives to the National Commission on the Public Service (Washington, D.C., 1989). See recommendations 1–6, pp. 180–185.

6. Heclo, "The In-and-Outer System: A Critical Assessment," 213.

7. Ibid., 214.

8. John DiIulio, Gerald Garvey, and Donald F. Kettl, *Improving Governmental Performance* (Washington, D.C.: Brookings Institution, 1993), 57.

9. Moe, "The Politicized Presidency," 269.

Sources Consulted

BOOKS

Abels, Jules. *Out of the Jaws of Victory*. New York: Henry Holt, 1959.

Adams, Bruce, and Kathryn Kavanagh-Baran. *Promise and Performance: Carter Builds a New Administration*. Lexington, Mass.: D.C. Heath, 1979.

Adams, Sherman. *First Hand Report*. New York: Harper, 1961.

Aldrich, John H. "Presidential Campaigns in Party and Candidate-Centered Eras." In Matthew McCubbins, ed., *Under the Watchful Eye*. Washington, D.C.: Congressional Quarterly, 1992.

Alexander, Herbert, ed. *Studies in Money in Politics*. 3 vols. Princeton, N.J.: Citizen's Research Foundation, 1965–1974.

———. *Financing the 1968 Election*. Lexington, Mass.: D.C. Heath, 1971.

———. *Financing the 1972 Election*. Lexington, Mass.: D.C. Heath, 1976.

———. *Financing the 1980 Election*. Lexington, Mass.: D.C. Heath, 1983.

Ambrose, Stephen. *Nixon: The Triumph of a Politician, 1962–1972*. 3 vols. New York: Simon and Schuster, 1987–1991.

Anderson, Martin. *Revolution*. New York: Harcourt, Brace, Jovanovich, 1988.

Anderson, Patrick. *The President's Men*. New York: Doubleday, 1968.

Arnold, Douglas. *The Logic of Congressional Action*. New Haven, Conn.: Yale University Press, 1990.

Arterton, F. Christopher. *Media Politics*. Lexington, Mass.: D.C. Heath, 1984.

Asher, Herbert. *Presidential Elections and American Politics*. 4th ed. Chicago: Dorsey Press, 1988.

Barrett, Lawrence. *Gambling with History*. Garden City, N.Y.: Doubleday, 1983.

Bartels, Larry M. *Presidential Primaries and the Dynamics of Public Choice*. Princeton, N.J.: Princeton University Press, 1988.

Bass, Harold F., Jr. "Presidential Responsibility for National Party Organization, 1945–1974." Ph.D. dissertation, Vanderbilt University, 1976.

Bell, Griffin. *Taking Care of the Law*. New York: William Morrow, 1982.

Bell, Terrell. *The Thirteenth Man*. New York: Free Press, 1988.

Bennett, W. Lance. *News: The Politics of Illusion*. 2d ed. New York: Longman, 1988.

Bernstein, Marver. *The Job of the Federal Executive*. Washington, D.C.: Brookings Institution, 1958.

Bone, Hugh. *Party Committees and National Politics*. Seattle: University of Washington Press, 1958.

Boyarsky, Bill. *The Rise of Ronald Reagan*. New York: Random House, 1968.

Brauer, Carl. *Presidential Transitions: Eisenhower through Reagan*. New York: Oxford University Press, 1986. Broder, David. *The Party's Over*. New York: Harper and Row, 1972.

Brody, Richard. *Assessing the President: The Media, Elite Opinion, and Public Support*. Stanford, Calif.: Stanford University Press, 1990.

Brownlow, Louis. *A Passion for Anonymity*. Chicago: University of Chicago Press, 1958. Burke, Vincent J., and Vee Burke. *Nixon's Good Deed: Welfare Reform*. New York: Columbia University Press, 1974.

Caesar, James. "Political Parties: Declining, Stabilizing, or Resurging?" in Anthony King, ed., *The New American Political System*. Rev. ed. Washington, D.C.: American Enterprise Institute Press, 1990.

Califano, Joseph. *A Presidential Nation*. New York: Norton, 1975.

———. *Governing America: An Insider's Report from the Cabinet and the White House*. New York: Simon and Schuster, 1981.

Campbell, Colin. *Managing the Presidency: Carter, Reagan, and the Search for Executive Harmony*. Pittsburgh, Pa.: University of Pittsburgh Press, 1986.

Carrol, Susan, and Barbara Geiger-Parker. *Women Appointed to the Carter Administration: A Comparison with Men*. New Brunswick, N.J.: Rutgers University, Eagleton Institute, 1983.

Chubb, John E., and Paul E. Peterson, eds. *The New Direction in American Politics*. Washington, D.C.: Brookings Institution, 1985.

Corson, John. *Executives for the Federal Service: A Program of Action in a Time of Crisis*. New York: Columbia University Press, 1952.

Cotter, Cornelius P., and Bernard Hennessy. *Politics without Power: The National Party Committees*. New York: Atherton, 1964.

Crabb, Cecil V., and Kevin V. Mulcahy. *American National Security: A Presidential Perspective*. Pacific Grove, Calif.: Brooks/Cole, 1991.

Cronin, Thomas. "The Swelling of the Presidency: Can Anyone Reverse the Tide?" In Peter Woll, ed., *Debating American Government*. 2d. ed. New York: Scott, Foresman, 1988.

David, Paul T., and Ross Pollock. *Executives for Government*. Washington, D.C.: Brookings Institution, 1962.

David, Paul T., Ralph M. Goldman, and Richard C. Bain. *The Politics of National Party Conventions*. Washington, D.C.: Brookings Institution, 1960.

David, Paul T., ed. *The Presidential Election and Transition of 1960–1961*. Washington, D.C.: Brookings Institution, 1962.

Davis, James W. *Presidential Primaries: Road to the White House*. New York: Crowell, 1967.

Day, Edward J. *My Appointed Round: 929 Days as Postmaster General*. New York: Holt, Rinehart, Winston, 1965.

Derthick, Martha. *Uncontrollable Spending for Social Service Grants*. Washington, D.C.: Brookings Institution, 1975.

———. *Policymaking for Social Security*. Washington, D.C.: Brookings Institution, 1978.

———. *Agency under Stress: The Social Security Administration in American Government*. Washington, D.C.: Brookings Institution, 1990.

Devine, Thomas M., William Dobrovir, and Joseph Gebhardt. *Blueprint for Civil Service Reform*. Washington, D.C.: Fund for Constitutional Government, 1976.

Dick, Jane. *Volunteers and the Making of Politics*. New York: Dodd, Mead, 1980.

DiIulio, John, Jr., Gerald Garvey, and Donald F. Kettl. *Improving Governmental Performance*. Washington, D.C.: Brookings Institution, 1993.

Docksai, Ronald. "Health." In Charles Heatherly and Burton Pines, eds., *Mandate for Leadership III*. Washington, D.C.: Heritage Foundation, 1989.

Downs, Anthony. *An Economic Theory of Democracy*. New York: Harper and Row, 1957.

Drew, Elizabeth. *American Journal*. New York: Random House, 1977.

————. *Politics and Money*. New York: Macmillan, 1983.

Dunlop, Becky Norton. "The Role of the White House Personnel Office." In Sanera and Rector, eds., *Steering the Elephant*. New York: Universe Books, 1987.

Eastland, Terry. *Energy in the Executive*. New York: Free Press, 1992.

Edsall, Thomas Byrne. *The New Politics of Inequality*. New York: W.W. Norton, 1984.

Ehrlichman, John. *Witness to Power: The Nixon Years*. New York: Simon and Schuster, 1982.

Evans, Roland, and Robert Novak. *Nixon in the White House: The Frustration of Power*. New York: Random House, 1971.

Fenno, Richard. *The President's Cabinet: An Analysis of the Period from Wilson to Eisenhower*. New York: Vintage Books, 1959.

Fiorina, Morris P. *Congress: Keystone of the Washington Establishment*. 2d ed. New Haven, Conn.: Yale University Press, 1989.

Frantzich, Stephen E. *Political Parties in a Technological Age*. New York: Longman, 1989.

Germond, Jack W., and Jules Witcover. *Blue Smoke and Mirrors: How Reagan Won and Why Carter Lost the Election of 1980*. New York: Viking Press, 1981.

Gosnell, Harold. *Truman's Crises: A Political Biography of Harry S. Truman*. Westport, Conn.: Greenwood Press, 1980.

Gray, Robert K. *One Hundred Acres under Glass*. New York: Doubleday, 1962.

Greenstein, Fred. *The Hidden-Hand Presidency: Eisenhower as Leader*. New York: Basic Books, 1982.

Grossman, Michael B., and Martha Joynt Kumar. *Portraying the President*. Baltimore, Md.: Johns Hopkins University Press, 1981.

Guttman, Daniel, and Barry Willner. *The Shadow Government*. New York: Pantheon Books, 1976.

Haig, Alexander. *Caveat: Realism, Reagan, and Foreign Policy*. New York: Macmillan, 1984.

Haldeman, H. R. *The Ends of Power*. New York: Times Books, 1978.

Hallin, Daniel. *The Uncensored War: The Media and Vietnam*. New York: Oxford University Press, 1986.

Hansen, John Mark. *Gaining Access: Congress and the Farm Lobby, 1919–1981*. Chicago: University of Chicago Press, 1991.

Harris, Joseph. *The Advice and Consent of the Senate: A Study in the Confirmation of Appointments by the U.S. Senate*. Berkeley: University of California Press, 1953.

Hart, John. *The Presidential Branch*. New York: Pergamon Press, 1987.

Heatherly, Charles, and Burton Pines, eds., *Mandate for Leadership III*. Washington, D.C.: Heritage Foundation, 1989.

Hechler, Ken. *Working with Truman: A Personal Memoir of the White House Years*. New York: Putnam, 1982.

Heclo, Hugh. *A Government of Strangers: Executive Politics in Washington*. Washington, D.C.: Brookings Institution, 1977.

———. "Issue Networks and the Executive Establishment." In Anthony P. King, ed., *The New American Political System*. Washington, D.C.: American Enterprise Institute, 1978.

———. "The Changing Presidential Office." In Arnold Meltzner, ed., *Politics and the Oval Office*. San Francisco: Institute for Contemporary Studies, 1981.

———. "The In-and-Outers: A Critical Asssessment." In G. Calvin Mackenzie, ed., *The In-and-Outers: Presidential Appointees and Transient Government in Washington*. Baltimore, Md.: Johns Hopkins University Press, 1987.

Heclo, Hugh, and Lester Salamon, eds., *The Illusion of Presidential Government*. Boulder, Colo.: Westview, 1981.

Heineman, Ben W., Jr., and Curtis A. Hessler. *Memorandum for the President: A Strategic Approach to Domestic Affairs in the 1980's*. New York: Random House, 1980.

Heller, Francis H. *The Truman White House: The Administration of the Presidency*. Lawrence: University Press of Kansas, 1980.

Henderson, Phillip G. *Managing the Presidency: The Eisenhower Legacy—From Kennedy to Reagan*. Boulder, Colo.: Westview Press, 1988.

Henry, Laurin. *Presidential Transitions*. Washington, D.C.: Brookings Institution, 1960.

———. "The Presidency, Executive Staffing, and the Federal Bureaucracy." In Aaron Wildavsky, ed., *The Presidency*. Boston: Little, Brown, 1969.

Hess, Stephen. *Washington Reporters*. Washington, D.C.: Brookings Institution, 1981.

———. *Organizing the Presidency*, 2d ed. Washington, D.C.: Brookings Institution, 1988.

Hess, Stephen, and David S. Broder. *The Republican Establishment*. New York: Harper and Row, 1967.

Hoxie, R. Gordon, ed. *The White House: Organization and Operations*. New York: Center for the Study of the Presidency, 1971.

Iyengar, Shanto, and Donald Kinder. *News That Matters: Television and American Opinion*. Chicago: University of Chicago Press, 1987.

Jacobson, Gary C. *The Politics of Congressional Elections*. New York: Harper Collins, 1992.

Johnson, Haynes. *In the Absence of Power: Governing America*. New York: Viking, 1980.

Johnson, Richard. "Presidential Style." In Aaron Wildavsky, ed., *Perspectives on the Presidency*. Boston: Little, Brown, 1975.

Jones, Charles O., ed. *The Reagan Legacy*. New York: Chatham House, 1990.

Kearns, Doris. *Lyndon Johnson and the American Dream*. New York: Harper and Row, 1976.

Kelley, Stanley. *Professional Public Relations and Political Power*. Baltimore, Md.: Johns Hopkins University Press, 1956.

Kernell,Samuel. "The Evolution of the White House Staff." In John Chubb and Paul Peterson, eds. *Can the Government Govern?* Washington, D.C.: Brookings Institution, 1989.

———. *Going Public: New Strategies of Presidential Leadership*. 2d ed. Washington, D.C.: Congressional Quarterly Press, 1993.

Kernell, Samuel, and Samuel L. Popkin. *Chiefs of Staff: Twenty-Five Years of Managing the Presidency*. Berkeley: University of California Press, 1986.

Kessel, John. *Presidential Campaign Politics*. 2d ed. Chicago: Dorsey Press, 1984.

Key, V. O. *Politics, Parties, and Pressure Groups*. 5th ed. New York: Cromwell, 1964.

King, Gary, and Lynn Ragsdale. *The Elusive Executive: Discovering Statistical Patterns in the Presidency*. Washington, D.C.: Congressional Quarterly Press, 1988.

Kissinger, Henry. *The White House Years*. Boston: Little, Brown, 1979.

Lake, Anthony. *Somoza Falling*. Boston: Houghton Mifflin, 1989.

Lieberman, Joseph. *The Power Broker*. Boston: Houghton Mifflin, 1966.

Lowi, Theodore J. *The Personal President: Power Invested, Promise Unfulfilled*. Ithaca, N.Y.: Cornell University Press, 1985.

McCubbins, Matthew D., ed. *Under the Watchful Eye: Managing Campaigns in the Television Era*. Washington, D.C.: Congressional Quarterly Press, 1992.

McFeeley, Neal D. *The Appointment of Judges: The Johnson Administration*. Austin: University of Texas Press, 1986.

Mackenzie, Calvin G. *The Politics of Presidential Appointments*. New York: Free Press, 1981.

Mackenzie, Calvin G., ed. *The In-and-Outers: Presidential Appointees and Transient Government in Washington*. Baltimore, Md.: Johns Hopkins University Press, 1987.

McMahon, Arthur W., and John D. Millet. *Federal Administrators*. New York: Columbia University Press, 1939.

Maltese, John Anthony. *Spin Control: The White House Office of Communications and the Management of Presidential News*. Chapel Hill: University of North Carolina Press, 1992.

Mann, Dean, and Jameson Doig. *The Assistant Secretaries: Problems and Processes of Appointment*. Washington, D.C.: Brookings Institution, 1965.

Mansfield, Harvey C. "Political Parties, Patronage, and the Federal Government Service." In Wallace Sayre, ed., *The Federal Government Service: Its Character, Prestige, and Problems*. Englewood Cliffs, N.J.: Prentice Hall, 1954.

Marmor, Theodore R. "Entrepreneurship in Public Management: Wilbur Cohen and Robert Ball." In Jameson W. Doig and Erwin C. Hargrove, eds., *Leadership and Innovation*. Baltimore, Md.: Johns Hopkins University Press, 1987.

Marmor, Theodore R., and Jerry L. Mashaw. *Social Security: Beyond the Rhetoric of Crisis*. Princeton, N.J.: Princeton University Press, 1988.

May, Ernest R., and Janet Fraser. *Campaign '72*. Cambridge, Mass.: Harvard University Press, 1973.

Mayhew, David. *The Electoral Connection*. New Haven, Conn.: Yale University Press, 1974.

———. *Placing Parties in American Politics*. Princeton, N.J.: Princeton University Press, 1986.

Menefee-Libey, David. "The Politics of Party Organization." Ph.D. dissertation, University of Chicago, 1989.

Michelson, Charles. *The Ghost Talks*. New York: G.P. Putnam's Sons, 1944.

Milkis, Sidney M. "The Presidency and Political Parties." In Michael Nelson, ed. *The Presidency and the Political System*. 3d ed. Washington, D.C.: Congressional Quarterly Press, 1989.

Miller, Warren E., and M. Kent Jennings. Parties in Transition: A Longitudinal Study of Party Elites and Supporters. New York: Russell Sage Foundation, 1986.

Moe, Terry. "The Politicized Presidency." In John Chubb and Paul Peterson, eds., *New Directions in American Politics*. Washington, D.C.: Brookings Institution, 1985.

———. "Presidents, Institutions, and Theory." In George Edwards, John H. Kessel, and Bert A. Rockman, eds., *Researching the Presidency: Vital Questions, New Approaches*. Pittsburgh, Pa.: University of Pittsburgh Press, 1993.

Moore, Jonathan, ed. *The Campaign for President: 1980 in Retrospect*. Cambridge, Mass.: Ballinger, 1981.

Moore, Jonathan, and Janet Fraser, eds. *Campaign for President: The Managers Look at 1976*. Cambridge, Mass.: Ballinger, 1977.

Mosher, Frederick, ed. *The President Needs Help*. Lanham, Md.: University Press of America, 1988.

Murphy, Thomas P., Donald E. Neuchterlein, and Ronald J. Stupak. *Inside the Bureaucracy: The View from the Assistant Secretary's Desk*. Boulder, Colo.: Westview Press, 1976.

Nathan, Richard. *The Administrative Presidency*. New York: John Wiley and Sons, 1983.

National Academy of Public Administration. *Recruiting Presidential Appointees: A Conference of Former Presidential Personnel Assistants*. Washington, D.C., 1984.

————. *Watergate: Its Implications for Responsible Government*. Report by the panel of the National Academy of Public Administration at the request of the Senate Select Committee on Presidential Campaign Activities. Washington, D.C.: Government Printing Office, March 1974.

National Commission on the Public Service. *See* Volcker Commission.

Neustadt, Richard. *Presidential Power: The Politics of Presidential Leadership from FDR to Carter*. New York: John Wiley and Sons, 1980.

————. "The White House Staff." In Francis H. Heller, ed., *The Truman White House*. Lawrence: University Press of Kansas, 1980.

Olien, Roger. *From Token to Triumph: Texas Republicans Since 1920*. Dallas, Tex.: Southern Methodist University Press, 1982.

Olesczek, Walter J., and Roger Davidson. *Congress against Itself*. Bloomington: Indiana University Press, 1977.

Orfield, Gary. *Must We Bus?* Washington, D.C.: Brookings Institution, 1978.

Osborne, John. *The Second Year of the Nixon Watch*. Washington, D.C.: New Republic Books, 1971.

Panetta, Leon, and Peter Gall. *Bring Us Together: The Nixon Team and the Civil Rights Retreat*. Philadelphia, Pa.: J.B. Lippincott, 1971.

Patterson, Bradley. *Ring of Power: The White House Staff and Its Expanding Role in Government*. New York: Basic Books, 1988.

Peterson, Mark. *Legislating Together: The White House and Capitol Hill from Eisenhower to Reagan*. Cambridge, Mass.: Harvard University Press, 1988.

Pfiffner, James. *The Strategic Presidency: Hitting the Ground Running*. Chicago: Dorsey Press, 1988.

Pfiffner, James, ed. *The Managerial Presidency*. Pacific Grove, Calif.: Brooks/Cole, 1991.

Polsby, Nelson. *The Consequences of Party Reform*. New York: Oxford University Press, 1983.

Rabkin, Jeremy. *Judicial Compulsions: How Public Law Distorts Public Policy*. New York: Basic Books, 1991.

Rae, Nicol. *The Decline and Fall of Liberal Republicans: From 1952 to the Present*. New York: Oxford University Press, 1989.

Redding, Jack. *Inside the Party*. New York: Bobbs-Merrill, 1958.

Redford, Emmette, and Richard T. McCulley. *White House Operations: The Johnson Years*. Austin: University of Texas Press, 1986.

Reedy, George. *The Twilight of the Presidency*. New York: New American Library, 1970.

Reichley, A. James. *The Art of Government: Reform and Organization Politics in Philadelphia*. New York: Fund for the Republic, 1959.

————. "The Rise of National Parties." In John Chubb and Paul Peterson, eds., *New Directions in American Politics*. Washington, D.C.: Brookings Institution, 1985.

Rockman, Bert. *The Leadership Question: The Presidency and the American System*. New York: Praeger, 1984.

————. "The Style and Organization of the Reagan Presidency." In Charles O. Jones, ed., *The Reagan Legacy*. New York: Chatham House, 1987.

Rose, Richard. *The Post-Modern President: George Bush Meets the World*. Chatham, N.J.: Chatham House, 1988.

Ross, Irwin. *The Loneliest Campaign: The Campaign of 1948*. New York: New American Library, 1969.

Salisbury, Robert H., "The Paradox of Interest Groups in Washington—More Groups, Less Clout." In Anthony King, ed., *The New American Political System*. 2d ed. Washington, D.C.: American Enterprise Institute Press, 1990.

Schlesinger, Arthur M., Jr. *A Thousand Days: John F. Kennedy in the White House*. Boston: Houghton Mifflin, 1965.

Schlozman, Kay Lehman, and John Tierney. *Organized Interests and American Democracy*. New York: Harper and Row, 1986.

Seidman, Harold. *Politics, Position, and Power*. 3d ed. New York: Oxford University Press, 1980.

Seligman, Lester. "The Presidential Office and the President as Party Leader." In Jeff Fishel, ed., *Parties and Elections in an Antiparty Age*. Bloomington: Indiana University Press, 1978.

Shafer, Byron. *Bifurcated Politics: Evolution and Reform in the National Party Convention*. Cambridge, Mass.: Harvard University Press, 1988.

————. *The Quiet Revolution: The Struggle for the Democratic Party and the Shaping of Post-Reform Politics*. New York: Russell Sage Foundation, 1984.

Shogan, Robert. *Promises to Keep*. New York: Crowell, 1977.

Skowronek, Stephen. *The Politics Presidents Make*. Cambridge, Mass.: Harvard University Press, 1993.

Smith, Steven S. *Call to Order: Floor Politics in the House and Senate*. Washington, D.C.: Brookings Institution, 1990.

Smith, Steven S., and Christopher Deering. *Committees in Congress*. 2d ed. Washington, D.C.: Congressional Quarterly Press, 1990.

Sorauf, Francis J. *Party Politics in America*. 3d ed. Boston: Little, Brown, 1976.

————. *Money in American Politics*. Glenview, Ill.: Scott, Foresman, 1988.

Sorauf, Francis J., and Paul Allen Beck. *Party Politics in America*. 6th ed. Glenview, Ill.: Scott, Foresman, 1988.

Sousa, David J. "Union Politics in an Era of Decline." Ph.D. dissertation, University of Minnesota, 1991.

Stanley, David T. *Changing Administrations: The 1961 and 1964 Transitions in Six Departments*. Washington, D.C.: Brookings Institution, 1965.

Stanley, Harold, Dean Mann, and Jameson Doig. *Men Who Govern*. Washington, D.C.: Brookings Institution, 1967.

Thayer, George. *Who Shakes the Money Tree?* New York: Simon and Schuster, 1973.

Thompson, Kenneth W., ed. *The Nixon Presidency: Twenty-Two Intimate Perspectives on Richard Nixon*. Lanham, Md.: University Press of America, 1987.

Tower Commission. *The Tower Commission Report: The Full Text of the President's Special Review Board*. New York: Bantam and Times Books, 1987.

Tuchman, Gaye. *Making News: A Study in the Construction of Reality*. New York: Free Press, 1978.

Tulis, Jeffrey. *The Rhetorical Presidency*. Princeton, N.J.: Princeton University Press, 1987.

U.S. Congress. *Final Report on Violations and Abuses of Merit Principles in Federal Employment Together with Minority Views (Violations and Abuses)*. House Subcommittee on Manpower and Civil Service of the Post Office and Civil Service Committee, Committee Print, 94-28, 94th Cong., 2d sess. Washington, D.C.: Government Printing Office, 1976.

―――. *Policy and Supporting Positions*. House/Senate and Post Office and Civil Service Committee. Washington, D.C.: Government Printing Office, 1952–1988.

―――. *Study on Federal Regulation: The Regulatory Appointments Process*. Committee on Government Operations, U.S. Senate. Vol. 1. Washington, D.C.: Government Printing Office, 1977.

Van Riper, Paul. *History of the United States Civil Service*. Evanston, Ill.: Row, Peterson, 1958.

Volcker Commission. *Leadership for America: Rebuilding the Public Service*. Report of the National Commission on the Public Service [the Volcker Commission]. Washington, D.C., 1989.

―――. *Promise and Performance: Strengthening the Executive Leadership System*. Report of the Task Force on the Relations between Political Appointees and Career Executives to the National Commission on the Public Service. Washington, D.C.: Government Printing Office, 1989.

Von Damm, Helene. *At Reagan's Side*. New York: Doubleday, 1989.

Ware, Alan. *The Breakdown of Democratic Party Organization 1948–1980*. Oxford: Oxford University Press, 1985.

Waterman, Richard. *Presidential Influence in the Administrative State*. Knoxville: University of Tennessee Press, 1990.

Wattenberg, Martin P. *The Decline of American Political Parties, 1952–1994*. Cambridge, Mass.: Harvard University Press, 1994.

Wayne, Stephen. *The Legislative Presidency*. New York: Harper and Row, 1978.

Weko, Thomas J. " 'A Good Man Is Hard to Find': Presidents and Their Political Executives." Ph.D. dissertation, University of Minnesota, 1991.

White, Theodore. *The Making of the President 1960*. New York: Atheneum, 1961.

―――. *The Making of the President 1964*. New York: Atheneum, 1965.

Witcover, Jules. *Marathon: The Pursuit of the Presidency, 1972–1976*. New York: Viking Press, 1977.

Williams, Walter. *Mismanaging America: The Rise of the Anti-Analytical Presidency*. Lawrence: The University Press of Kansas, 1990.

Wilson, James Q. *The Amateur Democrat*. Chicago: University of Chicago Press, 1960.

ARTICLES AND PAPERS

Aberbach, Joel D., and Bert A. Rockman. "Clashing Beliefs in the Executive Branch: The Nixon Administration Bureaucracy." *American Political Science Review* 70 (June 1976).

―――. "From Nixon's Problem to Reagan's Achievement—The Federal Executive Reexamined." Paper presented to Hofstra Conference on the Presidency of Richard Nixon. November 1987, Hempstead, N.Y.

―――. "Mandates of Mandarins? Control and Discretion in the Modern Administrative State." *Public Administration Review* 48 (March–April 1988).

Aldrich, John H. "A Downsian Spatial Model with Party Activism." *American Political Science Review* 77:4 (1985).

Barrett, Paul M. "Conservatives Tear a Page from Liberals' Book, Borking Clinton's Nominees for Legal Positions." *Wall Street Journal*, November 29, 1993.

Berke, Richard. "Time Bomb in the White House." *New York Times*, June 6, 1993.

Bonafede, Dom. "Carter Sounds Retreat from Cabinet Government." *National Journal*, November 18, 1978.

———. "Carter's Recent Staff Shakeup May Be More of a Shakedown." *National Journal*, June 17, 1978.

———. "Nixon's Executive Reorganization Plans Prompt Praise and Criticism." *National Journal*, March 10, 1973.

———. "Nixon's First Year Appointments Reveal the Pattern of His Administration." *National Journal*, January 24, 1970.

———. "Nixon Personnel Staff Works to Restructure Federal Policies." *National Journal*, November 12, 1971.

———. "Reagan and His Kitchen Cabinet Are Bound by Friendship and Ideology." *National Journal*, April 11, 1981.

———. "White House Report/Nixon Personnel Staff Works to Restructure Federal Policies." *National Journal*, November 12, 1971.

"Bowen Resists Cutbacks." *New York Times*, December 21, 1985.

Brownstein, Ronald. "Jobs Are the Currency of Politics, and the White House Is on a Spending Spree." *National Journal*, December 15, 1984.

———. "White House Personnel Office Struggles with More Vacancies, Less Influence." *National Journal*, June 15, 1985.

Clymer, Adam. "Staff Quietly Planning for a Reagan Presidency." *New York Times*, September 14, 1980.

Cole, Richard L., and David J. Caputo. "Presidential Control of the Senior Civil Service: Assessing Strategies of the Nixon Years." *American Political Science Review* 73 (1979).

Cook, Rhodes. "Carter and the Democrats: Benign Neglect?" *Congressional Quarterly Weekly Report*, January 14, 1978.

Cross, Mercer. "Interest Group Doubts Rise on Top Jobs." *Congressional Quarterly*, April 30, 1977.

Demkovich, Linda E. "Team Player Schweiker May Be Paying a High Price for His Loyalty to Reagan." *National Journal*, May 15, 1982.

Devroy, Ann. "Envoys without Experience; Bush Favors GOP Donors as Ambassadors." *Washington Post*, July 18, 1989.

———. "Late for Appointments: Presidential Hiring Process Slower Than Ever." *Washington Post*, March 2, 1993.

Dewar, Helen. "Envoy-Designate on Hold: There Is No There, There, Senator Says of Credentials." *Washington Post*, November 10, 1989.

Evans, Rowland, and Robert Novak. "Cleaning Out the Kitchen." *Washington Post*, March 20, 1981.

———. "GOP Job Chaos." *Washington Star*, March 9, 1969.

Fenno, Richard. "Observation, Context, and Sequence in the Study of Politics." *American Political Science Review* 80:1 (March 1986).

Ferguson, Ernest. "Women, Blacks, in Bottom Cabinet Drawer." *Los Angeles Times*, December 27, 1976.

Fowler, Dorothy. "Congressional Dictation of Local Appointments." *Journal of Politics* 7 (1945).

Friedman, Thomas L. "Clinton Taking Big Role in Picking Cabinet Aides." *New York Times*, November 18, 1992.

Frisby, Michael K. "While Some Clinton Changes Make Big Waves, Others Trickle Down to Lower Levels." *Wall Street Journal*, November 3, 1993.

Glad, Betty. "The Idiosyncratic Presidency." *Presidency Research* (Winter 1990–1991).

Haveman, Joel. "The TIP Talent Hunt: Carter's Original Amateur Hour?" *National Journal*, February 19, 1977.

Healy, Jon. "As Administration Fills Its Slots, Congress Plays Waiting Game." *Congressional Quarterly Weekly Report*, May 1, 1993.

Heclo, Hugh. "OMB and the Presidency—The Problem of Neutral Competence." *Public Interest* (Winter 1975).

Herrnson, Paul. "Political Parties, Campaign Finance Reform, and Presidential Elections." Paper presented to the American Political Association, 1990.

Hicks, Nancy. "Women's Groups Want More Women Named to High Positions, Citing Expectations Raised in the Campaign." *New York Times*, February 8, 1977.

Iglehart, John. "Diffuse Nature of HEW Mission Challenges Republicans' Management Goals." *National Journal*, August 5, 1970.

"Integrity in Numbers." *Washington Post*, May 26, 1973.

Jacobs, Bruce. "The Recoil Effect: Public Opinion and Policymaking in the U.S. and Britain." *Comparative Politics* 24:2 (January 1992).

Jacobs, Bruce, and Robert Y. Shapiro. "Leadership and Responsiveness: Some New Evidence on the Johnson Presidency." Paper presented to the Annual Meeting of the American Political Science Association, 1992.

Jehl, Douglas. "Clinton Nominations Come Slowly and with Many Setbacks." *New York Times*. January 30, 1994.

———. "High-Level Grumbling over Pace of Appointments." *New York Times*, February 25, 1993.

Johnston, David. "GOP Official Made a Census of Jews at Agency." *New York Times*, September 11, 1988.

Kaiser, Robin G. "The 2,000 Carter Administration Jobs: Who Got Them?" *Washington Post*, June 6, 1977.

Kamen, Al. "Administration Still Walking On Egg Shells." *Washington Post*, April 19, 1993.

———. "Banker's Ours: Clinton Snares Atlanta Executive." *Washington Post*, January 12, 1994.

———. "Personnel Trend Pleases Women's Groups." *Washington Post*, April 5, 1993.

Kaufman, Herbert. "Emerging Conflicts in the Doctrines of Public Administration." *American Political Science Review* 50 (December 1956).

Kelly, Michael, and Maureen Dowd. "The Company He Keeps." *New York Times*, January 17, 1993.

Kernell, Samuel. "Explaining Presidential Popularity." *American Political Science Review* 72 (June 1978).

Kirschten, Dick. "Cabinet Power." *National Journal*, June 28, 1986.

———. "Wanted: 275 Reagan Team Players: Empire Builders Need Not Apply." *National Journal*, December 6, 1980.

Klutz, Jerry. "New U.S. Job Set Up Planned." *Washington Post*, December 20, 1953.

Korb, Lawrence J. "The President and the Military at Odds." *Brookings Review* (Summer 1993).

Lynch, Edward J. "No, We Don't Have Too Many Political Appointees." *Bureaucrat* (April, 1991).

Lyons, Richard D. "Richardson Says He'll Fight Cuts: Asserts Job Reductions Will Trim 'Muscle.'" *New York Times*, December 18, 1971.

———. "U.S. Health Aide Is Out in Dispute." *New York Times*, June 3, 1970.

MacKenzie, G. Calvin. "The Reaganites Come to Town: Personnel Selection for a Conservative Administration." Paper presented to the annual meeting of the American Political Science Association, New York City, 1981, revised, January 1982.

Malek, Frederick V. "Mr. Businessman Goes to Washington." *Harvard Business Review* (September–October, 1972).

Manegold, Catherine S. "Clinton's Ire on Appointments Startles Women." *New York Times*, December 23, 1992.

Maranto, Robert. "Still Clashing after All These Years: A Political Geography of Ideological Conflict in the Reagan Executive Branch." Unpublished paper, 1990.

Marcus, Ruth. "Clinton Berates Critics in Women's Groups." *Washington Post*, December 22, 1992.

Neustadt, Richard E. "The Constraining of the President: The Presidency after Watergate." *British Journal of Political Science* 4 (April 1974).

———. "On Patronage, Power, and Politics." *Public Administration Review* (Spring 1958).

Ostrom, Charles, and Dennis Simon. "Promise and Performance: A Dynamic Model of Presidential Popularity." *American Political Science Review* 79 (June 1985).

Pear, Robert. "Nominee for Social Security Defends Decisions on Grants." *New York Times*, May 15, 1986.

Peterson, Mark, and Walker, Jack. "The Effect of the Reagan Administration on National Interest Group Politics." Paper presented to the annual meeting of the American Political Science Association, New Orleans, 1985.

Pfiffner, James P. "Cutting Staff No Easy Task for Clinton." *Maine Sunday Telegram*, December 12, 1993.

Pianin, Eric. "Budget Gives City a Sweetened Setback." *Washington Post*, February 8, 1982.

Pierson, John. "Nixon Talent Hunt Off to Good Finish." *Wall Street Journal*, May 5, 1969.

Pika, Joseph. "Moving beyond the White House: Problems in Studying the Presidency." *Congress and the Presidency* 9:1 (Winter 1981–1982).

"Politics without Patronage." *Time*, June 7, 1954.

Radcliffe, Donnie. "The Women's Hour: Clinton Appointees Revel in Their First Year in Power." *Washington Post*, February 9, 1994.

Raines, Howell. "Conservatives Cite Gains in Top Posts." *New York Times*, March 8, 1981.

Rich, Spencer. "Elite Medical Corps Is Facing Budget Survey by Stockman." *Washington Post*, April $7, 1981.

———. "Phase-Out of Head Start Proposed by Stockman." *Washington Post*, December 12, 1981.

"Richardson Threatens to Resign Over Rejection of his Austin Texas Desegregation Plan." *New York Times*, August 10, 1971.

Richie, Martha Farnsworth. "The Bean Count Is In! A Promise Fulfilled: Clinton's Appointees Really Are as Diverse as America." *Washington Post*, January 23, 1994.

Rosen, Bernard. "Effective Continuity of U.S. Government in Jeopardy." *Public Administration Review* (September/October 1983).

Rourke, Francis. "Executive Responsiveness to Presidential Policies: The Reagan Presidency." Paper presented to the annual meeting of the American Political Science Association, Atlanta, 1989.

Scott, Austin. "Jobs Found for Carter Supporters." *Washington Post*, February 13, 1977.

Shafer, Ronald G. "Washington Wire." *Wall Street Journal*, February 11, 1994.

Shalit, Ruth. "Unwhite House." *New Republic*, April 12, 1993.

Sherrill, Robert. "Hatchman and Hatchetmyth." *Washington Post*, February 6, 1972.

Smith, Terence. "It's Carter Folk vs. Regular Democrats." *New York Times*, December 11, 1977.

Solomon, Burt. "Scrimping on White House Staff Could Damage Clinton's Fortunes." *National Journal*, August 14, 1993.

Sorauf, Francis. "The Silent Revolution in Patronage." *Public Administration Review* 20 (Winter 1960).

Sundquist, James. "Jimmy Carter as Public Administrator: An Appraisal at Mid-Term." *Public Administration Review* (January–February 1979).

"Thousands Seek a Niche in Reagan Administration." *New York Times*, November 23, 1980.

Tolchin, Martin. "Carter Takes Hands Off Approach to Patronage, Irking Some in Party." *New York Times*, May 22, 1977.

Walker, Jack. "The Origins and Maintenance of Interest Groups in America." *American Political Science Review* 77 (June 1983).

Watson, James. "Is Patronage Obsolete?" *Personnel Administration* (July 1955).

Weaver, Warren, Jr. "National Committee Scolds Carter for Bypassing State Party Chiefs." *New York Times*, April 2, 1977.

Index